AF597797

The series
"Historical Dimensions of European Integration"
is edited by

Prof. Dr. Guido Thiemeyer | Dr. Christian Henrich-Franke

Founding editor:
Prof. Dr. Gerold Ambrosius

Volume 34

Valentine Aldebert | Christian Henrich-Franke
Léonard Laborie | Sabrina Proschmann
Guido Thiemeyer [Eds.]

Conflict in Cooperation

Crossborder Infrastructures in Europe Facing the Second World War

The series "Historical Dimensions of European Integration" was edited by Nomos up to volume 29 on behalf of the Institut für Europäische Regionalforschungen (Institute for European Regional Research) by Prof. Dr. Gerold Ambrosius and was published under the title "Institut für Europäische Regionalforschungen – Institute for European Regional Research".

The Deutsche Nationalbibliothek lists this publication in the Deutsche Nationalbibliografie; detailed bibliographic data are available on the Internet at http://dnb.d-nb.de

ISBN 978-3-8487-8885-9 (Print)
978-3-7489-2940-6 (ePDF)

British Library Cataloguing-in-Publication Data
A catalogue record for this book is available from the British Library.

ISBN 978-3-8487-8885-9 (Print)
978-3-7489-2940-6 (ePDF)

Library of Congress Cataloging-in-Publication Data
Aldebert, Valentine | Henrich-Franke, Christian | Laborie, Léonard
Proschmann, Sabrina | Thiemeyer, Guido
Conflict in Cooperation
Crossborder Infrastructures in Europe Facing the Second World War
Valentine Aldebert | Christian Henrich-Franke | Léonard Laborie
Sabrina Proschmann | Guido Thiemeyer (Eds.)
257 pp.
Includes bibliographic references.

ISBN 978-3-8487-8885-9 (Print)
978-3-7489-2940-6 (ePDF)

1st Edition 2022

Published by
Nomos Verlagsgesellschaft mbH & Co. KG
Waldseestraße 3–5 | 76530 Baden-Baden
www.nomos.de

Production of the printed version:
Nomos Verlagsgesellschaft mbH & Co. KG
Waldseestraße 3–5 | 76530 Baden-Baden

ISBN 978-3-8487-8885-9 (Print)
ISBN 978-3-7489-2940-6 (ePDF)
DOI https://doi.org/10.5771/9783748929406

Onlineversion
Nomos eLibrary

Table of Content

Conflict in Cooperation – Some Introductory Words

Johan Schot and Philip Scranton, the editors, oppose technological co-operation and circulation, on the one hand, and war, on the other, as two different ways to narrate the history of contemporary Europe in their introduction to the six-volume series *Making Europe. Technologies and Transformation, 1850-2000.*

> We offer a European history viewed through the lens of technology rather than war. We believe that a European history with technology at its core can help to understand the continuities that have endured despite the rupture of wars.[1]

While we agree generally that less visible cross-border connections have long been overlooked in historiography, we think it is timely to go even a step further and write a history of Europe where technological co-operation and conflict are thought of together, not in opposition.

From the Crimean war to the Cold War, technologies that so many engineers, industrialists and commentators presented as new ways to bind peoples together across borders proved to be decisive tools in military confrontations. The subtitle of the volume devoted to infrastructures in the *Making Europe* series rightly thematizes 'war' in between 'economy' and 'nature'.[2] Railways transported soldiers, guns, animals and food for the regiments, communication lines forwarded commands and intelligence, and energy networks fed war factories. It seems common sense to conclude that wars resulted in destruction and disintegration.[3] Yet, the capacity to connect and co-ordinate these means became key among allied countries. Co-operative and integrative dynamics appeared to serve the needs of the "logistics of war."[4] The experience was to be formative for the peacetime reordering of

1 Schot, Johan / Scranton, Philip: "Making Europe: An Introduction to the Series", in: Oldenziel, Ruth / Hard, Mikael (eds.): *Consumers, Tinkerers, Rebels. The People who Shaped Europe,* Basingstoke 2013, p. ix – xv, here p. ix.

2 Högselius, Per / Kaijser, Arne / van der Vleuten, Erik: *Europe's Infrastructure Transition. Economy, War, Nature*, Basingstoke 2016.

3 Kleinschmidt, Christian: "Review: Infrastructure, Networks, (Large) Technical Systems: The 'Hidden Integration' of Europe", in: *Contemporary European History* 19 (2010), pp. 275 – 284.

4 Högselius / Kaijser / van der Vleuten: Europe's Infrastructure Transition, p. 183 – 228.

transnational relations. It is well-known that people in charge of co-ordinating French, British, Italian and American maritime transport capacities during the First World War become subsequently deeply involved in the League of Nations and also in the first European communities after the Second World War – Jean Monnet embodied such a trajectory.[5] That said, we know far less about the situation from the side of those who eventually lost the wars, the Second World War in particular. What happened to infrastructural co-ordination in continental Europe under German domination? Which lines of continuity can be drawn and which marks of rupture can be underlined during the war, from 1939 to 1945, and the pre- and post-war periods?

A Historiographical Blind Spot

Transnational co-operation in the area of infrastructures during the Second World War can, at the moment, be described as a research desideratum. It appears counter-intuitive to suggest that the time of the Second World War would be one of continuity and perhaps even a deepening and widening of European co-operation within any area. Thus, the inter-war and the after-war time have been researched, while the war time is generally viewed as a caesura. This applies to the different strands of research that this publication touches upon, such as infrastructure history, the history of European integration and Franco-German relations.

The impact of technical co-operation on European integration since the 19th century had long been overlooked but has been the focus of several publications in recent years. Thus, what Misa and Schot in 2005 called the "hidden integration of Europe"[6] is today no longer hidden – with the exception of the Second World War, which might well be characterised as the era of the most hidden integration. Co-operation was characterised by the strong role of the experts in different fields of infrastructure, such as postal services, telecommunications, rail and navigation. These experts (often engineers or lawyers) came in large numbers from the respectively responsible national administrations, built cross-border epistemic communities and de-

5 Kaiser, Wolfram / Schot, Johan: *Writing the Rules for Europe: Experts, Cartels, and International Organisations*, London 2016, pp. 63 – 66.

6 Misa, Thomas / Schot, Johan: "Inventing Europe: Technology and the Hidden Integration of Europe", in: *History and Technology* 21 (2005), S. 1 – 19.

veloped a self-image that Lagendijk and Schot labelled "technocratic internationalism"[7]: At the heart of this concept was the idea that international infrastructure governance was best done by experts who decided rationally upon standards and regulations. Political interference (or what experts considered as political interference) in these negotiations should be avoided as far as possible. Behind this idea of the technocratic governance of international infrastructure issues, stood the more political ideal that peace could only be upheld if peoples from different countries were connected.

In May and June 1914, telephone engineers and railway experts could be optimistic. The former had a convention signed enabling direct telephone conversations between Paris and Vienna through German territory, while the latter met in Bern at a 'European Timetable Conference'. A few weeks later though, the outbreak of a four-year war proved that international co-ordination on so-called administrative or technical issues had created bonds that were not strong enough to prevent deadly conflicts within Europe. War interrupted connections between fighting blocs. During the war and its immediate aftermath, experts on the French side struggled hard to link up Europe again, this time bypassing or marginalising Germany. German telephone engineers, for instance, were not invited to the preliminary meeting of the "Comité technique préliminaire pour la téléphonie à grande distance en Europe"[8] in Paris in 1923. The Weimar Republic, on the contrary, fought hard and managed to restore the central place of Germany on the European scene through infrastructure. German engineers were invited to the second founding conference on European telephony in 1924. Remarkably, the organisation bears the official Franco-German denomination 'Comité consultatif international (for) Fernschreiben'.

All in all, while many observers and politicians argued for more political co-operation to maintain durable peace with the League of Nations, experts and technicians found a new reason to believe in technocratic internationalism in the experience of the conflict and this new international environment. Against the background of high political instability during the interwar years, technocracy was seen as:

7 Schot, Johan / Lagendijk, Vincent: "Technocratic Internationalism in the Interwar Years. Building Europe on Motorways and Electricity Networks", in: *Journal of Modern European History* 6 (2008), pp. 196 – 217.

8 Henrich-Franke, Christian / Laborie, Léonard: "Technology Taking over Diplomacy? The 'Comité consultatif international (for) Fernschreiben' (CCIF) and its Relationship to the ITU in the Early History of Telephone Standardization, 1923–1947", in: Balbi, Gabriele / Fickers, Andreas (eds.): *History of the International Telecommunication Union*, Berlin 2019, pp. 193 – 216.

> The way of business leaders, engineers, politicians, intellectuals and their respective organisations and parties to create a new societal order for nation-states in Europe plagued by huge problems of instability, social conflict, unemployment and economic depression.[9]

While this self-image was not propagated officially, research in the fields of postal services and telecommunications shows that the experts had, in fact, a high level of autonomy from national political and diplomatic actors.[10] Therefore, Ambrosius and Henrich-Franke coined the term "epistemic expert regulation"[11] to describe how international standards were set within infrastructures. These standards were necessary to make the transnational circulation of people, goods and services possible.

Given the long-term fragilization of Europe after the First World War, some individuals and communities refocused their internationalism explicitly on Europe, developing what Schipper and Schot called "infrastructural Europeanism."[12] During the inter-war period, this vision – building Europe on infrastructures – clashed with or at least tried to go beyond all 'border builders' that tried, first and foremost, to build nations on infrastructures. "International-system builders" worked for more fluid and denser transnational connections, but with different visions of Europe – while some were pan-European, others focused on central Europe or Latin countries.[13] Grand plans flourished to fight under-employment and integrate Europe, at the same time, through electric, automobile or airmail networks, but all failed. National and imperial approaches prevailed. How did the Second World War reshuffle the deck in this respect?

Due to the fact that experts usually enjoyed long-lasting careers within the administrations, the organisations that they built turned out to be crisis-proof: both the Universal Postal Union and the International Telegraph (later on Telecommunication) Union resumed their work rapidly after the First and the Second World War. Co-operating on an international level for

---

9 Lagendijk, Vincent / Schot, Johan: "Technocratic Internationalism in the Interwar Years: Building Europe on Motorways and Electricity Networks", in: *Journal of Modern European History* 6 (2008), p. 196 –217, here p. 197.

10 Laborie, Léonard: *L'Europe mise en réseaux. La France et la coopération internationale dans les postes et les télécommunications (années 1850-années 1950)*, Bruxelles 2011.

11 Ambrosius, Gerold / Henrich-Franke, Christian: *Integration of Infrastructures in Europe in Historical Comparison*, New York 2016.

12 Schipper, Frank / Schot, Johan: "Infrastructural Europeanism, or the Project of Building Europe on Infrastructures: An Introduction", in: *History and Technology* 27 (2011), pp. 245 – 264.

13 Högselius / Kaijser/ van der Vleuten: Europe's Infrastructure, p. 40.

decades also led to solidified institutions, such as international congresses and study groups that were held regularly, and forged the personal and professional relationships between the experts.[14] Against this background, it seems reasonable to assume that the way of working together before and after the war did not change fundamentally during the war and the circles of agents remained extant as well.

While we often understand European integration as the process starting with the European Coal and Steel Community in 1952, the research on processes of infrastructure integration shows that these developments have to be put into context with the internationalist practices in the 19th century[15] as well as of the inter-war time.[16] Additionally, studies around the Nazi concepts of a "New Europe" underline that the term was conceptually rather vague,[17] which gave room for individual initiatives. This tendency was enhanced by the support for Italian-German projects at the beginning of Axis co-operation.[18] However, this Italian-German co-operation was often conflictual because both sides saw themselves as superior to the other.[19] The ideas to fill the term 'New Europe' were partially based on inter-war ideas of Europe, both on spatial elements (*Lebensraum*[20]) and organisational ones

14 Laborie: L'Europe mise en réseaux.

15 Henrich-Franke, Christian / Hiepel, Claudia / Türk, Henning / Thiemeyer, Guido (Hg.): *Grenzüberschreitende institutionalisierte Zusammenarbeit von der Antike bis in die Gegenwart. Strukturen und Prozesse*, Baden-Baden 2019; Thiemeyer, Guido: *Europäische Integration*, Köln 2010.

16 Schirman, Sylvain: *Quel ordre européen? De Versailles à la chute du IIIe Reich*, Paris 2006.

17 Mazower, Mark: *Hitler's Empire. Nazi Rule in Occupied Europe*, London 2008.

18 Fehlhaber, Nils: *Netzwerke der ‚Achse Berlin-Rom'. Die Zusammenarbeit faschistischer und nationalsozialistischer Führungseliten 1933 – 1943*, Köln 2019.

19 Fioravanzo, Monica: "Italian Fascism from a Transnational Perspective: The Debate on the New European Order (1930 – 1945)", in: Bauerkämper, Arnd / Rossoliński-Liebe, Grzegorz (eds.): *Fascism without Borders. Transnational Connections and Cooperation between Movements and Regimes in Europe from 1918 to 1945*, New York 2017, pp. 243 – 263.

20 Concept of the 'living space' in the East which provided grounds for the war in the East of Europe where this living space was supposed to be established for German settlers.

(*Mitteleuropa*,[21] International Paneuropean Movement[22]).[23] Elevating issues to a European level was seen as a tool to benefit national purposes – not only from the Italian and the German side but also from other Fascists in occupied countries. They supported (partially) the ideas for a united Europe of fascist states under Axis supremacy – similar to a European federal state – because this concept would have protected their nation from communist forces and provide at least some independence from dominating Nazi Germany or fascist Italy.[24] Thus, despite, or maybe due to, the fact that the "New Europe" was a mere propaganda term with no actual decided plan for the after-war Europe,[25] concrete projects were developed, for example, in the areas of culture,[26] social policy,[27] infrastructures[28] and youth.[29] In addition, groups were founded both in Italy and Germany whose aim it was specifically to spread fascist ideas among international organisations as well as make plans regarding which of those organisations should be upheld, replaced or terminated.[30]

Technocratic internationalism, with its focus on the political independence of experts and the different ideas of a fascist "New Europe", might seem, at first glance, contradictory, but as different scholars have pointed out, the two internationalisms could also be seen as two sides of the same

21 "Middle Europe": a concept that foresaw a deeper integration within central Europe with a strong German dominance.

22 Founded in 1923 under the leadership of Richard Nikolaus Coudenhove-Kalergi, the movement envisioned a unified European state.

23 Kletzin, Birgit: *Europa aus Rasse und Raum. Die nationalsozialistische Idee der Neuen Ordnung*, Münster 2000.

24 Grunert, Robert: *Der Europagedanke westeuropäischer faschistischer Bewegungen 1940 – 1945*, Schöningh 2012.

25 Bauer, Raimund: *The Construction of a National Socialist Europe During the Second World War: How the New Order Took Shape*, London 2020; Pohl, Dieter / Dafinger, Johannes (eds.): *A New Nationalist Europe Under Hitler: Concepts of Europe and Transnational Networks in the National Socialist Sphere of Influence, 1933 – 1945*, Routledge 2019.

26 Martin, Benjamin G.: *The Nazi-fascist New Order for European Culture*. Cambridge, Massachusetts 2016.

27 Kott, Sandrine / Patel, Kiran Klaus (eds.): *Nazism across Borders. The Social Policies of the Third Reich and Their Global Appeal*, Oxford 2018.

28 Henrich-Franke, Christian / Laborie, Léonard: "European Union by and for Communication Networks: Continuities and Discontinuities during the Second World War", in: *Comparativ* 28 (2018), pp. 82 – 100.

29 Fehlhaber, Nils: *Netzwerke der „Achse Berlin-Rom"*, Köln 2019.

30 Herren, Madeleine: "Fascist Internationalism", in: Sluga, Glenda / Clavin, Patricia (eds.): *Internationalisms. A Twentieth-century History*, Cambridge, United Kingdom, New York 2017, pp. 191 – 212

coin.[31] Van der Vleuten and Kaijser underline that National Socialists combined the idea of unifying Europe by building transnational infrastructure networks, that was on the rise in the 1930s, with the idea of a "New Europe."[32] Kaiser and Schot emphasise that technocrats supported the authoritarian regimes partially due to ideological overlaps and because they ensured faster processes.[33] All in all, the easy transit between different regimes by the experts "highlighted the ambivalence and pitfalls of the experts' preference for depoliticising policy-making."[34] The 'Comité consultatif international (for) Fernschreiben' was founded in the inter-war, reflected the Franco-German relations at that time, was realigned within the European Postal and Telecommunications Union (EPTU) and adapted to the post-war international relations in 1947. Thus, international co-operation in the area of infrastructures was not generally hindered by fascist regimes, but might even have been intensified. Understanding how actors, institutions, practices and knowledge travelled from the inter-war to the post-war through the war time is generally key for those who want to seize "the concrete nuts and bolts of cooperation and integration in Europe as much neglected carriers of continuity". In this book, we uncover what was mostly "covered up" at the time – not only continuities between war time and post-war co-operation, but also, already previously, continuities between pre-war and war time co-operation.[35] There are, thus, important links between the European integration projects in the Second World War and the post-war period. However, this does not mean, as Kaiser and Patel have rightly emphasised, that European integration was built on the debates and concepts surrounding the "New Europe". What is decisive is that, in addition to the continuities, the discontinuities in terms of structure, content and personnel are also worked out and analysed.

---

31 Herf, Jeffrey: *Reactionary Modernism. Technology, Culture, and Politics in Weimar and the Third Reich,* Cambridge, Massachusetts 1984.

32 van der Vleuten, Erik / Kaijser, Arne: *Networking Europe. Transnational Infrastructures and the Shaping of Europe. 1850 – 2000*, Sagamore Beach, Massachusetts 2006.

33 Kaiser, Wolfram / Patel, Kiran: "Continuity and Change in European Cooperation during the Twentieth Century", in: *Contemporary European History* 27 (2018), p. 165 – 182.

34 Kaiser / Schot: Writing the Rules, p. 74.

35 "When analysing such continuities at the level of knowledge, it is productive to distinguish between 'celebrated' and 'covered up' continuities. In some cases, actors and organisations invoked connections to legitimise their ends. In other cases continuities existed that actors were loath to discuss in public. This holds particularly true for continuities from wartime cooperation into the post-war era." Kaiser / Patel: Continuity and Change.

Regarding the history of Franco-German relations, the research interest has delved into questions of co-operation, collaboration, "accommodement" (accommodation) and resistance during the occupation of France by Nazi Germany[36]. When discussing the co-operation between the German and the French postal and telecommunications administration during World War II on the issue of the EPTU, Laborie focuses on the question whether the decisions taken could be a form of (passive) resistance or reluctance to collaborate by some high civil servants.[37] While the narrative of German-French relations during the Second World War is generally often one underlining the caesura the war meant in the relations – two hereditary enemies who started a reconciliation process after the war necessary for European integration and the European Union we know today – studies have also shown the impact that personal contacts during the war had on German-French reconciliation, for example, when it comes to the establishment of twin cities.[38]

Aim and Guiding Questions

This book, which is one result of the research project EUROPTT between the CNRS (French National Centre for Scientific Research) and the universities of Sorbonne, Düsseldorf and Siegen, has the aim of tackling the historiographical blind spot and filling part of the research desideratum regarding transnational co-operation in infrastructures during the Second World War.[39] By analysing the EPTU, founded in Vienna in 1942, and placing it in the broader framework of co-operation and conflict in infrastructure sectors in general, it sheds light on the years often simply seen as a break between the inter-war and post-war time. It examines how an international organisation led by the Axis powers functioned during a total war and looks at how inter-war processes shaped the war time co-operation. The end of the Second World War did not mean a complete change in international

36 Martens, Stefan / Vaïsse, Maurice (Hg.): *Frankreich und Deutschland im Krieg (November 1942 – Herbst 1944): Okkupation, Kollaboration, Résistance*, Paris 2000; Aglan, Ayla: *La France à l'envers: La guerre de Vichy (1940-1945)*, Paris 2020.

37 Laborie: L'Europe mise en réseaux.

38 Defrance, Corine u.a. (Hg.): *Wege der Verständigung zwischen Deutschen und Franzosen nach 1945*, Tübingen 2010.

39 Europtt (ANR- 16-FRAL-0013-01) was an ANR/DFG funded research project on 'Infrastructures, infrastructural cooperation and the continuity of European Integration: The European Postal and Telecommunication Union (1942 – 1944)'.

technocratic co-operation either, which is why the research project also attempts to discuss continuities and discontinuities in the postal services and telecommunications sector up until the 1960s. The EPTU was, on the one hand, part of the long-term development paths of technical co-operation and, on the other hand, a component of the political concepts of Europe. It reflects the long-term transformation of intergovernmental relations in Europe.

Against this background, this volume aims to supplement the common perspective on confrontation and collaboration during the Second World War with the dimensions of co-operation and integration in infrastructure sectors. In addition to the field of postal services and telecommunications, it also examines the extent to which these new dimensions can be found in other infrastructure sectors. It does not primarily address the Nazis' diverse infrastructural plans for the future of Europe. It focuses instead on the actual practices for maintaining and developing cross-border connections in continental Europe among Axis powers, occupied territories and neutral countries. Remarkably, since The Hague convention of 1907, neutral countries also defined themselves in terms of their ability to keep their telecommunication infrastructure connected with those of the belligerents.[40] By analysing co-operation in the field of infrastructures, this volume aims to provide a new element for a more precise understanding of infrastructure and European integration history as a whole.

Questions that all contributions raise both directly and indirectly are: What role did political, social, technical, economic, societal and similar reasons play in co-operation, non-co-operation and integration? What contents were discussed? Was there a German or Italian dominance? Did the Axis powers, Germany and Italy, co-operate? What role did war and foreign policy considerations play? Was it possible to separate technical co-operation from political goals?

This volume places a particular focus on Franco-German relations because of the key role these had for the history of Europe. The interplay of co-operation, collaboration and competition between the two states had proven to be a decisive engine of European integration since the 19th century. Hence the following questions: How did the tension between *de facto* co-operation/collaboration and *de iure* non-co-operation/confrontation develop? What role did the specific Franco-German constellation (Occupying forces, Vichy government) play in co-operation? What was the importance

40 Druelle-Korn, Clotilde: "Miserable Souls Who Lived without Infamy and without Paradise. Les neutres pendant la Grande Guerre", in: *Les Cahiers Sirice* 26 (2021), pp. 73 – 83.

of the French public administration, and what roles did the Vichy government and the German military administration play in France? Where did the boundary between co-operation and collaboration lie? What continuities and discontinuities existed in Franco-German co-operation before and after the war? Did German leaders try to contest the traditional French leadership role on the international stage?

Structure and Contributions to this Volume

This volume is structured along the lines of two main parts: one on 'postal services and telecommunications' and the other on 'inland transport'. Both parts contain a mix of chapters on institutional aspects of 'co-operation' within the different infrastructure sectors and shorter contributions which highlight particular aspects of infrastructural 'co-operation', such as actors and representation.

a) War Time and Postal Telecommunications

The first part of the volume has two focus areas. The first is on the EPTU itself as a newly found organisation during war time. It consists of two chapters on postal services (Sabrina Proschmann) and telecommunications (Valentine Aldebert). Both pay tribute to the particular wartime role of France and Germany, however, from different angles. Regarding postal services, it is asked whether the EPTU was a creation to promote German hegemony or if the pressure of path dependency and technocratic traditions led to an organisation without (geo-)political influence. Regarding telecommunications, the focus is on the role of the administration in occupied France, which was officially not part of the EPTU but at the insistence of Germany, participated in the organisation's work from 1943. Both chapters show that unambiguous assignments are not possible. Instead, there were signs of hegemony and path dependency in both cases, however, the EPTU hardly had a lasting effect on working routines. These chapters also show that the EPTU, as an international organisation, was not set once and for all. Though brief in time due to the fate of the war, it evolved along its own dynamics. The focus on organisations is supplemented by a contribution on the Swiss-based International Broadcasting Union (Christian Henrich-Franke), which was founded in the inter-war period to co-ordinate broadcasting and the use of broadcasting frequencies. The Union tried to continue 'objective operations' during war time under the protection of Swiss neutrality. However, it is shown that the Union did not succeed in maintaining a Pan-European approach to broadcasting co-operation due to war tensions, the importance of radio propaganda and the monitoring of radio transmissions. The inability to remain objective and neutral during the war greatly discredited the Union when it tried to restart its activities in June 1945.

The second focus is on key actors which, in one way or another, shaped or were shaped by the EPTU. The actors portrayed show how war time co-operation was embedded into long continuities of individual participation in international organisations and committees, such as the Universal Postal Union or the International Telecommunication Union. The three chapters on Giuseppe Gneme (Valentine Aldebert), Pierre Marzin (Pascal Griset) and Friedrich Risch/Helmut Bornemann (Sabrina Proschmann/Christian Henrich-Franke) discuss the personal motivations and mechanisms behind continuities and discontinuities in European postal and telecommunication co-operation.

The contributions on institutions and actors are supplemented by one on the representation of EPTU by postage stamps (Sabrina Proschmann). The stamps that were emitted by four postal administrations across Europe were quite different in style and motif. Remarkably, the EPTU failed to issue one common stamp for Europe due to financial or technical problems and the potentially lacking will to do so by almost all sides.

b) Comparison with Inland Transport Infrastructures

The second part of the volume offers a view on co-operation and non-co-operation in inland transport infrastructures. It starts with a contribution on the impact of the war on inland navigation on the Rhine (Guido Thiemeyer). The Central Commission for Navigation on the Rhine became inactive after Germany had invaded all riparian states and put the entire Rhine region under German control. German authorities were put into a position to unilaterally set new standards. However, the contribution demonstrates that the rules and standards of the Rhine commission were hardly changed by the Germans. This allowed for a number of continuities in the sector. A similar picture can be drawn for the canalisation of the Moselle as part of an improvement of inland navigation in the Rhine region (Martial Libera). Libera's contribution uses a diachronic approach to focus on German war time projects in order to explore continuities to earlier projects as well as to the realisation of the Moselle's canalisation in the 1960s. Nazi policy took its place in the longue durée of Moselle improvement projects, however, during the war it was a project of domination instead of co-operation among neighbouring countries. Central European rivers were less intensely used and integrated as transnational waterways than the Rhine (Jiří Janáč). Although the issues were the same when it came to the governance and regulations, the transnational cartelization of companies operating transport, and the material standardisation and connection through international canals. The rise of Germany as a leading power in the region already in 1938 signed the end of an international liberal regime born out of the First World War and the League of Nations, and the return to a form of governance closer to the one in place before 1919. The new regulatory framework combined with the strengthening of cartels served the war economy needs of Germany. Traffic on the Danube, the Oder and the Elbe indeed peaked during the war. Unsurprisingly, this revived projects to integrate further Central European rivers through river development and new connecting waterways. Czechoslovak experts were associated and actively supported this agenda. Neither the governance regime favouring riparian states and bilateral agreements, the taming of competition through deep cartelization nor the experts' support of large public works projects disappeared after Germany collapsed and was replaced by USSR as the dominant power in the region.

That the continued application of inter-war agreements by German authorities could even strengthen international co-ordination is discussed concerning the railways (Leonard Laborie). International pre-war railway agreements, such as the International Wagon Regulation about the international use of goods wagons in Europe, which were hardly altered, made cross-border traffic possible throughout the war. Wartime experiences not only kept the International Railway Union, which had formally suspended its activities, untouched but more than that fostered the coming into being of advanced projects, such as the European Freight Wagon Pool. On the other hand, the German-centred, century-old Verein Mitteleuropischer Eisenbahnverwaltungen (Association of Central European Railway Administrations) did not survive the war. From this point of view, the end of the war, not the war itself marked a rupture. Regarding motorways the developments were completely different. There was no active co-operation in the road sector and the inter-war congresses on European highways did not meet again during the war (Mathieu Flonneau). Motorways were a hotly debated topic at a national level even in war time. Motorways spread across Europe between 1935 and 1955 and with them, the European models for road traffic and techniques which were often inspired by German and Italian models. The war years made a decisive contribution to the development of the technical object that is the 'motorway', whose national, social, political and geopolitical impact should, under no circumstances, be obscured.

Advances of existing projects of co-operation and other institutional reforms were often as a consequence of war time experiences of key figures, such as the Dutch banker Karel van der Mandele (Martial Libera). Van der Mandele was the director of the Rotterdam Chamber of Commerce and Industry during the war, which was a challenging position at the interface of the city, the occupiers and the interest groups along the Rhine. Being shaped by the wartime experiences, van der Mandele stood up for functional reforms after the war. He had drawn the lesson that Europe had to be built from the bottom up by responsive economic actors that could produce results quickly. Therefore, he became the driving force behind the founding of the Rhine Union Chamber of Commerce.

Claire Aslangul-Rallo emphasises the key role of infrastructure projects in the sociotechnical imaginary and propaganda of German authorities in order to get support for their view of a "New Europe" (under German leadership). She zooms in on the reports on the actual or desired building of transnational infrastructure networks which were presented as 'European' achievements within the bimonthly magazine *Signal*. The magazine, which was launched in French in April 1940 and spread widely across Europe, served to legitimise the war effort and the occupation of Europe by painting the picture of a 'European Economic Community' that would drive exchange, prosperity and unity. It willingly placed the developments it portrayed in the continuity of a well-established international co-operation, reinterpreted as the fruit and prodrome of German technical and organisational leadership. By a singular cognitive inversion, some articles in the magazine gave the idea that the war was the world before 1939, and that political unity would allow this technical integration dynamic to finally give its full measure.

In sum, the book shows that the maintenance and development of transnational infrastructures were compatible with different visions and discourses supported by very diverse actors: the economic exploitation of the continent in favour of the Reich; the unity of a reborn Europe enlightened by the German torch; the pursuit of a practice of international co-operation, guided by the utility of standardization, for more efficient networks for the public; and the insertion of dominated countries into a semblance of an egalitarian multilateral structure.

Chapter I: Wartime Postal and Telecommunications

European Postal Services During the Second World War – German Hegemony vs. Technocratic Traditions

Sabrina Proschmann

Table of Content

1. Introduction

At the time of the German invasion of Poland in September 1939 and the official military beginning of the Second World War, the national postal and telecommunications administrations had been cooperating as part of a global organisation for six decades. The Universal Postal Union (UPU) was established in 1874 – the leading figure in founding the union was Heinrich von Stephan, a German postal expert.[1] The strength of the participating administrations' cooperation had already been tested by the First World War, but the postal experts nonetheless succeeded in protecting and restoring the UPU during times of great division in Europe.[2]

The Second World War foreshadowed by European postal relations; this is especially applicable to the relations between Germany and other

1 Sasse, Horst: *Der Weltpostverein. französischer und deutscher Text des Weltpostvertrages und anderer grundlegender Bestimmungen mit einer Einführung*, Metzner 1959, S. 11.

2 Laborie, Léonard: *L'Europe mise en réseaux. La France et la coopération internationale dans les postes et les télécommunications (années 1850 – années 1950),* Bruxelles 2011, p. 250.

administrations due to censorship issues. Germany began censoring foreign mail as early as 1933. Despite complaints of and fear among the *Reichspost* that this would cast a poor light on Germany among other administrations, censorship continued to be reported and the number of censorship cases rose.[3] The German postal administration started preparing for war in 1935 and the first tests of wartime protocol for the field and civil post took place in 1937.[4] Postal protection[5] was reinforced in "the time of tension"[6] before the war in September 1935.[7]

High politics found their way into the UPU's affairs during the Postal Union Congress in Buenos Aires in 1939. The question of representation for the annexed territories of Czechoslovakia and their continued recognition in the agreement of 1939 led to the refusal to sign and *de facto* exit of not only Germany but Italy, Spain and Hungary as well. The *Reichspost* did not favour this withdrawal but had no power to challenge the Führer's decision. To overcome this isolation within the UPU, in 1940 the *Reichspost* resolved to apply the conditions agreed upon in the 1939 congress in services with non-hostile countries. Despite the fact that German delegate Karl Ziegler reported that no political questions were discussed during the congress,[8] pre-war German aggressions influenced the discussions nevertheless.

The beginning of the war in military terms entailed a worsening of European postal relations and a further weakening of the UPU as well as other regional postal unions such as the Nordic Postal Union, which had to pause its activities between 1941 and 1946.[9] Repercussions of war for the UPU included limiting its services to member administrations only and

---

3 Ueberschär, Gerd R.: *Die Deutsche Reichspost 1933 – 1945. Eine politische Verwaltungsgeschichte* (Bd. 2), Berlin 1999, p. 201.

4 Bundesarchiv, Berlin-Lichterfelde, R470-154 and R4701-12132.

5 The postal protection was a service to ensure that the send items reached their goals unharmed.

6 Writer's own translation: „Spannungszeit". Bundesarchiv, Berlin-Lichterfelde, R4701-11161, Anweisung für den verstärkten Postschutz, p. 2.

7 Ebd.

8 Ueberschär: Die Deutsche Reichspost, p. 281 – 284.

9 Riksarkivet, Oslo, S-1342 Samferdselsdepartementet, 1. postadministrasjonskontor A, F Konvensjoner og overenskomster med utlandet, 1946 – 1948, F 0042.

censorship, prompting the office to request that its mailing activities become protected as diplomatic mail.[10]

Despite being restored after the First World War, traditional technocratic cooperation strategies and organisations, such as the UPU, were challenged by the fact that the Second World War was driven by National Socialist and fascist ideologies and that the Axis powers occupied large parts of Europe for certain periods of the war. This difficulty applied not just for the administrations of the occupied countries but for the German postal administration as well. The European Postal and Telecommunications Union (EPTU), founded in October 1942 in Vienna, is an example of the reaction to such a challenge. Despite multiple attempts, a European postal union had never been created before because numerous administrations, particularly the British administration, opposed it. One proponent of such a union in the 1930s, Karolý von Forster, served as the Hungarian delegate to the EPTU congress in 1942.[11]

The EPTU (1942 – 1945) was thus a first in European postal services, but it did not mark the beginning of international cooperation in the area of postal services. The Axis powers had prepared the union's founding intensively with bilateral agreements, a fully drafted agreement, and regulation proposals for both postal services and telecommunications. Delegates from 17 administrations were officially present at the congress in 1942, and 13 later signed the agreement and became members in April 1943 when the agreement came into force. The four other administrations were observers from Switzerland, Spain, Turkey and the Vatican. The 13 signatories were Germany, Italy, Norway, Denmark, Finland, the Netherlands, Slovakia, Hungary, Romania, San Marino, Albania, Croatia and Bulgaria.[12] The main question explored in this paper regarding the newly founded union is as follows: *Was the EPTU created to promote German hegemony in the European continent and to dictate the continent's postal rules, or did the pressure of path dependency and technocratic traditions lead to an organisation without (geo)political influence?*

In order to answer this question, the EPTU will be analysed from three perspectives: 1) the processes of cooperation, 2) the scope of standardisa-

---

10 PTT Archives, Bern, P-00C_0128_11, Expédition des documents de service par le bureau international aux Administrations de l'Union, 05.1943.

11 Laborie, Léonard: „Enveloping Europe. Plans and Practices in Postal Governance, 1929 – 1959", in: *Contemporary European History* 27 (2018), p. 305 –310.

12 Europäischer Postkongress, p. 10 – 103.

tion and 3) the use of hegemonic force by the German postal administration. Each section explores the ways in which the balance between the two influences (technocracy and politics) was renegotiated. The paper ends with a conclusion.

2. Processes of Cooperation

The new geopolitical situation, caused by the early wins of the Axis powers within Europe despite Mussolini's reluctance to join the war, gave Germany and Italy the opportunity to lay new grounds for PTT (Post, Telephone and Telegraph) cooperation and European postal services – at least within the boundaries of occupied and allied territories.

The postal administration of the Reich and particularly Dr Friedrich Risch, who served as the head of the foreign department within the *Reichspost*, worked continuously to conclude bilateral agreements with other European administrations. To do this, Risch and his colleagues had to convince the responsible parties of the idea of a European postal union in (at least) three other institutions: the German Foreign Ministry, the targeted postal administration and its respective government or foreign ministry. After an initial agreement between the Axis powers on 8 October 1941,[13] agreements with Bulgaria, Croatia, Denmark, Finland, Hungary, the Netherlands, Norway, Romania and Slovakia were signed and came into force between April and September 1942.[14] The success of the representatives of the *Reichspost* was mixed. Importantly, when it came to the abolition of the transit fee,[15] the other administrations – including the Italian administration – did not agree. In the beginning, only three out of nine administrations agreed to a complete abolition,[16] while a reduction of 50%

13 Bundesarchiv, Berlin-Lichterfelde, R4701-25935, Abkommen zwischen der Deutschen Reichpost und der Königlichen Italienischen Post- und Telegraphenverwaltung, 08.1941.

14 Bundesarchiv, Berlin-Lichterfelde, R4701-25935, Bilaterale Abkommen.

15 For example, when sending a letter from Copenhagen to Rome in 1942, the sending person would pay for the transport services provided by the Danish, German and Italian postal systems. Because Germany would neither be the country of origin nor the country of destination of the letter, it would be a transit country; thus, the fee that the German post would receive was called the transit fee.

16 Bundesarchiv, Berlin-Lichterfelde, R4701-25935, Bilaterale Abkommen.

was negotiated with all the other administrations.[17] In the end, agreements with Denmark and Finland were also adapted to abolish the transit fee,[18] which meant that five out of nine administrations had agreed upon it prior to the congress of 1942.

Cooperation during the congress itself seems to have been marked by continuities of the habitus of international postal conferences, such as the hoisting of every administration's national flags,[19] the occupation of the posts within the presidium and committees, the committee structure itself, regular meetings and their scheduling, references to the UPU and the financial contribution system to the international organisation.[20] All these aspects suggest an effort to present the EPTU as a simple regional union of the UPU and legitimised it not only to the other member administrations but also to the respective foreign offices[21] and administrations outside the union. For the newly founded organisation in the area of cultural policy, Benjamin Martin stated,

> Ironically, these institutions were built on the practices of the kind associated with precisely the internationalism that Nazis and fascists rejected. Founding multilateral institutions with regular conferences, subcommittees, and multi-language journals, Nazis and fascists deftly deployed what have been called *the mechanics of internationalism* for political ends antithetical to the internationalist spirit.[22]

This can easily be applied to the PTT as well. The key issue for the German *Reichspost* might have not been to change these mechanisms but rather to be in control of them.

The two delegates from the Swiss PTT administration both confirmed that their reception had been welcoming, but Hans Keller, the Swiss delegate for telecommunications, also reported that "despite all friendliness and form one had the feeling of an invisible power that steered the con-

17 Bundesarchiv, Berlin-Lichterfelde, R4701-25935, Abkommen zwischen der Deutschen Reichpost und der bulgarischen, ungarischen, kroatischen, und rumänischen Postverwaltung.

18 Bundesarchiv, Berlin-Lichterfelde, R4701-25935, Abkommen zwischen der Deutschen Reichpost und der norwegischen sowie dänischen Postverwaltung.

19 Politisches Archiv, Berlin, R106301, Bericht des Legationsrats Stahlberg, 20.10.1942, p. 2.

20 Europäischer Postkongress, p. 98 – 103.

21 The argument could have been that the EPTU was not a political union but a simple continuation of technocratic work.

22 Martin, Benjamin George: *The Nazi-fascist new order for European culture*, Cambridge, Massachusetts 2016, p. 6.

gress from the beginning to the end"[23] and that private conversations with other delegates that he had met before were difficult. Ernest Bonjour, the Swiss delegate for postal affairs, designated the bilateral agreements as the last barrier to joining the union: "If adhering to the new European postal order would cause hesitations within one administration or the other, they would have to be expressed before the conclusion of the bilateral accord".[24] This comment underlined the ambition of the *Reichspost* to create a new European postal regime on the basis of the changed geopolitical situation. Ernest Bonjour noted the comparatively short duration of the congress and the few discussions due to the intensive preparation by the *Reichspost.*[25] These hints within the reports of the Swiss delegates point to an important question: was the new European postal order mainly a German one?

In terms of the processes of cooperation, it is worth mentioning that some countries' administrations might not have been *de jure* part of the EPTU framework but were rather *de facto* participants and would thus constitute examples of *hidden integration*;[26] this was the case for Belgium and France as well as for Spain, Switzerland and Sweden to varying degrees.

France never officially joined the EPTU, but French officials felt adherence was imminent in May 1944.[27] In the report for May – June 1945, the military commander of Germany in France states that the French government had declared to apply the provisions of the EPTU agreement on the 8

23 Writer's own translation: „Trotz aller Freundlichkeit hatte man das Gefühl einer unsichtnaren Macht, die den Kongress von Anfang bis Ende beherrschte.", Archives des PTT, Berne, P-00C_0108_01, 1. Bericht über den europäischen Postkongress, 04.11.1942, p. 12.

24 Writer's own translation: „Si l'adhésion au nouvel ordre postal européen pouvait susciter des hésitations chez une administration ou chez l'autre, c'est avant la conclusion d'un accord bilatéral qu'elles devaient se faire jour." Archives des PTT, Berne, P-00C_0108_01, Congrès postal européen de Vienne, p. 1.

25 Archives des PTT, Berne, P-00C_0108_01, Congrès postal européen de Vienne, p. 2.

26 Misa, Thomas J. / Schot, Johan: „Introduction. Inventing Europe: Technology and the hidden integration of Europe", in: *History and Technology* 21 (1), pp. 1 – 19. DOI: 10.1080/07341510500037487, 2005.

27 Archives diplomatiques, La Courneuve, Vichy Guerre 245, p. 157, Ouvertures des relations postales entre l'Allemagne et le territoire français non-occupé.

June 1943,[28] which could be interpreted as France unofficially joining the union.

The Belgian administration was – like the French administration – first invited as an observer at the congress of 1942 but then was uninvited; this may have been because the head of the Belgian telecommunications administration declined the invitation, though the head of postal services had accepted.[29] The Belgian administration nevertheless signed a bilateral agreement with the *Reichspost* in December 1942 that contained the exact provisions of the EPTU agreement.[30] As such, from a German perspective, Belgium was part of the European postal area. However, from a Belgian point of view, there were simply favourable conditions for German-Belgian postal relations. Being part of the union therefore had the advantage that favourable (and equal) conditions were valid with a number of countries at once.

In the case of Spain and Switzerland, the *Reichspost* tried to sign a bilateral agreement but failed.[31] Both countries' administrations sent observers to the congress of 1942. The Spanish administration sent six delegates, while the Swiss sent two. Nonetheless, the two administrations remained outside of the union; it seems as though political arguments[32] were the decisive factor, even though both administrations also named more technical obstacles.[33] The *Reichspost* nevertheless maintained contact with the two administrations by continuing negotiations with them at least

---

28 Lagebericht April – Juni 1943 (MBF), AN, AJ 40/444, http://www.ihtp.cnrs.fr/prefets/fr/content/lagebericht-april-juni-1943-mbf (20.10.2019).

29 Politisches Archiv, Berlin, R106301, Kurier an den Reichsaußenminister, 08.10.1942.

30 Bundesarchiv, Berlin-Lichterfelde, R4701/25935, Abkommen zwischen der Deutschen Reichspost und der belgischen Postverwaltung, 09.12.1942.

31 Bundesarchiv, Berlin-Lichterfelde, R901/116970, Aufzeichnung Martius, 12.11.1943.

32 Political arguments included the ongoing war, the neutrality of Switzerland and the interests of Spain in South America rather than in Europe.

33 Technical arguments included loss of revenue due to the abolition of the transit fee and the non-entry of France that Spanish delegates cited as a hindrance. If France did not join the union, the transit fee between Spain and the rest of the EPTU would not be entirely abolished, leading to higher costs but also operational difficulties.

up until the beginning of 1944.[34] The *Reichspost* also informed the Swiss administration of developments within the EPTU and even extended an invitation to a conference planned for October 1944 in Vienna, but the Swiss administration declined.[35] Thus, though out of the EPTU formally, the Spanish and Swiss administrations remained connected to the project through the work of the *Reichspost.*

The Swedish PTT administration was invited to the congress in 1942 and serves as an example of an attempt at hidden cooperation. After careful discussions with the Swedish Foreign Ministry, which closely monitored what the Swiss administration would do,[36] the head of the Swedish postal administration declined to send any observers or experts to the conference, whereas the head of the telecommunications administration announced that it would send experts who were not official observers to the 1942 congress in Vienna,[37] which the German side refused.[38] The Swedish case thus also illustrates the rift between the PTT administrations and foreign ministries.

The *Deutsche Reichspost* aimed at integrating the PTT services through its representatives abroad or the *Armeefeldpostmeister.*[39] Their work was defined as building connections to the PTT administrations of other countries and reporting back information to the *Reichspost.* Representatives of the *Reichspost* were therefore part of the German diplomatic mission to other countries.[40] These representatives were also present during the congress of 1942.[41]

This kind of cooperation let to attempts of knowledge transfer, such as in the visit by a delegation of the Dutch postal administration in Germany from 24 November to 5 December 1942. In addition to dinners, cultural

34 Bundesarchiv, Berlin-Lichterfelde, R4701-11628 and Archives des PTT, Berne, T-00B_0148_09.

35 Archives des PTT, Berne, T-00B_136_02 and P-00C_0143_03.

36 Riksarkivet, Stockholm, UD 1920 års doss HP 3258, Kungl. Utrikes Departemente ang. postkonferens i Wien, 03.08.1942.

37 Riksarkivet, Stockholm, UD 1920 års doss HP 3258, Kungl. Utrikes Departemente ang. postkonferens i Wien.

38 Riksarkivet, Stockholm, UD 1920 års doss HP 3258, Söderblom an Chargé d'Affaires E. von Post, Berlin, 07.10.1942.

39 Depending on the status of occupation of the country.

40 Bundesarchiv, Berlin-Lichterfelde, R4701/13657, Richtlinien für die Leiter deutscher Abordnungen im Ausland, ohne Datum.

41 Europäischer Postkongress, p. 326.

events and meetings with the heads of the *Reichspost*, this visit also included appointments at post offices; training centres, such as the prestigious training centre Zeesen; and (recreational) establishments for the staff of the *Reichspost*.[42] Furthermore, the *Reichspost* concluded or offered help with concluding contracts for the delivery of PTT material to other countries, for example with the administrations of Romania[43] or Croatia[44].

Lastly, the role of foreign ministries within these processes of cooperation is noteworthy. Both in Germany as well as in Italy, the foreign ministries did not seem convinced of the idea to create a postal union in wartime.[45] Several times, the *Reichspost* and the German Foreign Ministry did not agree on certain elements of the project, such as flags, languages and/or the invitation of ministers. Similarly, it remained uncertain up until the end of September 1942 whether Mussolini would allow Minister of Transport Host Venturi to participate in the congress.[46]

Hence, European postal cooperation was embedded in a larger context of high politics, and conflicts and cooperation depended upon these factors. What is unquestionable is that all administrations – regardless of their belonging to a neutral, occupied or allied country – were or seemed interested in this kind of European postal cooperation[47] and its proclaimed benefits, and the fact that a war was raging at the same time sometimes appeared to have been of smaller importance. However, the war seems to have been the most important point for the foreign ministries, which might also partially explain the small scope of standardisation within the EPTU regarding postal services.

42 Nationaal Archief, Den Haag, 2.16.09.993, Verslag Reis naar Duitschland, 24.11. – 05.12.1942.

43 Bundesarchiv, Berlin-Lichterfelde, R901-112730, Junker an Reichwirtschaftsministerium, 08.07.1940.

44 Bundesarchiv, Berlin-Lichterfelde, R901-110878, Hudecezk an HaPol Iva 4465/42, 19.05.1942.

45 Politisches Archiv, Berlin, R60609, Bericht Wiehl, 15.07.1942, p. 3.

46 Politisches Archiv, Berlin, R106301, Telegramm Mackensen, 29.09.1942.

47 One can see for instance that the Swiss administration calculates the costs of joining the union. Archives des PTT, Berne, P-00C_0108_01, Bonjour an Generaldirektor der PTT, 27.03.1942.

3. Standardising Services in Times of Constraints

The administrations successfully concluded an agreement for the EPTU within three sessions, and the postal committee negotiated the provisions for postal services within the EPTU over four sessions.[48] As stated, the Swiss delegates justified attributed the speed with which agreements were made to the preparations made by the *Reichspost*, but another reason can be added, namely the limited scope of the agreements. Within this scope, however, the progress in terms of establishing a single European postal area was notable and remains – concerning the transit fee in particular – unparalleled up to today.

The postal service agreements included provisions for letters and postcards sent via land. The weight categories for letters were significantly enlarged[49] in comparison with the 20g steps that the UPU provisions foresaw.[50] Sea and air mail were initially excluded.[51] All the bilateral agreements that were concluded before the EPTU contained additional aspects of postal services, such as journals, printed material and business papers.[52] The whole division of packages and postal cheques was not mentioned in any of the negotiations;[53] there could be several explanations for this, including that a further cheapening of the services would have meant even higher financial losses for the administrations. Additionally, the time for discussions during the congress was very limited. It was thus important to focus on the more pressing aspects of the (German) standardisation agenda. The EPTU was intended to function fully in the post-war peacetime period when postal services would run without disruptions, which made the advantages of further standardisation questionable. On the other hand, this meant that Germany was further integrated into this postal network than the other countries – including Italy.

However, it does not seem uncommon to start with only a few standardised aspects. Since the creation of the UPU, the process of technocratic postal cooperation was built upon the idea of incrementally facilitating international communication. In a sense, this incremented approach repre-

48 Europäischer Postkongress 2013.
49 Up until 20g, 20g – 250g, 250 – 500g, 500g – 1000g.
50 Sasse: Der Weltpostverein, p. 19.
51 Europäischer Postkongress, p. 98 –103.
52 Bundesarchiv, Berlin-Lichterfelde, R4701-25935, Bilaterale Abkommen.
53 Europäischer Postkongress, p. 104 – 144.

sents the use of old strategies in new times. For example, the Danish delegate mentioned during negotiations that it would be desirable to wave the sea transit fees as well, but the Italian administration did not judge this to be financially practical; the president, Heinrich Poppe, asked almost immediately to restrict the discussion to land transit fees. The question of see transit fees could then be discussed in a later session of the permanent postal committee.[54]

The two crucial postal service successes of the *Reichspost* with the creation of this union were the new larger weight categories that were introduced and – even more importantly – the abolition of the transit fee for land post within the territory of the member administrations.[55] Both points had the potential to reduce the bureaucratic burden of the PTT administrations immensely and thus also reduced the staff needed, and they manifested two goals of the German postal administration ever since the creation of the UPU in the previous century.[56] The standardising was not supposed to stop after the congress in 1942 but should have been continued by the permanent committees.

The permanent postal committee met for the first and last time in Copenhagen in June 1943 to further work on the postal provisions of the EPTU. A total of 12 proposals to enlarge and specify the existing provisions were discussed.[57] Among other things, these proposals treated the extension of the weight levels up to 2,000g, inclusion of more postal services such as the transport of journals, extension of the abolition of the transit fee to sea mail, a maximum weight for journals and a system for dealing with insufficiently franked letters. The proposals came from Germany (3), Finland (1), Italy (5) and Croatia (3).[58] They were discussed in the order presented here. The latter eight proposals were – according to the report by undersecretary Risch – of practical and operational nature and were all either deferred or rejected. The German proposal concerning the extension of the weight levels for letters was accepted, augmenting the foreseen

---

54 Ibid., p. 126.

55 Ibid., p. 118.

56 Bundesarchiv, Berlin-Lichterfelde, R4701-11248, Vortrag auf der Gesamtsitzung des Reichspostministeriums von Oberpostrat Timm, 07.09.1940, S. 4 – 14.

57 Bundesarchiv, Berlin-Lichterfelde, R4701-25935, Vorschläge der Vereinsverwaltungen für die 1. Tagung des Europäischen Postausschusses (Ständiger Ausschuss), Kopenhagen, Juni 1943.

58 Bundesarchiv, Berlin-Lichterfelde, R4791-25935.

prices. The second proposal, which would have included journals, printed material, samples and mixed shipments, was generally accepted but deferred until various concerns, including legal concerns,[59] were addressed. The abolition of transit fees for sea mail was similarly accepted but deferred due to Italian opposition. The Finnish proposal to render correspondence between the administrations free of charge was accepted.[60] In total, two out of 12 proposals were accepted, while further decisions were postponed. Risch explained this outcome by referring to the administrations' wish not to differentiate the provisions too much "in order to give the administrations not yet belonging to the union the possibility to integrate into the coming reorganisation without difficulties".[61] By *reorganisation*, he probably alluded to the new order of Europe after the victory of the Nazi-Fascist Axis. One could argue that the outcome also might have been the expression of the heavy restrictions that the administrations faced due to the ongoing war, uncertainty about who would win the war and the lack of unity between the Axis powers. Indeed, Risch himself reported to Georg Martius[62] that the Germans "have to always take into consideration the sensitivity of Italy".[63] This sensitivity was likely also heightened by the Allies' victories in Italy and the country's subsequent division in September 1943. As the *Reichspost* internally claimed the obviousness of German leadership of the EPTU[64] from the beginning, the question is how German the union really was.

---

59 For instance, whether or not the provisions were in compliance with UPU rules.

60 Bundesarchiv, Berlin-Lichterfelde, R4901-116969, Bericht des Ministerialdirektors Risch über die Kopenhagener Tagung des Europäischen Postausschusses, 18.08.1943.

61 Writer's own translation: „um den heute noch nicht dem Verein angehörenden Verwaltungen die Möglichkeit zu bieten, sich ohne Schwierigkeiten in die kommende Neugestaltung einzugliedern". Bundesarchiv, Berlin-Lichterfelde, R4901-116969, Bericht des Ministerialdirektors Risch über die Kopenhagener Tagung des Europäischen Postausschusses, 18.08.1943, p. 3.

62 Martius was responsible for different international organisations, also for inland navigation, within the German Foreign Ministry.

63 Writer's own translation. Bundesarchiv: „immer auf die Empfindlichkeit Italiens Rücksicht nehmen müssen"., Berlin-Lichterfelde, R4901-116969, Risch to Martius, 09.04.1934, p. 2.

64 Bundesarchiv, Berlin-Lichterfelde, R4701-11248, Vortrag auf der Gesamtsitzung des Reichspostministeriums von Oberpostrat Timm, 07.09.1940, p. 17.

4. A European Postal Union – German Style?

There are several aspects that lead to the hypothesis that the EPTU might have been a German-European postal union, including the *constructed* line of continuity with Heinrich von Stephan, the integration of the EPTU into the *New Europe* discourse, the changing of long-standing international rules and the EPTU's use as a tool for different national administrations.

The frequent references to Heinrich von Stephan by different German actors[65] underline the *Reichspost*'s aim to establish a link between the UPU and the EPTU both for an inner-German as well as for an international audience. Von Stephan was credited with the creation of the UPU in 1874 and represented as a national hero. The EPTU symbolised the continuation of his work and the fulfilment of his dreams, which were the abolition of the transit fee and a unified postal area.[66] As such, the postal branch of the EPTU was, despite its international character, Germanised in order to fit into the National Socialist vision of German greatness. The line of argument surrounding the continuation of Heinrich von Stephan's work could be used as a legitimisation for other postal administrations: The idea that the same cooperation would be continued in a regional organisation might have been utilised to assuage fears of a National Socialist and fascist organisation that was less technocratic and more politically charged.

The political bent of the EPTU leads to the second point: whether or not the EPTU was integrated into the larger discourse of the *New Europe*. It must be noted that this was not one coherent discourse but rather a melting pot of different ideas of how to organise the future Europe that Adolf Hitler himself showed little interest in.[67] Nevertheless, the foundation of the EPTU may have been rhetorically linked to this vague concept. For instance, Postal Minister Wilhelm Ohnesorge did mention the fight against bolshevism in a letter inviting the Slovakian administration to bilateral ne-

---

65 cf. Bundesarchiv, Berlin-Lichterfelde, R4701/11248, Vortrag auf der Gesamtsitzung des RPM von Oberpostrat Dr. Timm; Bundesarchiv, Berlin-Lichterfelde, R4701/11263, Rede Dr. Risch über: „Gedanken zu einer Reform des Post- und Fernmeldewesens", S. 9 – 15; Risch even wrote a book about him after the war (Risch, Friedrich Adolf: *Heinrich von Stephan: die Idee der Weltpost*, Hamburg 1948).

66 Sasse: Der Weltpostverein, p. 11.

67 Kletzin, Birgit: *Europa aus Rasse und Raum. Die nationalsozialistische Idee der Neuen Ordnung*, Münster 2000, p. 5 – 10.

gotiations prior to the congress in 1942.[68] The opening speeches of the conference by Ohnesorge and Venturi underlined the intention of creating ever-closer cooperation between the European PTT administrations that would eventually lead to a united continent.[69] If Ohnesorge remained more vague about the connection between the war and the foundation of a European postal union, Venturi explicitly linked them in his speech: "This congress, the aim of which is the organisation of European PTT services, is another proof of our certainty regarding the final result of the tremendous conflict that currently takes place".[70] The vagueness of the German postal minister seems to have been a strategy. In internal documents and correspondence, the responsible people in the *Reichspost* were more direct about certain objectives and the political aspects of the union. This might have been a strategy to gain domestic support but leaves a question mark as to which approach reflected the real intentions. For example, in a letter to Hitler, Ohnesorge justified the need for a European Postal Union by arguing that it would provide the means to economically exploit occupied countries.[71] He further stated that the exact design of the union depended upon the political reorganisation of Europe after the war.[72] The idea of said reorganisation can also be identified in some organisational aspects of the newly founded union.

Within the EPTU, long-standing international rules concerning the official language, reference currency and the location of an official office were changed. French had been the international language not just in the UPU but in other international organisations as well. Language is power, and the change from French to German and Italian as official languages of an international union is significant because it represents the translation of a hegemonic status into the institutions of the EPTU. It is also important to

---

68 Bundesarchiv, Berlin-Lichterfelde, R4701-11627, Der Reichpostminister an das Ministerium für Verkehr und öffentliche Arbeiten, Postverwaltung, 03.03.1942.

69 Europäischer Postkongress, p. 12 – 20.

70 Writer's own translation: „Dieser Kongreß, dessen Ziel die Organisirerung der europäischen Post-, Telegraphen- und Fernsprechdienst ist, ist ein weiterer Beweis unserer Gewißheit in Bezug auf das Endergebnis des ungeheuren Konflikts, der sich gegenwärtig abspielt", Europäischer Postkongress 2013, p. 16.

71 Bundesarchiv, Berlin-Lichterfelde, R4701-11200, Reichspostminister an den Führer des Großdeutschen Reichs, 21.06.1941. He mentions more technocratic arguments and a union's possible contribution to international understanding as well.

72 Ibid.

mention that the original draft of the treaty did not include Italian as an official language – the German Foreign Ministry in cooperation with its Italian counterpart and the Italian PTT administration lobbied successfully to change this in order to show full parity between the Axis powers during the congress.[73] However, the language spoken during the negotiations seems to have been predominantly German.[74]

Similarly to the change in official language, the reference currency was changed from French gold francs to the *Reichsmark*.[75] Concerning the choice of currency, inequality between Germany and Italy again emerged and appears to have been consistent throughout the different institutions of the EPTU. The French PTT administration together with other French ministries tried to fight against this deprivation of international standing and power. "an agreement was made [between the French Finance Ministry and the French PTT administration] about the necessity of keeping the gold francs as reference currency".[76]

The UPU had its office in Berne,[77] Switzerland, a politically neutral and comparatively small country. This was different in the case of the EPTU: the choice of Vienna with an office in a building of the *Reichspost* (thus under the supervision of the *Reichspost*)[78] represented a power grab by Germany. Original plans even foresaw the office in Berlin.[79] The two-man team of the official union office was staffed by German and Italian employees, which only reinforced the hierarchies within the union.

Given all of the points presented thus far, the idea that the first-ever European postal union was heavily shaped by German hegemony and thinking seems justifiable. However, in addition to contextual and institutional aspects, the EPTU also needs to be analysed from the perspective of a

---

73 Politisches Archiv, Berlin, R106301, Aufzeichnung Bericht des Legationsrats Stahlberg, 20.10.1942, p. 1.

74 Ibid.

75 Europäischer Postkongress, p. 314.

76 Writer's own translation: „Un accord se réalisait sur la nécessité de maintenir coûte que coûte le franc-or comme monnaie d'étalon". Archives nationales, Pierrefitte, 19870773/33, Historique des pourparlers concernant la Conférence de Vienne, p. 5.

77 Sasse: Der Welpostverein, p. 12.

78 Europäischer Postkongress, p. 101.

79 Bundesarchiv, Berlin-Lichterfelde, R4701-11248, Vortrag auf der Gesamtsitzung des Reichspostministeriums von Oberpostrat Timm, 07.09.1940, p. 17.

day-to-day war situation: what advantages did the EPTU bring to the different member administrations in this particular moment of World War II?

Starting again with the German point of view, the EPTU presented a possible solution to deal with loss of staff resulting from military mobilisation that could not be compensated by foreign PTT workers in Germany.[80] If one did not have to weigh every letter due to the larger weight categories agreed upon in 1942, it promised a more efficient service despite the reduction of staff. Additionally, territorial wins meant an enlarged area of responsibility for the *Reichspost*, ergo additional work that the administration needed to cope with as well.[81] Against this background, the EPTU can be interpreted as a tool for the facilitation of everyday postal services.

Furthermore, the EPTU can be understood as a tool for propaganda. Not only could the unity of the Axis powers be presented to the outside,[82] but the EPTU could also be used as an illustration of how the *New Europe* would look. The *Reichspost* used both stamps to circulate the news of the foundation of the EPTU[83] as well as its own journal to present a unified postal Europe to the outside.[84] The German administration even planned the publication of two new and multilingual journals, *The European Post* and *Wire and Ether*, in order to integrate the PTT administrations even more. Due to the lack of paper because of the war, these plans had to be stopped.[85]

From the perspective of other European PTT administrations, the EPTU could be viewed as a tool to improve their own particular situations. The Danish government had chosen a politics of cooperation to appease the German occupiers,[86] and their cooperation within the EPTU fits into this

---

80 Ueberschär: Die deutsche Reichspost, p. 302.

81 Ibid, p. 296.

82 Politisches Archiv, Berlin, R106301, Aufzeichnung Bericht des Legationsrats Stahlberg, 20.10.1942, p. 1.

83 Bundesarchiv, Berlin-Lichterfelde, R4701/11445, Bulletin No.1 du Bureau International de l'UPU, 16.01.1.942.

84 For example: Ohne Verfasser: Der Erste Europäische Postkongress und seine Ergebnisse, in Postarchiv: Zeitschrift für das gesamte Post- und Fernmeldewesen, 70 (1941/1942), pp. 468ff.

85 Bundesarchiv, Berlin-Lichterfelde, R4701/13438.

86 Lund, Joachim: „Denmark and the 'European New Order' 1940 – 1942“, in: *Contemporary European History* 13 (3), p. 305 – 321. DOI: 10.1017/S0960777304001742, 2004, p. 320.

strategy. The Norwegian administration used the foundation of the EPTU for state-building or rather to legitimise their new leader, Vidkun Quisling. A stamp showing his head next to the motive of the first stamp ever emitted by a Norwegian state[87] was published to commemorate the congress in 1942. However, despite the heading "European Postal Union",[88] this stamp has virtually no connection to the PTT sector or any idea of Europe. Rather, it seems that Norwegian membership in the EPTU was used to try to convince the Norwegian public of the benefits of the new leadership. With Quisling, Norway would have a place in the *New Europe*.

The French PTT administration tried to eliminate the demarcation line that divided the territory of France and thus also the French postal services in two. In July 1943, when discussing the possibility of a French entry into the EPTU, the director of postal services within the French PTT administration, M. Moignet, argued: "It would be otherwise not understandable if facilitations were introduced for interstate services, while the exchange of messages within the French territory would be subject to the strongest obstruction in the area of inner French service".[89] One can detect the use of the EPTU as an argument to revise the condition of postal services under German occupation.

These examples demonstrate that while the EPTU was a useful tool for the *Reichspost*, other PTT administrations utilised it as well to improve their postal services in wartime despite the first impression that the EPTU was mainly a German construction, at least for the field of postal services. Nevertheless, their room for manoeuvring was limited, and every improvement had the price of integrating the administrations more deeply into a European postal union that was heavily dominated by representatives of a National Socialist *Reichspostministerium*.

---

87 Lion with a double paw.

88 Writer's own translation, „Europeisk Postforening". Riksarkivet, Oslo, Postens sentralledelse, Fa-008, 309-310 Postforening, Merknader, not dated.

89 Writer's own translation: „Es wäre andernfalls nicht zu verstehen, wenn Erleichterungen für den zwischenstaatlichen Dienst eingeführt werden sollen, während andererseits im Bereich des inneren französischen Dienstes der Nachrichtenaustausch innerhalb des französischen Gebiets schwersten Behinderungen unterworfen ist.". Bundesarchiv, Berlin-Lichterfelde, R4701-11618, Niederschrift über die Eröffnungssitzung der deutsch-französischen Besprechung am 20. Juli 1943 im Reichspostministerium zu Berlin, p. 2.

5. Conclusion

In summary, the footprint of the wartime experience in postal services cannot be described in a simple way. It bears witness to hegemony but also the agency of occupied countries' administrations, to continuities and discontinuities in technocratic postal cooperation, to Axis powers whose cooperation was conflictual because the foreign ministries and postal administrations did not always work hand in hand, and to big achievements in the standardisation of European postal infrastructure and yet strong constraints due to the war. The two poles described in the introduction – an organisation dominated by Germany or an apolitical, technocratic one – were not necessarily opposites but rather were often two sides of the same coin. After all, German interests and technocratic ideals overlapped regarding certain issues, such as the cheapening of international postal services by abolishing the transit fee.

It is difficult to define what remained of the EPTU after the war. The idea to create another regional union was not buried with the end of the Nazi dictatorship. In fact, multiple plans arose in the 1950s within different frameworks, such as the Council of Europe and the European Coal and Steel Community.[90] Here, Hans Schuberth's – the first Western German postal minister – strong engagement in the creation of a new union in the beginning of the 1950s is interesting: Dr Friedrich Reiss was responsible for foreign affairs in Schuberth's ministry.[91] Dr Reiss had worked in the foreign department of Dr Friedrich Risch during the Second World War.[92] Though Schuberth's plans failed, the end of the 1950s saw the creation of two European PTT unions. In the Eastern Bloc, the Organisation of Cooperation between the Socialist Countries in the Field of Postal Services and Telecommunications was founded in 1958.[93] In the Western Bloc, the Eu-

---

90 Laborie: Europe mise en réseaux, S. 347 – 367.

91 Bundesarchiv, Sankt Augustin, B257/ORG4, Organisationsplan des Bundesministeriums für das Post- und Fernmeldewesen, 01.08.1951.

92 Bundesarchiv, Berlin-Lichterfelde, R4701/11256, Geschäftsplan des Reichspostministeriums, Abteilung Min-A, 04.1942.

93 Henrich-Franke, Christian: „Die Gründung europäischer Infrastrukturorganisationen im Ost/West-Vergleich: die PTT-Organisationen OSS und CEPT", in: Ambrosius Gerold / Neutsch, Cornelius / Henrich-Franke, Christian (eds.): *Internationale Politik und Integration europäischer Infrastrukturen in Geschichte und Gegenwart*, 1. Auflage, Baden-Baden 2010, S. 113 – 142.

ropean Conference of Postal and Telecommunications Administrations (CEPT) was created in 1959. Though the members of the CEPT underlined their technocratic traditions and continued working in similar structures as the pre-war experts had done,[94] the very fact that two organisations were founded and that the UPU had a clause that new members needed to be approved by a two-thirds majority[95] and the CEPT had a waiting period before accepting new members[96] shows that the political surroundings had gained significant influence international postal cooperation. However, this development did not start after the Second World War but during it.

6. *References*

Benz, Andreas: *Integration von Infrastrukturen in Europa im historischen Vergleich.* Band 3. Post, Baden-Baden 2013.

Europäischer Postkongress. Wien 1942; Original-Nachdruck zur postgeschichtlichen Forschung in deutscher (ohne italienische) Sprache = Congresso Postale Europeo (2013). Lizensierte ed., [Nachdr.] der Ausg., Berlin, Reichsdr., 1942. Berlin-Schönefeld: Morgana-Ed (Moderne Postgeschichte, GG 77).

Henrich-Franke, Christian: „Die Gründung europäischer Infrastrukturorganisationen im Ost/West-Vergleich: die PTT-Organisationen OSS und CEPT", in: Ambrosius Gerold / Neutsch, Cornelius / Henrich-Franke, Christian (eds.): *Internationale Politik und Integration europäischer Infrastrukturen in Geschichte und Gegenwart*, 1. Auflage, Baden-Baden 2010, S. 113 – 142.

Kletzin, Birgit: *Europa aus Rasse und Raum. Die nationalsozialistische Idee der Neuen Ordnung*, Münster 2000.

Laborie, Léonard: *L'Europe mise en réseaux. La France et la coopération internationale dans les postes et les télécommunications (années 1850 – années 1950),* Bruxelles 2011.

Ueberschär, Gerd R.: *Die Deutsche Reichspost 1933 – 1945. Eine politische Verwaltungsgeschichte* (Bd. 2), Berlin 1999.

94 Laborie: L'Europe, pp. 378 – 381; Benz: Integration, p. 197.

95 Sasse: Weltpostverein, p. 26.

96 Amtsblatt des Bundesministers für das Post- und Fernmeldewesen 1960 (5), Nr.6/1960 Europäische Konferenz der Verwaltungen für das Post und Fernmeldewesen, p. 22.

Lund, Joachim: „Denmark and the 'European New Order' 1940 – 1942", in: *Contemporary European History* 13 (3), p. 305 – 321. DOI: 10.1017/S0960777304001742, 2004.

Martin, Benjamin George: *The Nazi-fascist new order for European culture*, Cambridge, Massachusetts 2016.

Misa, Thomas J. / Schot, Johan: „Introduction. Inventing Europe: Technology and the hidden integration of Europe", in: *History and Technology* 21 (1), pp. 1 – 19. DOI: 10.1080/07341510500037487, 2005.

Sasse, Horst: *Der Weltpostverein. französischer und deutscher Text des Weltpostvertrages und anderer grundlegender Bestimmungen mit einer Einführung*, Metzner 1959.

“Cooperate!” – The Occupied French Administration, European Telecommunications and War: A Fragile Balance

Valentine Aldebert

Table of Content

1. Introduction

“We know [...] that the PTT Administration dragged things out and raised objections, and that in the end, when the Germans left, the Convention had not yet been applied.”[1] This statement was made by the French historian André Paul while reviewing the wartime relations between the French PTT administration and German occupying forces. In the years following the war, France’s official position was to minimize its participation in the

---

1 „[...] Nous savons d’autre part, que l'Administration des PTT fit traîner les choses en longueur, suscita des objections, et que finalement, au départ des Allemands, la Convention n'avait pas encore été appliquée“, in: Paul, André (ed.): *Histoire des PTT pendant la Deuxième Guerre mondiale*, p. 264. Paul was a retired history professor charged with writing a history of the PTT by the War History Committee, returned to this idea after the war.

European Postal and Telecommunications Union (EPTU),[2] and to show a united front despite the multiple positions the French administration held with respect to this organisation. One may nevertheless ask whether the situation was so clear-cut.

France was first invited to participate in the founding congress of the EPTU[3] in Vienna (12-24 October 1942), but was turned down by the *Reichspostministerium*[4] a month before the event in September 1942 (due to France's continuous hesitation). In fact, during the EPTU's last days (1944-1945), France apparently had not applied its agreements—in spite of Germany's follow-ups[5]—as the available documentation mentions either refusals or delays. However, France was no longer marginalized in 1943 when, at Germany's insistence, it participated in two working groups on telecommunications, to the detriment of the Italian administration (which was nevertheless a founding member of EPTU). The interest of studying the EPTU through the prism of a non-signatory state is to understand the interrelationships between the organisation and third parties, namely the dynamics that bear witness to the organisation's constant transformation, which is the main topic of our chapter.

The EPTU was a postal and telecommunications organisation (originally German-Italian) ideologically defined by the *Reichspostministerium* — notably by the Ministerial Director Friedrich Risch (head of the Department of Foreign and Colonial Affairs at the *Reichspostministerium*) — as having a new and broad unifying role in Europe. During the EPTU's developmental phase (1942-1943), the postal dimension dominated the propaganda surrounding this Union (often referred to as the "European Postal Union"), and served as the framework for defining it. In fact, from 1942 onward the EPTU's telecommunications side was seemingly less marked ideologically, or at least symbolically (EPTU propaganda focused less on telecom than on the postal sector). Telecommunications experts sought to continue technical discussions at meetings by continuing the work of the

---

2 In German *Europäische Post- und Fernmeldeverein.*

3 See the contribution by Sabrina Proschmann in this volume.

4 The German Post Ministry.

5 "The German authorities returned to the charge [...] General Von Stulpnagel unofficially insisted to the French Government that France's accession to the European Postal Union be given as soon as possible [...]", Archives Nationales, Pierrefitte-sur-Seine, 19960439/8. Undated.

former pre-war advisory committees[6], but also moving toward harmonizing telecommunications services (by making tariffs homogenous).

Most of the negotiations between France and Germany were conducted in the field of telecommunications, seemingly leading to "a broad German-French agreement on all technical issues."[7] In reality, the talks concerning France's entry into the EPTU and the development of European telecommunications would always be tinged with ambiguity, a fact that can be explained by the pre-war relationship between the French and German PTT administrations.[8] Following the First World War, the French administration chose to rely on American industry to develop its telecommunications service, giving birth in 1920 to a French-American industrial consortium (*Les Lignes télégraphiques et téléphoniques*). At the same time, a preliminary technical committee for international telephony in Europe was created in 1923, driven by the French Ministry of PTT. This committee refused the participation of German experts, and promoted the American Bell standards on the European scale. Although German experts were invited in 1924 to join the CCIF (*Comité Consultatif International des Communications Téléphoniques*, headed by the Frenchman Georges Valensi until 1956), it proved impossible to form a French-German technical alliance on the European continent. Despite these setbacks, Germany's interest[9] in involving French experts in this organisation did not wane with WWII. France's entry in the EPTU would help legitimize this Union,

---

6 *Comité Consultatif International Téléphonique* (CCIF), *Comité Consultatif International Télégraphique* (CCIT), *Comité Consultatif International de Radio* (CCIR). See also note 40.

7 Bundesarchiv, Berlin-Lichterfelde, R4701/12286 Band 2, Letter (probably from Friedrich Risch) to the Federal Foreign Office, to the attention of (Georg) Martius (Chief of Transports Division, Department of Economic Policy at the Ministry of Foreign Affairs), Berlin, 16.09.1943. The letter concerns the meeting of Committee 2 in Vienna during September 1943.

8 Henrich-Franke, Christian / Laborie, Léonard: "Technology taking over diplomacy? The 'Comité consultatif international (for) Fernschreiben' (CCIF) and its relationship to the ITU in the early history of telephone standardization, 1923 – 1947" in: Balbi, Gabriele / Fickers, Andreas (ed.): *History of the International Telecommunication Union*, Berlin 2020, p. 215 – 242.

9 In September 1942, Armeefeldpostmeister Müller considered "the presence of French delegates to be indispensable", Archives Nationales, Pierrefitte-sur-Seine, 19960439/8, Letter of the Services of the Armistice to the General Secretary of the Posts, Telegraphs and Telephones (Cabinet), 05.09.1942.

a symbolic aspect that worked in Germany's favour. One could also imagine that Germany wanted to ally itself with France in the technical field of telecommunications in order to counter Anglo-American domination.

To give an account of the dynamics surrounding the EPTU, I will first focus on EPTU activity in the field of telecommunications, and then analyse the interactions between French telecommunications experts and EPTU members. The central question will be the meaning of European cooperation during the war? I will discuss the EPTU's German-Italian origin in order to better understand its bias toward telecommunications. I will also analyse the position of telecommunications experts in relation to the EPTU, in an effort to identify the continuities and discontinuities with techno-diplomacy. I will then take a closer look at the French case, as well as the issue of European cooperation in the field of telecommunications. Finally, I will conclude with a study of the ultimate deadlock between the EPTU and the French PTT administration.

2. *The EPTU, a German-Italian Project?*

While the EPTU had a European focus[10], its institutional origin was indeed German-Italian, as it emerged from German-Italian postal[11] and telegraphic arrangements[12] signed in Rome on 8 October 1941. The telegraphic arrangement was part of a special agreement[13] between Germany (*Deutsche Reichspost*) and Italy (*Amministrazione delle Poste e dei Telegrafi*) that had been in force since 1 January 1939. These agreements concluded before October 1941 were the logical continuation of negotiations carried out earlier, for instance during meetings held in Bolzano on 30 November 1940 and in Munich on 16-18 January 1941 between Italian[14] and German[15] delegations. At the outset, each party seemingly gave

10 "The network of Universal Postal Union and International Telecommunication Union services is still far too large for a relatively small Europe", Risch, Friedrich: "Probleme und Ziele eines Europäischen Postvereins", in: *Postarchiv* 70 (1942), p. 81 – 103.

11 Entry into force on 1 January 1942.

12 Entry into force after activation of the international Brennero telegraph cable.

13 *Poste e Telecomunicazioni* 5 (1942), p. 137 – 138.

14 Dr. Bleiner, Dr. Capanna, Dr. Albanese, Dr. Ing. Baldini, Dr. Vasio, and Dr. Ing. Pepe.

importance to telecommunications in this new European project. A general meeting of the *Reichspostministerium* was held on 9 September 1940, with the presentation of a programme ascribing the *Reichspost* a central and pioneering role in the new construction of Europe. Emphasis was placed on creating a "European Information Association,"[16] as well as the role of the *Reichspostforschungsanstalt* (Research Institute) and the *Reichspostzentralamt* (Head office) as future "training and research centres for global information technology, and hence as the centre of the European telecommunications system."[17] On the Italian side, the decennia of Constanzo Ciano[18] (Italian Admiral), which lasted from 1924-1934 under his Ministry, saw a profound reorganisation of telecommunications. Italy's entry into the war in June 1940 reinforced its interest in developing telecommunications. The Italian perception of the EPTU after the congress is of interest: in December 1942, the Italian engineer Giuseppe Gneme indicated that the initial German project only mentioned a European Postal Union, but that in the Italian proposal, this concept was abandoned in favour of including telecommunications within this European project.[19] Was the *Reichspostministerium* less involved in telecommunications during the development phase of the EPTU (1942-1943)? Was there a decline in interest resulting from too many constraints? In any event, the German-Italian axis clearly materialized in the EPTU as early as 1941.

At least half of the participants at the Munich meeting (January 1941) were experts who had participated in the pre-war meetings of the Consultative Committees for Telecommunications.[20] Most of them therefore had broad experience in the technical telecommunications problems of the

15 Dr. Jaeger, Gladenbeck, Ehlers, and Bornermann.

16 „Um alle diese Ziele zu erreichen, empfahl Flanze mit Billigung Ohnesorges die Bildung eines neuen europaischer Nachrichtenvereins, der auf dem Kontinent an die Stelle des Weltnachrichtenvereins treten solle […]" in: Ueberschär, Gerd: *Die Deutsche Reichspost 1933 – 1945. Eine politische Verwaltungsgeschichte, Band II: 1939-1945*, Berlin 1999, p. 161.

17 Ibid.

18 Also the father of Galeazzo Ciano, who became the Minister of Foreign Affairs.

19 Gneme, Giuseppe: "Il Congresso europeo postale e delle telecomunicazioni di Vienna (12 – 24 ottobre 1942)", in: *Poste e Telecomunicazioni* 12 (1942), p. 317 – 328.

20 CCIF (*Comité consultatif international téléphonique*), CCIT (*Comité consultatif international télégraphique*), and CCIR (*Comité consultatif international des radiocommunications*).

time, and knew each other very well. This meeting of technicians reflected the field's importance for the Ministries of Foreign Affairs of these two countries, as they approved the possible participation of other European countries in the future Vienna Congress.[21] What's more, validation was required by the supreme command of the German armed forces, the OKW (*Oberkommando der Wehrmacht*): "The OKW is requested to agree to the foundation of the working group."[22] The 1941 meetings were therefore already politicized, or were at least under the control of Foreign Affairs.

Resolving the technical problems inherent in telecommunications was discussed immediately. This decision was quickly followed by the adoption of German and Italian as the official languages for the 1942 Congress. The choice of these two languages would have a profound effect on the EPTU and its relationship with certain PTT administrations, such as the French administration, which clearly viewed this as a mark of Axis dominance. The following excerpt shows that this idea was also present with *Armeefeldpostmeister*[23] Müller in Paris, during his conversation with General Girodet, head of the French Delegation for Transmissions:

> At the end of this meeting, Colonel Dr. Müller gave me the attached copy of the volume printed in Berlin, in German and Italian, to report on the progress of the Congress and the various provisions adopted by the participating States. I did not fail to point out to the Armeefeldpostmeister that this document, written in German and Italian only, did not include a French text, which is a most regrettable innovation. To a remark that it was an agreement between the Axis Powers, I replied that the organisers of the Congress had aimed to go further than an Italian-German agreement, since they were inviting all of the States of Europe to adhere to the provisions agreed in Vienna between the participating countries.[24]

---

21 "However, for the countries listed below b) [Denmark, Finland, the Netherlands, Norway, Portugal, Russia, Spain, Switzerland, Vatican City], the approval of the two ministries for foreign affairs remains to be obtained", Bundesarchiv, Berlin-Lichterfelde, R4701/12284.

22 Bundesarchiv, Berlin-Lichterfelde, R4701/12284, 12.09.1941.

23 The direct intermediary between the postal services of the occupied country and the German administration. He was a postal commissioner of the German Reichspost seconded to a German mission abroad and subrogated to the Foreign Affairs Department of the Reichspostministerium (headed by Risch). See also note 45.

24 Archives Nationales, Pierrefitte-sur-Seine, 19960439/8, L'Inspecteur Général Girodet, Chef de la Délégation française pour les transmissions auprès du *Militärbefehlshaber* en France à M. le Secrétaire Général des PTT, 16.06.1943.

This German-Italian dimension was also present at another preparatory meeting, namely a visit by the Italian delegation[25] to Berlin, Munich, and Vienna on from 8 – 14 January 1942, which included the Minister of Communications, Giovanni Host-Venturi. A number of visits to post offices and telegraph offices were organised. Of the fifteen members[26] of the Italian delegation from January 1942, made up of PTT experts and Foreign Affairs representatives, more than half[27] were present in Vienna in October 1942. This shows a real willingness on the part of the Italian delegation, as well as a permanence in its structure. The German-Italian foundations for the Congress of Vienna had thus been established.

However, there are elements that call this bilateral dynamic into question. Two months before the start of the Congress, there was apparent discordance on the Italian side:

> As was also indicated to the Reich Foreign Minister, a discussion was to take place on 20 July in Cortina between Ministerial Director Risch and the Director General of the Italian Post Office Pession, on the further handling of the problem of the European Postal Union [...] However, on the evening of 14 July, the Reich Ministry of Posts was informed by Rome that the conference could not take place in Cortina because the Italian Ministry of Foreign Affairs was causing difficulties.[28]

The Italian Minister of Communications, Giovanni Host-Venturi, was hindered in his work by Foreign Minister Galeazzo Ciano, Mussolini's son-in-law. Ciano seemed very reluctant to the idea of this "European" union led by Germany, and was undoubtedly influenced by his scepticism toward Germany. The German Post Office Minister Wilhelm Ohnesorge, who was a personal friend of the Führer, did not have similar problems. German preponderance was demonstrated in the preliminary phase by the fact that the majority of the arrangements prior to the Vienna agreements

25 Half of the 1941 delegation took part in the January 1942 trip, including Dr. Bleiner, Dr. Capanna, and Dr. Vasio.

26 The members were Giovanni Host-Venturi, Giuseppe Pession, Giuseppe Capanna, Pasquale Vasio, Benedetto Caldara, Vito Saracista, Tullio Gorio, Ferdinando Bagnoli, Alessandro Hiver, Michele Auteri, Giuseppe Bleiner, Leonardo Vannata, Arturo Ricci, Franco Salvi, and Mirko Antonelli.

27 The members were Giovanni Host-Venturi, Giuseppe Pession, Giuseppe Capanna, Pasquale Vasio, Benedtto Caldara, Vito Saracista, Tullio Gorio, Ferdinando Bagnoli, Leonardo Vannata, and Arturo Ricci.

28 Politisches Archiv, Berlin, R 160301, Postverein, 23.07.1942.

were bilateral arrangements between Germany and a neighbouring country.[29] Italian delays continued after the preliminary phase, because after the Vienna Congress in October 1942, Italy signed the Final Agreement of the Congress, but with the note "subject to subsequent validation." This particularity, which was due to Italian domestic legislation, subjected the Agreement's coming into force to conditions.[30] The Agreement was validated by a 18 March 1943 decree[31] by the King of Italy, Victor-Emmanuel III. However, 1943 left its mark on Italy, which was now under Allied fire following the landing in Sicily 10 June 1943 and the start of the Italian Campaign. Thanks to a German intervention in September 1943, the north of the peninsula remained under fascist rule (actually under German domination), under the name of the Italian Social Republic. This troubled context obviously disrupted the organisation of EPTU-related events. The continuation of the war forced Minister Ohnesorge to cancel the Congress planned in Rome in 1943, and to replace it with a meeting planned in Vienna on 4 October 1944[32], a development that of course weakened the Italian PTT administration.

The year 1943 was thus marked by progressive German pre-eminence over the EPTU. At the same time, the French PTT administration enjoyed renewed interest from the Reichspostministerium, which invited it to at-

29 Arrangements between Germany and the Netherlands signed on 4 December 1941 and 15 – 21 April 1942; arrangements between Germany and Finland signed on 12 December 1941, arrangements between Germany and Hungary signed on 2 June 1942, etc.

30 Europäischer Postkongress, p. 102.

31 Regio Decreto 18 marzo 1943 – XXI, n. 392. *Approvazione degli atti del Congresso europeo postale e delle telecomunicazioni, stipulati in Vienna, fra l'Italia ed altri Stati il 19-24 ottobre 1942.*

32 "At the invitation of the Italian Postal and Telegraph Administration, the next meeting of the Association was scheduled for October 1943 at the Postal and Telecommunications Congress 1942 in Rome. Unfortunately, both the warlike events and the progress of the Association's work prevented the meeting from being held on time. The Italian Postal and Telegraph Administration therefore felt obliged to approach the German Reich Post Office with the request for the Association to hold the meeting on its own initiative. [...] Pending the agreement of all the administrations, the Deutsche Reichspost has the honour of inviting the European Post and Telecommunications Association to a meeting in Vienna, beginning on 4 October 1944.", Riksarkivert, Oslo, A 22 Journalsaker, Der Reichspostminister Ohnesorge an die Generaldirektion der Norwegischen Posten, 12.09.1944.

tend a French-German working meeting in July 1943 (20-22 July 1943, in Berlin), as well as to participate in the meeting of the EPTU's Second Standing Committee in September 1943 (1-7 September 1943, Vienna). In addition, Minister Ohnesorge addressed the French Minister of Production and Communications Jean Bichelonne directly, praising the "rich experience of the French administration."[33] I will now examine this evolution, with a focus on the continuities and discontinuities of techno-diplomacy in the relations between the EPTU and European telecommunications experts. This analysis will provide a deeper understanding of the particular relations between the French PTT administration, its experts, and the Reichspostministerium.

3. *Telecommunication Experts and the EPTU: The Continuities and Discontinuities of Techno-diplomacy*

Prosopographical analysis of the EPTU highlights continuities with pre-war techno-diplomacy, which was intimately linked to the tradition of major international scientific congresses.[34] Since the end of the nineteenth century, PTT experts and their governments had been "putting the continent in order" through technology and the establishment of intergovernmental treaties. With regard to the EPTU, there were continuities with the pre-war period, as some experts such as Giuseppe Pession were already involved before 1939. Pession[35], who was the Vice President of the Vienna Congress and a member of Standing Committees 1 and 2 in 1942, was a leading expert[36] in the field of radiotelegraphy and electromagnetism.

33 Archives Nationales, Pierrefitte-sur-Seine, 19960439/8, 16.09.1943.

34 Schot, Johan / Lagendijk, Vincent: "Technocratic Internationalism in the Interwar Years: Building Europe on Motorways and Electricity Networks", in: *Journal of Modern European History*, vol. 6, no. 2 (2008); Laborie, Léonard: "De quoi l'universel est-il fait? L'Europe, les empires et les premières organisations internationales", in: *Les cahiers Irice*, vol. 9, no. 1 (2012), pp. 11 – 22.

35 In 1942, *Direttore Generale Poste e Telegrafi* (Director of PTT service).

36 He was the author of many books on the subject, such as *Lezioni sulle radiocomunicazioni. Vol I. Studio degli elementi dei circuiti*, Raffaele Pironti, Napoli 1930, p. 154.

Before the German Government rejected[37] the participation of the French delegation in the Congress of Vienna (September 1942), the *Reichspostministerium* drew up a list[38] of French experts[39] it would like to see participate in the Congress of October 1942. All these experts were recognized for their experience in the field of telecommunications, and the vast majority of them had already participated in International Telecommunication Congresses (ITU) and the meetings of Consultative Committees.[40] For example, Malézieux, the Chief Engineer in charge of long-distance underground lines, participated in CCIF meetings in Cairo and Oslo in 1938. Schneider, who was the head of the office in the telecommunications directorate, and who was sent in 1943 to the meeting of the second permanent commission of the EPTU, participated in the CCIT meeting in Warsaw in 1936. These examples show that the EPTU was not simply a political and ideological construction desired by the Axis, but also an opportunity to perpetuate a tradition of exchange between European PTT experts, which is clearly demonstrated by the study of individual paths. Techno-diplomacy seemed to be following its course, as in the fol-

37 "On 22 September, during an interview, the Armeefeldpostmeister informed Mr Inspector General Girodet that he had received a telegram that morning from Berlin advising him that the higher authorities of the Reich saw no reason to invite the French PTT Administration to the Congress of Vienna.", Archives Nationales, Pierrefitte-sur-Seine, 19960439/8, Historique des pourparlers concernant la conference de Vienne et l'application, par la France, des Accords issus de cette conference, 17.06.1944.

38 This list, which was transmitted on 5 September 1942 by the Armistice services to the French General Secretary of the PTT, was both an innovation and a result of the war.

39 The Reichspostministerium would be pleased to appoint one or two of the following officials: Sirs. Aguillon, Malézieux, Bigorgne, Leroi, Schneider, and Dauphin.

40 CCIF, CCIT, CCIR (see notes 6 and 20). As a reminder, the Consultative Committees were independent of, but connected to, the ITU. This intermediate status avoided diplomatic pitfalls. Telecommunication Consultative Committees issued recommendations that were transmitted to the ITU and invited its members to comply with them as far as possible. See Henrich-Franke, Christian / Laborie, Léonard: "Technology taking over diplomacy? The 'Comité consultatif international (for) Fernschreiben' (CCIF) and its relationship to the ITU in the early history of telephone standardization, 1923 – 1947", in: Balbi, Gabriele / Fickers, Andreas (ed.): *History of the International Telecommunication Union*, Berlin 2020, p. 215 – 242.

lowing episode from August 1943, when Colonel Müller, who was *Armeefeldpostmeister* in France, thanked the French PTT delegation[41] for a stamp album offered during the French-German meeting of July 1943:

> Finally, I would like to express my deepest thanks for the beautiful and precious stamp album I received during the Berlin session. This album will remain for me a lasting memory of the trip to Berlin made with the representatives of your Ministry in an atmosphere of camaraderie.[42]

On the German side, there is no doubt there was political interference in EPTU affairs.[43] This was reflected in the decision, prior to the Vienna Congress, to have delegations from foreign postal administrations be accompanied by a German Postal Commissioner previously sent to the country in question.[44] Such "*Postbeauftragten im Auslande*"[45] were present in many European countries.[46] During the EPTU congress in Vienna in 1942, postal commissioners met to exchange experiences with the official representatives of the *Reichspost*. Their functions involved three central areas: deepening relations between the *Reichspost* and foreign postal and telegraphic administrations, providing intelligence advice to German Wehrmacht services abroad, and promoting the dissemination of German telecommunications technology abroad.[47] During 1943, this interference again manifested itself in the decision to involve the French delegation in discussions of the EPTU's Second Standing Committee, which took place

41 The French delegation at the French-German meeting in July 1943 consisted of Moignet (Director of the Post Office at PTT headquarters, head of the French delegation), Bernard (Head of the Post Directorate), Schneider (Head of the Telecommunications Directorate), Malézieux (chief engineer at the Long-distance Underground Lines Directorate), Marzin (chief engineer at the Technical Research and Control Directorate), and Hilbert (chief engineer, technical adviser in the minister's office).

42 Archives Nationales, Pierrefitte-sur-Seine, 19960439/8, *Armeefeldpostmeister* auprès du *Militärbefehlshaber* en France à M. le Ministre, Paris, 23.08.1943.

43 "Since last year, the *Reichspostminister* has personally signed all bilateral agreements on the approximation of tariffs in Europe.", Berlin, Politisches Archiv, R 106301, Postverein, Note for the Reich Foreign Minister, 29.09.1942.

44 Berlin, Politisches Archiv, RAV Pressburg 233, Letter dated 08.10.1942 to the German Legation in Pressburg (Bratislava).

45 See note 23.

46 Croatia, France, Romania, Spain, Italy, Hungary, Sweden, Bulgaria, Slovakia, the Netherlands, Greece (and Serbia), Norway, Denmark, Finland, and Turkey.

47 Ueberschär: Deutsche Reichspost, p. 180

in Vienna in September 1943. Indeed, at the EPTU Plenary Assembly on 24 October 1942, it was decided that "Representatives of administrations which are not members of the European Postal and Telecommunications Union may also be admitted to the deliberations with the agreement of the members of the Committees."[48] This was clearly the case for France, which was quite simply excluded from the Congress in 1942, and therefore could not sign the agreements. As a result, all member delegations would have to approve the participation of the French delegation in the September 1943 meeting. The *Reichspostministerium* ignored this:

> I would therefore like to suggest, if you agree with my opinion, that Mr. Gneme, as chairman of Commission 2, invite the French PTTs to participate in the committee's discussions. I think that, given the short time available, it may not be necessary to consult the members of the committee beforehand.[49]

However, what actually constituted a real break with pre-war technocratic internationalism was the German administration's internal denunciation of the role of telecommunications advisory committees, which it considered to be "under strong American and British influence."[50] Moreover, this denunciation was marked by anti-Semitism (by some members of Foreign Affairs and Post Ministry), which was directed against the secretary general of the CCIF, the Frenchman Georges Valensi.[51] Friedrich Gladenbeck (president of the *Reichspostforchungsanstalt*[52]) continued in his 1941 letter addressed to the OKW (Supreme Command of the German armed forces):

> In order to prevent the 3 CCIs from recapturing their former importance, I intend to found a working group of the European telecommunications administrations in the course of the European reorganisation. [...] I would also like to strengthen

48 Europäischer Postkongress, p. 294.

49 Bundesarchiv, Berlin-Lichterfelde, R4701/12286 Band 2, Letter to the Italian General Directorate of Posts and Telegraphs, 30.07.1943.

50 "These committees, whose work is practically suspended for the time being, were under strong American and English influence.", Bundesarchiv, Berlin-Lichterfelde, R4701/12284, 20.10.1941.

51 "Also the Secretary General of the CCIF in Paris was Jewish.", Bundesarchiv, Berlin-Lichterfelde, R4701/12284, 20.10.1941.

52 Reichspost Research Institute. The letter is not signed, but several elements suggest that the author is Gladenbeck.

German influence over the technical development of civil communications in European countries, especially neutral ones, as much as possible.[53]

This position was quite disturbing when compared with the opening speech by the President of the EPTU's Third Standing Committee, the German engineer Karl Herz, who in October 1942 explained that the Committee's purpose was to consider the technical arrangements to maintain alongside the recommendations of the International Advisory Committees.[54] One may legitimately wonder what the German administration's real motives were in setting up this European Post and Telecommunications Union.

Germany had an ambiguous position vis-à-vis other European delegates, or at the very least there was a difference between its administration (Post Office and Foreign Affairs) and its experts (from the PTT). This ambiguity was very well perceived by French experts and the French PTT administration, hence their mistrust and denunciation of "Germanic hegemony in Europe."[55] France nevertheless participated in this ambiguity.

4. France and European Cooperation in the Field of Telecommunications

In 1942, the European particularity of the EPTU, and the fact that its postal branch operated independently[56] of the UPU (Universal Postal Union) office in Berne, blocked France: "The French Administration cannot lend its support to a European Postal Union that would operate outside the Universal Postal Union."[57] European cooperation already existed in the

53 Bundesarchiv, Berlin-Lichterfelde, R4701/12284, 20.10.1941.

54 Europäischer Postkongress, p. 220 – 224.

55 "Germany's attitude showed an intention to establish German hegemony over Europe rather than to conclude postal or economic arrangements in the interest of all European countries.", Archives Nationales, Pierrefitte-sur-Seine, 19960439/8, Note from the Directorate of Posts and Buildings for the State Secretary, 19.09.1942.

56 A "permanent body independent of the International Bureau operating in Berne", Archives Nationales, Pierrefitte-sur-Seine, 19960439/8, Organisation et fonctionnement d'une union postale européenne (1942?).

57 Archives Nationales, Pierrefitte-sur-Seine, 19960439/8, Organisation et fonctionnement d'une union postale européenne (1942?).

field of telecommunications, but was developed in relation to the ITU office.[58] This secondment of the Reichspostministerium to the EPTU initially led to France's rejection, before its ultimate exclusion from the Congress by the German administration in September 1942. The French PTT administration used the term "dissidence"[59] vis-à-vis the UPU.

However, in September 1942 there was a change in the French administration, which indicated that it was ready to participate in negotiations "exclusively in the technical field,"[60] but not to the initial agreements, noting that the language used for the deliberations would not be French, and that the gold franc would be replaced by the *Reichsmark* as a standard. It is clear that this was a reversal of both the practices and symbols from prewar congresses. French caution could also be explained as a reaction to the ambiguous attitude of the German administration, which had not provided a formal written invitation to France for the Congress in Vienna.[61] Internal German documents from September 1941 show that France's invitation to the Congress was put on hold by the German Ministry of Foreign Affairs.[62] One year later, on 22 September 1942, France was excluded from the Union by order of the *Reichspostministerium*. This decision was once again surprising, given that the *Reichspostministerium* had, through *Armeefeldpostmeister* Müller, considered "the presence of French delegates to be indispensable,"[63] and wished to designate French officials (on a list) as participants. Was this refusal a political choice on the part of the

58 See Henrich-Franke / Laborie: Technology taking over diplomacy?

59 "[...] it would be desirable for the French administration [...] to ensure that the creation of the new body does not appear to constitute an act of dissent or affect the prestige of the Universal Postal Union.", Archives Nationales, Pierrefitte-sur-Seine, 19960439/8, Note for the Secretary of State for Communications, 22.09.1942.

60 Archives Nationales, Pierrefitte-sur-Seine, 19960439/8, Note from the Direction of Posts and Buildings to the Secretary of State, 19.09.1942.

61 Archives Nationales, Pierrefitte-sur-Seine, 19960439/8, Note from the Direction of Posts and Buildings to the Secretary of State, 19.09.1942.

62 "When asked whether France, Belgium, Serbia and Greece should be invited to join the Association of European Telecommunications Administrations, Mr Martius replied that the question should remain unresolved.", Bundesarchiv, Berlin-Lichterfelde, R4701/12284, 12.09.1941.

63 Letter from the Armistice Services to the Secretary General of Posts, Telegraphs and Telephones (Cabinet), Archives Nationales, Pierrefitte-sur-Seine, 19960439/8, 05.09.1942.

Reich? Was it symbolic punishment, a backlash against French demands (use of Golf franc and the French language) reminiscent of pre-war practices? Was the danger of protest by the French delegates during the debates too pronounced?

This fear on the part of the *Reichspostministerium* is understandable, as opposition from European experts also appeared with the Belgian administration in the weeks leading up to the Congress:

> [...] The senior official of the Belgian postal administration had agreed to respond to the conference invitation, indicating that he would attend as an observer. However, the head of the telegraph administration apparently refused for political reasons. The head of the postal administration also later indicated that he would like to make as few external appearance as possible. Under these circumstances, the Minister of Post preferred not to involve the Belgian postal administration at all.[64]

Despite the French "setback" of September 1942, the *Reichspostministerium* finally invited French experts to a French-German working meeting in Berlin from 20-22 July 1943, to reflect on "the conditions of France's application of the Vienna provisions."[65] At that meeting in July 1943 (preceding the meeting of the EPTU's second Standing Committee in September 1943), French experts expressed doubts about the usefulness and effectiveness of the EPTU's third Standing Committee (dedicated to telecommunications technology), whose meeting date had not yet been fixed[66]:

> Mr Moignet said that the existence of the 3rd Committee was undoubtedly useful for the present. However, he questioned whether the existence of the 3rd Committee was appropriate in the long term. [...] The French delegation asked whether, by setting up the Third Committee, the Congress of Vienna had not prepared to some extent the unification of European technology, which would give European industry protection against foreign industry. The German side replied that the establishment of the Third Committee was not a fight in any direction [...].[67]

---

64 Berlin, Politisches Archiv, R 106301, Postverein, Ministerial Director Wiehl to the Reich Foreign Minister, 08.10.1942.

65 Archives Nationales, Pierrefitte-sur-Seine, 19960439/8, Letter from Inspector General Girodet, Head of the French Delegation for Transmissions to the Militärbefehlshaber in France, addressed to Mr Secretary General of Posts, Telegraphs and Telephones (Cabinet), 16.06.1943.

66 Bundesarchiv, Berlin-Lichterfelde, R4701/11618, 21.07.1943.

67 Ibid.

Here French experts were potentially implying that the German administration was attempting to pull European telecommunications away from Anglo-American influence, and simultaneously subjecting them to the German technological model. The last quotation should be put into perspective with the *Reichspostministerium*'s 1940 programmes, which outlined the goal of "creating a European telecommunications system" in which "the German cable network is at the heart of Europe's telecommunications development."[68] Internal documents from the *Reichspostministerium* seem to confirm that during the preliminary phase of the Congress, interest in technical telecommunications issues was strategic (economic and political), and even ideological. This motivation was of course hidden from the other EPTU partners at the Congress. A relevant question is whether the German administration gave the same importance to technical telecommunications issues during the EPTU's developmental phase (after the 1942 Congress). The ambiguity was actually maintained, as telecommunications seemingly took a back seat. It is safe to assume that until the French administration formally joined the EPTU, the *Reichspostministerium* and the German Foreign Ministry would relegate telecommunications and its technical aspect to the background. This relegation was present at the 1942 Congress, namely in how the EPTU's Committee 3 was managed. The treatment of the issues of Commission 3 (telecommunications technology) were postponed following the Congress:

> The 3rd Commission, due to time constraints, was not able to deal with any of the issues in Vienna, but was only concerned with the precise and complete formulation of these issues and the practical system for their study. [...] The above organisation seems very complicated, and perhaps it would have been more appropriate to adopt the existing rules for the International Telecommunications Consultative Committee, according to which committees of rapporteurs are appointed and grouped as and when the need arises. In any case, the above distribution must be considered as provisional, and the 1943 Rome Conference could amend and renew it according to what the first experiences will suggest.[69]

Once again, this particular situation surrounding telecommunications was accentuated by the scepticism of French experts, who were key players in European telecommunications at the time. While they were of course not the only important players, since the Germans and Italians had a high level

68 Ueberschär: Deutsche Reichspost, p. 161.

69 Gneme: Il congresso, p. 317 – 328.

of expertise, it was difficult to conceive of genuine European synergy without the help of French experts and industry. This has been confirmed by the historian Gerd Ueberschär, who has commented on what *Armeefeldpostmeister* Müller said at the meeting of postal commissioners in March 1943:

> The French production potential for the needs of the German post office was permanently exploited by means of transfer orders [...] the construction of telephones parts and alternating current devices was ordered by German industry in France, and used in Germany to set up telecommunications installations. Likewise, the Research Institute and the *Reichspost* Central Office [...] ordered shortwave transmitters and receivers [...] from French industry [...]. The French postal administration had been influenced to adapt to German standards as much as possible, and to build the equipment in such a way that it required as little raw material as possible. [...] The former French telecommunications companies were working on a large scale for Germany, whereas German companies had only taken orders for military installations in France.[70]

Scepticism among French experts was probably heightened after Germany insisted on continuing negotiations for the European telecommunications network, which had been practically inoperative during the war. This was expressed by the head of the French delegation Moignet in July 1943 (French-German meeting):

> France's application of the Vienna Convention is of little practical significance at present, as almost all telegraphic connections between France and other countries are cut off. It would therefore be necessary to improve this situation noticeably beforehand.[71]

Dr. Risch (German delegation) then defended the German position, which was laying the groundwork for the development of European telecommunications in times of peace.[72] The peace argument is disturbing, because as early as 1940 the president of the central post office, Günter Flanze, internally defended the exploitation of occupied territories to establish telecommunications domination in Europe, supported by the unlimited power

70 Ueberschär: Deutsche Reichspost, p. 182 – 183.

71 Bundesarchiv, Berlin-Lichterfelde, R4701/11618, 21.07.1943.

72 "With regard to this, Ministerial Director Dr. Risch remarked that the communication of almost all countries was subject to great restrictions during the war, but that in preparation for the peace work, the regulations should already be made now.", ibid.

of the Wehrmacht, "which would not continue after the peace negotiations."[73]

Dr. Risch's preponderance in the discussions (between French and German experts in July 1943 in Berlin, and in the meeting of Commission 2 in September 1943 in Vienna) proved to be a hindrance, as he was the ideologist of this new European organisation of the Post and Telecommunications.[74] He was a lawyer and a member of the NSDAP, but most importantly the ministerial director responsible for foreign affairs at the *Reichpostministerium*. Points of view were therefore exchanged within a politicized context. This great mistrust of French experts is a key to understanding the minimal propaganda surrounding this meeting. The specialized journals of the time, such as Die Deutsche Post, provide evidence of real propaganda regarding the *Europäische Post und Fernmeldeverein* in 1941-1942, mostly on the front page of newspapers. However, in 1943 the announcement of the French-German working meeting of July 1943 was the subject of six lines in the "*Petits messages*" section of the magazine.[75] This French mistrust was a thorn in the Reich's side, and illustrated the difficulty it had in subjugating the French PTT administration.

The discrepancies between the French and German delegations of course continued at the meeting of the EPTU's Second Standing Committee (on telecommunications service and tariffs), which brought together member delegations and the French delegation in September 1943. Three points of tension emerged very clearly, and would persist until 1945: the question of the French language at the EPTU (entailing the French delegation's influence in decision-making), the use of the *Reichsmark* as a standard currency, and postal and telegraphic restrictions (and their impact on the entry into force and implementation of EPTU agreements by France).

73 Ueberschär: Deutsche Reichspost, p. 160 – 161.

74 Risch: Probleme und Ziele eines Europäischen Postvereins, p. 81 – 103.

75 *Die Deutsche Post, Zeitschrift für das Post- und Fernmeldewesen*, no. 21 (07.08.1943), p. 209.

5. The EPTU and the French PTT Administration: The Deadlocks

Shortly before the Vienna Congress, the French PTT administration, which was in the midst of negotiations[76] with the *Reichspostministerium*, internally raised the problem of the language to be used during the deliberations:

> Drawing a link between the old and the new continent, Mr Arnal[77] has every reason to suppose that, like the United States of America, Germany wishes to play the role of arbiter between States in the new Europe, both politically and economically, and it is for this reason that it is seeking the preponderance of its currency by designating it as the standard. The adoption of a draft European Postal Convention, which would include the use of the German language for deliberations, and the *Reichsmark* in place of the gold franc for the fixing of postal rates, would be a first success of the Reich towards its goal.[78]

This "regrettable innovation" discouraged the French administration from initiating potential agreements.[79] The French position did not prevent the simultaneous constitution of a delegation of French experts. French hesitations abruptly ended with the exclusion of 22 September 1942. Following its exclusion from the Congress, the French administration renewed its questions about the EPTU's working language during the French-German meeting of July 1943.[80] The French experts present at the meeting clearly stressed that the use of French was a sine qua non condition for France's entry into the EPTU:

> The Head of the French delegation also stressed the interest that the European Union itself would find in this, since France's decisions with regard to the European

---

76 "Finally, he (Dr. Müller) added that in order to easily follow the discussions, which had to be held mostly in German, it was desirable for him (a French expert) to speak German, without this condition being obligatory," (21.08.1942), Archives Nationales, Pierrefitte-sur Seine, 19960439/8, Historique des pourparlers concernant la conférence de Vienne et l'application, par la France, des Accords issus de cette conférence, 17.06.1944.

77 Pierre Arnal, Deputy Director of Economic and Political Affairs, Ministry of the Economy

78 Archives Nationales, Pierrefitte-sur Seine, 19960439/8, 19.09.1942

79 Ibid.

80 "It was on this occasion that Mr Moignet, Head of the French Delegation, raised the question of the use of French as an official language, in the same manner as the two other languages already admitted by the Vienna Agreements.", Archives Nationales, Pierrefitte-sur Seine, 19960439/8, 24.09.1943.

> Union were likely to influence those of other countries. Finally, he stated that the French Administration attached the greatest importance to this question, and he had doubts about the French Administration's attitude in the future if satisfaction was not given.[81]

To justify its request, the French delegation praised the precision of its language, and offered reminders of pre-war international scientific congresses (where French was predominant).[82] The German delegation, through Dr. Risch, reassured the French experts, although there was already a divergence of German and French sentiment regarding the admission of French at the EPTU. In internal German documentation, the principle remained uncertain[83], while on the French side the hope of the French language being accepted justified French participation at the meeting of the Second Permanent Committee in September 1943.[84] The political dimension of this choice was clearly expressed.

The recognition of French as an official language also raised another question, namely the role of French representation in the deliberations. In July 1943, Dr. Risch promised "that he would propose that the French Administration take part in the work of the Union's commissions 'as an active member with full rights,' which is to say with the right to vote in particular."[85] However, the French delegates Schneider and Marzin noted that their voice was in reality only advisory.[86] This statement is also ex-

81 Archives Nationales, Pierrefitte-sur Seine, 19960439/8, Historique des pourparlers concernant la conférence de Vienne et l'application, par la France, des Accords issus de cette conférence, 17.06.1944.

82 Ibid.

83 "Dr. Risch explains that the language issue is a political issue, and that the German position is therefore determined by the Federal Foreign Office. He wanted to start the negotiations concerned, but could not make any promises about the outcome.", Bundesarchiv, Berlin-Lichterfelde, R4701/11618, 21.07.1943.

84 "During the month of August, the Administration was assured that, according to senior German officials, the principle of the use of French as an official language was accepted and, on the basis of these indications, the French delegation went to Vienna to attend the meeting of the Second Committee scheduled for 1 September," Archives Nationales, Pierrefitte-sur Seine, 19960439/8, 24.09.1943.

85 Archives Nationales, Pierrefitte-sur-Seine, 19960439/8, Rapport sur la mission de M.M. Scheider, Chef du Bureau et Marzin, Ingénieur en Chef, Désignés pour représenter l'Administration française à la première réunion à Wien, de la deuxième commission de l'Union européenne des postes et des télécommunications.

86 Ibid.

plained by the fact that French was not accepted as the language of the deliberations:

> As the interventions of German- and Italian-speaking delegates did not need to be translated into French, the head of the French delegation declared and confirmed in the minutes of the 3rd meeting that he could, under these conditions, only play the role of observer.[87]

The refusal to use French isolated French experts from the deliberations: "The French delegation was unable to follow the committee's work in detail, as the interpreter could only provide very partial translations of foreign delegates' speeches."[88] Once again the German view of the situation was different:

> The meetings were informally distributed to them in French translation. In addition, the two French representatives had a personal meeting with the unprecedented opportunity to express their views [...] with broad French-German agreement on all technical matters, so that the subsequent entry of the French administration into the European Union of Posts and Telecommunications would not give rise to many differences of opinion or difficulties in a specialized field.[89]

Another point of tension between the French and German administrations in the context of the EPTU was the issue of the benchmark currency. The German choice of using the *Reichsmark* as the standard currency was justified by Dr. Risch: "[...] in the jurisdiction of the European Postal Union, a living currency, the mark, had been chosen instead of a fictitious currency, the franc-or."[90] This justification did not carry much weight; while the issue could be seen as being exclusively ideological, it posed real economic problems for the French administration (and also raised political issues), as did the decision to bring postal (and telegraph) rates in line with German rates.[91] The French administration was not the only one reluctant to

87 Archives Nationales, Pierrefitte-sur Seine, 19960439/8, 24.09.1943.

88 Ibid, Rapport sur la mission de M.M. Scheider et Marzin.

89 Bundesarchiv, Berlin-Lichterfelde, R4701/12286 Band 2, 16.09.1943.

90 Archives Nationales, Pierrefitte-sur Seine, 19960439/8, Historique des pourparlers concernant la conférence de Vienne et l'application, par la France, des Accords issus de cette conférence, 17.06.1944.

91 "[...] the substitution of the Reichsmark for the international franc-or for the fixing of basic charges raised objections, [with] the gold franc as determined at the Madrid Congress being the monetary standard adopted by the Universal Postal Union on which the international tariffs of all the countries of the Union are based. The coexistence of two monetary standards could therefore only be a source of difficulty. On the other hand, the French rates, if they were aligned with

replace the gold franc by the Reichsmark, as this was also the case with the Romanian delegation at the Congress of Vienna in October 1942.[92]

The final condition (and impasse) in France's acceptance of the EPTU agreements were the restrictions affecting French posts and telecommunications within the national territory, especially the removal[93] of the demarcation line in France:

> As far as the telegraph is concerned, only official and commercial telegrams between authorized correspondents and family telegrams reporting the death or serious illness of a close relative shall be admitted. With regard to the telephone, posts capable of exchanging interzone communications must be authorized in advance, and the number of circuits available to the French services is so small that it imposes waiting times of several hours, and even prevents a large part of the communications requested from being carried out.[94]

This French particularity prevented it from having a "normal regime" for PTTs, and was even the cause of discrimination.[95] Improvements were certainly made between the zones and the outside world: in late 1942, telegraph communications were re-established between Northern France and various European countries that were members of the EPTU (Bulgaria,

---

German rates, would become dependent on variations in the value of the Reich currency or the value of German internal prices. It is therefore to be feared that our country would have to undergo tariff changes unrelated to its monetary situation or the level of its own prices, or would not be able to raise its rates in line with the evolution of its own situation.", ibid.

92 "The Romanian PTT administration declares itself in agreement with the German proposals for the unified fees and the other fees provided for in these Regulations, but on the condition that the unified fees and fee rates, which are expressed in Reichsmark or Lire, are calculated and applied to Romania on the basis of the franc-or parity of the Romanian currency.", Europäischer Postkongress, p. 198.

93 Archives Nationales, Pierrefitte-sur Seine, 19960439/8, The Minister State Secretary for Production and Communications, to Mr President Dr. Michel Head of the Economic Department of the German Military Administration in France, 09.06.1943.

94 Ibid.

95 "The Head of the French delegation gave details of the consequences of the current situation not only with regard to trade between the two zones, but also between each zone and foreign countries. He pointed out, in particular, that from a postal point of view, French workers in Germany are not treated in the same way depending on whether they come from Northern or Southern France.", Archives Nationales, Pierrefitte-sur Seine, 19960439/8, Historique des pourparlers concernant la conférence de Vienne et l'application, par la France, des Accords issus de cette conférence, 17.06.1944.

Finland, Italy, Croatia, Romania, Slovakia, Hungary)[96]; in May 1944 general postal traffic between Germany and Southern France was resumed.[97] However, there was no unification within the national territory, since the demarcation line was maintained until 1944.

The abolition of the demarcation line could actually be seen as an illustration of the genuine equality of treatment to which France aspired within the EPTU:

> I have the honour of informing you that the Government of France authorizes the Secretariat General of Posts, Telegraphs and Telephones to make the necessary arrangements with the countries concerned on the basis of full reciprocity. Without making it a precondition for the application of this decision, it urges that the considerable restrictions still affecting postal, telegraphic, and telephone services within French territory be terminated at the same time.[98]

In fact, the removal of the demarcation line and the equal treatment of French PTTs vis-à-vis the *Reichspostministerium* were inseparable, and forcefully emphasized conditions for France's accession to the EPTU: considering that it might "make the necessary arrangements with the countries concerned on the basis of full reciprocity," it was imitating the *Reichspostministerium*, which had signed bilateral agreements with future member countries. However, in a letter dated 21 April 1943, *Armeefeldpostmeister* Müller indicated that French accession could be done by a simple written note to the *Reichspostministerium*.[99] Still, the French administration decided to send letters to the various EPTU member administrations on 16 July 1943.

The German administration justified maintaining the demarcation line for military reasons, independent of questions of communications.[100] Noting that the German authorities brushed aside the French request to abolish

96 Archives diplomatiques, la Courneuve, Vichy Europe 245, 28.11.1942.

97 Ibid., 12.06.1944.

98 Archives Nationales, Pierrefitte-sur Seine, 19960439/8, The Minister State Secretary for Production and Communications, to Mr President Dr. Michel Head of the Economic Department of the German Military Administration in France, 09.06.1943.

99 Archives Nationales, Pierrefitte-sur Seine, 19960439/8, Inspector General Girodet Head of the French Delegation for Transmissions to the Militärbefehlshaber in France, to Mr Secretary General of Posts, Telegraphs and Telephones, 21.04.1943.

100 Ibid.

the demarcation line[101], and that its mode of accession still posed difficulties and delays[102] in early 1944, the French PTT administration postponed[103] the implementation of the Vienna agreements until 1 June 1944:

> Finally, on 19 April, the Minister replied that instructions had been given for the necessary legal text to be submitted to the relevant ministerial departments, but that he was obliged to postpone until 1 June 1944, the date of France's application of the new regulations.[104]

Five days after the expected date of implementation of the Vienna Agreements, the Normandy Landing took place. The Allied advance in June 1944 put an end to this "unifying" project for European PTTs, and instituted amnesia within the French PTT.

6. *Conclusion*

In this study, I highlighted the German-Italian origin of the EPTU, which had a Europe-wide mission. This origin was reflected in symbolic practices, such as the use of German and Italian as the official languages of the congress. In the EPTU's preparatory phase (1940-1941), both countries showed notable interest in telecommunications technology, although Germany gradually prioritized the postal component in the development of the EPTU project during 1942.

---

101 "However, a few days later Colonel Dr. Müller informed the Delegation for Transmissions that the Berlin authorities had refused their authorization in this regard.", Archives Nationales, Pierrefitte-sur Seine, 19960439/8, Inspector General Girodet Head of the French Delegation for Transmissions to the Head of Government Minister, Secretary of State for Foreign Affairs.

102 "[...] the Minister did not make it known on February the 19th (1944) that, contrary to what Colonel Bienko (new *Armeefeldpostmeister*) thinks, the Romanian Postal Office has not yet responded to our proposal of 16 July 1943, nor has the Italian administration", Archives Nationales, Pierrefitte-sur Seine, 19960439/8, Historique des pourparlers concernant la conférence de Vienne et l'application, par la France, des Accords issus de cette conférence, 17.06.1944.

103 Ueberschär also refers to an agreement signed on 25 August 1944. See Ueberschär: Die deutsche Reichspost, p. 174. Given the context, it is safe to assume that an earlier implementation was highly uncertain.

104 Archives Nationales, Pierrefitte-sur Seine, 19960439/8, Historique des pourparlers concernant la conférence de Vienne et l'application, par la France, des Accords issus de cette conférence, 17.06.1944.

The Ministries of Foreign Affairs of the two founding countries played an important role during the preparatory phase, although on the Italian side the Ministry of Foreign Affairs sometimes ironically proved a hindrance to developing the project. This was a first difference between the parties, which became more pronounced with the Italian defeat in 1943. This new situation, in which Italy had become a puppet state, legitimately raised questions about the country's real role in the EPTU (the congress planned for 1943 in Rome was postponed). In 1943, Germany emerged as the EPTU's sole leader. However, this new situation coincided with renewed interest in French participation, leading to questions about the union's direction, specifically whether it was a political strategy, or whether it marked a desire to return to pre-war practices.

Focus on the continuities and discontinuities of techno-diplomacy within the EPTU revealed that the careers of telecommunications experts continued during the war, as did its network. The telecommunications experts who participated in various EPTU meetings had a long history of working together. What's more, a scientific sociability seemed to persist despite the war, as demonstrated by the stamp album given as a gift.

The war disturbed this balance, and the occupation of territories was a form of pressure on European delegates. French delegates in 1943 were relegated to the role of observers, with no decision-making power.

The ambiguity of the German position prompted suspicion within the French PTT administration, thereby contributing to France's ambivalence toward the EPTU. On-going talks between the French and German administrations demonstrate the mistrust of French experts, as well as the interest of the Reichspostministerium in the EPTU's long-term development. Also, from a symbolic point of view, it was difficult to see the EPTU as a European achievement without France.

What should be remembered in this case study is that the sticking points between the German and French PTT administrations stemmed from the context of war, namely the debate surrounding the lifting of restrictions on telecommunications services within the national territory, and challenges to the gold standard and the use of French as an official language. However, these demands represented nothing less than a return to the ITU's pre-war practices, and hence by definition were not compatible with the context of war and occupation in which France found itself. Efficient and "sincere" cooperation on the part of French experts was therefore unlikely. As a result, even though the EPTU was created and developed in a context of war, and discussions regarding telecommunications technology intensified, its long-term existence in times of conflict did not allow for real European synergy, and had limited effectiveness. European telecommunications under German hegemony were a failure.

In 1945, acknowledging the collapse of the Third Reich, several EPTU member administrations decided to leave the organisation. Two examples symbolize the end of the "European Project": a reply letter from the Italian PTT administration to the Postmaster General in Oslo (August 4, 1945, see citation below) and a letter from the Dutch Postmaster General to the Norwegian Postmaster General confirming the decision to exit the EPTU. In both examples, the letters were written in French.

> Dear Postmaster General, I have the honour of informing you that I duly noted your letter no. 2454 from 5 June past, in which you informed me that your Administration considers the Convention concluded in Vienna on 19 October 1942 between countries belonging to the European Postal and Telecommunications Union cancelled [...].[105]

This Italian response to the Norwegian request testifies to the willingness to end the agreement "officially and properly." I would add that the Norwegian request was made to Italy, because Italy had reworked its Ministry of Communications on 12 December 1944. Germany, at the same time, was subject to the Allied Control Council (since 30 July 1945).

Members of European PTT administrations reconnected with the old tradition of international congresses from the interwar period, and preferred using French rather than German or Italian. This symbolic reversal went even further, as the Italian PTT Administration—an official founding member of the EPTU—preferred shifting back to French rather than using the Italian language in its correspondence. Six years of war and occupation, as well as the propaganda hammered home since 1941 during the implementation of the EPTU, had not defeated the old customs of postal and telecommunication experts.

After 1945, one could imagine the return of French influence in European telecommunications. However, the victory of Allied Forces disrupted the habits of European telecommunication experts (including their work-

105 "Monsieur le Directeur Général, J'ai l'honneur de vous communique d'avoir pris bonne note de votre lettre n°2454 du 5 juin écoulé par laquelle vous m'avez informé que votre Administration considère comme annulée la Convention conclue à Vienne le 19 octobre 1942 entre les pays faisant partie de l'Union européenne des postes et des télécommunications. [...]" Riksarkivert, Oslo, A 22 Journalsaker, Postmaster General in Rome to Postmaster General in Oslo, 04.08.1945.

ing language), confirming in fact the American influence that had been developing since the aftermath of the First World War. At the end of the Second World War, in spite of efforts to build a European Community, talks during ITU and standing committees proved this American hegemony in European telecommunications.[106]

7. *References*

Die Deutsche Post, Zeitschrift für das Post- und Fernmeldewesen, n° 20 (17.05.1941), p. 305 – 311.

Die Deutsche Post, Zeitschrift für das Post- und Fernmeldewesen, n° 21 (07.08.1943), p. 209.

Europäischer Postkongress. Wien 1942; Original-Nachdruck in deutscher (ohne italienische) Sprache, Morgana Edition, Berlin-Schönefeld, 2013.

Gneme, Giuseppe: "Il Congresso europeo postale e delle telecomunicazioni di Vienna (12 – 24 ottobre 1942)", in: *Poste e Telecomunicazioni* 12 (1942), p. 317 – 328.

Henrich-Franke, Christian / Laborie, Léonard: "Technology taking over diplomacy? The 'Comité consultatif international (for) Fernschreiben' (CCIF) and its relationship to the ITU in the early history of telephone standardization, 1923 – 1947", in: Balbi, Gabriele / Fickers, Andreas: *History of the International Telecommunication Union*, Berlin 2020, p. 215 – 242

Journal des Télécommunications, Vol. 41 – VII (07.1974), p. 416 – 417.

Laborie, Léonard: "De quoi l'universel est-il fait? L'Europe, les empires et les premières organisations internationales", in: *Les cahiers Irice*, vol. 9, no. 1 (2012), pp. 11 – 22.

Paul, André: *Histoire des PTT pendant la Deuxième Guerre mondiale: 1939 – 1945. Ministère des Postes et Télécommunications, Direction du Budget et de la Comptabilité*, Paris 1968.

Poste e Telecomunicazioni, n°5 (01.03.1942), p. 137 – 138.

Risch, Friedrich: "Probleme und Ziele eines Europäischen Postvereins", in *Postarchiv* 70 (1942), p. 81 – 103.

Schot, Johan / Lagendijk, Vincent: "Technocratic Internationalism in the Interwar Years: Building Europe on Motorways and Electricity Networks", in: *Journal of Modern European History*, vol. 6, n° 2 (2008).

---

106 See Aagaard Jensen, Sanne: *Nuclear-proof communications? The Cold War and the governance of telecommunications security in NATO and Denmark*, 2018.

Ueberschär, Gerd: *Die Deutsche Reichspost 1933-1945. Eine politische Verwaltungsgeschichte, Band II: 1939-1945*, Berlin 1999.

‘Objective Operation’ under Swiss Neutrality? The International Broadcasting Union during WWII

Christian Henrich-Franke

Table of Content

> [The] continued activities in Geneva during the war must be seen as a guarantee that the IBU was in a good shape to immediately solve the problem of broadcasting after the war.[1]

1. Introduction

This observation about the International Broadcasting Union’s (IBU) activities during the Second World War, made in a letter written by its secretary general Alfred Glogg to the member broadcasting stations in December 1944, conveys the picture that it successfully continued to operate during the war years. Glogg was convinced that the IBU was in a good shape to restart its full services as soon as the hostilities ceased. In fact, the opposite was the case. Members accused the IBU of collaboration with the Nazis. They believed staff were unable to avoid being influenced by political tensions. Ultimately, the IBU was dissolved in 1950 and replaced by two new European broadcasting organisations, the ‘Organisation Interna-

1 Quote taken from: Hahr, Henrik: *Televisionens och radios internationellt samarbete.* (unpublished manuscript taken from Sveriges Radios Arkiv, Stockholm). Henrik Hahr was the head of the Swedish broadcasting organisation’s international department in the 1940s.

tionale Radiodiffusion' (OIR) and the European Broadcasting Union (EBU).

In this short piece, I will discuss the IBU's choice of a 'third way' of dealing with the wartime tensions. Rather than ceasing its activities like the Universal Postal Union (UPU) or the International Telecommunication Union (ITU) or being replaced by a new organisation like the European Postal and Telecommunication Union (EPTU), set up to promote European unification and cooperation under the leadership of Nazi Germany and Fascist Italy, the IBU continued its existence and work during the war. It was hoping to maintain objective operations under the protection of Swiss law and neutrality. The case of the IBU is made even more interesting by the fact that the EPTU never attempted to address the radio transmission sector and in particular broadcasting, although these topics had been discussed and regulated previously within the ITU.

Below I will focus on the difficulties of balancing neutral operations and the maintenance of a pan-European approach to broadcasting cooperation in wartime. My argument is primarily (but not solely) based on secondary literature as the archives of the IBU are no longer accessible to the public.

2. *The IBU's Origins*

Broadcasting was a new and unique telecommunication service in the first half of the 20th century. Spreading rapidly across Europe in the 1920s, it became one of the key information channels for the general public and political leaders within a decade. On the one hand, it connected individual households to the world, offering news, culture and entertainment. On the other, it enabled political leaders to reach the general public (domestically and abroad), sharing their messages with unprecedented effectiveness. Broadcasting became an effective tool for propaganda several years before the outbreak of the war in 1939.[2]

From a technical point of view, broadcasting was just one of many aspects to consider in the regulation and standardisation of radio frequencies and equipment. These activities were the responsibility of the national postal and telecommunications (PTT) authorities under the auspices of the

2 Tworek, Heidi: *News from Germany. The Competition to Control World Communications*, Cambridge 2019.

ITU and the International Consultative Committee for Radio (CCIR) set up in 1927.[3] The national broadcasting stations, operating under licences granted by their governments, also participated actively in technical regulation, in particular by monitoring broadcast transmissions and interferences from the beginning of regular broadcasting services in Europe. Their aim was to avoid interferences, which were caused by an increasing and uncoordinated number of transmissions, through voluntary cooperation.[4]

To this end, in 1925 the broadcasters founded the IBU with headquarters in Geneva. The new organisation soon designed frequency plans, which allocated broadcasting 'waves' to different stations, including technical specifications such as wavelength, power etc. Only two years later, in 1927, the IBU established a Checking Centre in Brussels to test and monitor the use of broadcasting frequencies and to analyse the origins of interferences in Europe. The Checking Centre became a technically advanced hub that served the purposes of both the member stations and the authorities.[5]

By the outbreak of the Second World War, the IBU had developed into a complex international organisation with three committees (technical, legal and programming), which continually discussed broadcasting issues. They exchanged radio programmes and organised cross-border music festivals to promote peace and mutual understanding among the people of Europe.[6] The IBU defended the interests of its member broadcasting stations and was subsequently recognised as an expert for frequency allocation plans and the monitoring of transmissions by the national postal and telecommunications administrations. The organisation was even allowed to participate in ITU conferences, where government representatives (mainly from the PTTs and the foreign offices) negotiated and signed broader international frequency plans. The last of these conferences was

3 Codding, George A.: *The International Telecommunication Union. An Experiment in International Cooperation*, Leiden 1952.

4 Wormbs, Nina: "Technology-dependent commons: The example of frequency spectrum for broadcasting in Europe in the 1920s", in: *International Journal of the Commons* 1 (2011), pp. 92 – 109.

5 Lommers, Suzanne / Hahr, Henrik: *Europe – On Air*, Amsterdam 2013.

6 Fickers, Andreas / Lommers, Suzanne: "Eventing Europe: Broadcasting and the mediated performance of Europe", in: Badenoch, Alexander / Fickers, Andreas (eds.): *Materializing Europe. Transnational Infrastructures and the Project of Europe*, New York 2010, pp. 225 – 251.

held in Montreux in 1939, but it was already overshadowed by the growing political tensions.[7]

3. The IBU during Wartime[8]

Like all international organisations, the outbreak of the Second World War forced the IBU to decide whether it should continue or suspend its activities. In November 1939, Antoine Dubois, the IBU's president called for a full closure of its secretariat for financial reasons. He expected a decline in funds and wanted to prioritise the Brussels Checking Centre in order to maintain at least some of the IBU's activities. However, the IBU's secretary general at the time, Arthur Burrows, voted for a continuation of the operations in both Brussels and Geneva. In his opinion, the Geneva office could provide a platform for exchanging views unaffected by political tensions. At a plenary assembly in Lausanne in April 1940, two weeks before the Nazis invaded the Western European countries, the representatives decided to continue its activities on a reduced scale, but under the protection of Swiss neutrality. The majority of members was still present at the assembly, even though it was relocated from Italy to Switzerland due to the war. The office staff was subsequently reduced from 13 to 5 and the secretary general and his deputy were replaced by the Swiss officials Alfred Glogg and Rudolphe von Reding. The IBU also planned to continue operations in its Checking Centre in Brussels (which was protected by Belgian neutrality). These steps were meant to ensure the IBU's existence for the duration of the war. The daily working routines were already at a standstill. All three committees (technical, legal and programming) had ceased meeting and the programme exchange had also stopped completely.

7 Report of the German PTT administration on the Montreux conference to the foreign office, Politisches Archiv des Auswärtigen Amts, Berlin, R116990; see also: Fickers, Andreas / Griset, Pascal: *Communicating Europe*, Basingstoke 2019.

8 The chapters III and IV are mainly based on a synoptic analysis of the following literature: Eugster, Ernest: *Television Broadcasting Across National Boundaries. The EBU and OIRT experience*, New York 1983; Wallenborn, Leo: "From IBU to EBU: The Great European Broadcasting Crisis", in: *EBU Review* 1 (1978), pp. 25 – 34 and 2 (1978), pp. 22 – 30; Hahr, Henrik: *Televisionens och radios internationellt samarbete*. (unpublished manuskript taken from Sveriges Radios Arkiv, Stockholm); Degenhardt, Wolfgang / Strautz, Elisabeth: *Auf der Suche nach dem europäischen Programm: Die Eurovision 1954 – 1970*, Baden-Baden 1999.

The IBU chose a remarkable third way to navigate wartime tensions. While the ITU postponed all its conferences and activities in April 1940, the IBU in the same month decided to continue with its operations. The IBU saw its role in providing a neutral link between warring countries at a time when psychological warfare in radio propaganda broadcasts increased dramatically.

The viability of this 'third way' was challenged just one month later, when the Checking Centre in Brussels came under renewed pressure. In May 1940, Nazi Germany invaded neutral Belgium. The Checking Centre's director, the Frenchman Raymond Braillard, immediately evacuated the equipment to Geneva as he wanted to prevent the Germans from using the technical equipment for military purposes such as the monitoring of allied transmissions. This decision, however, put the IBU into a difficult diplomatic position. Nazi Germany and the German Reich Broadcasting Corporation – the *Reichs-Rundfunk-Gesellschaft* (RRG) – that had remained an active member of the IBU, demanded the immediate return of the technical equipment to Brussels. The RRG argued this would demonstrate the full existence and continued 'objective operation' of the IBU as intended by the plenary assembly's decision just one month earlier. According to this view, the IBU was unable to serve as a neutral platform if it allowed such politically motivated steps. The IBU's neutrality was seriously challenged by the German organisation that threatened to withdraw from the IBU and to put diplomatic pressure on Switzerland. In a 'semi-diplomatic' mission, von Reding travelled to Berlin to convince the RRG to rescind the demand, but without success. Nazi Germany had reached the peak of its military success and took advantage of the political status quo in Europe to put pressure on the IBU's general secretariat. Finally, in January 1941, the secretary general gave in to the pressure and allowed the return of the equipment to Brussels. Afterwards, Glogg justified this decision as a necessary step to keep the IBU alive and to avoid diplomatic tensions between Switzerland and Germany. In March 1941, the equipment was retrieved from Geneva by the German engineers Braunmühl and Schweiger, who were also appointed by the RRG and the German authorities as the new heads of the Brussels Checking Centre and replaced Braillard, who had been put in charge by the IBU. The Checking Centre immediately restarted its activities, but the measurements and documents provided to IBU members differed considerably from those previously received. Unsurprisingly, the occupying military authorities also used the equipment to unofficially monitor allied transmissions.

It was obvious that the IBU had considerable difficulties maintaining objective operation under the protection of Swiss law. Neutrality was no guarantee for a full and unchallenged protection. Instead, Nazi Germany misused the IBU and instrumentalised neutrality for its own purposes. Beyond this, the member broadcasting stations in occupied countries like Belgium, Denmark, France, Norway and the Netherlands were either subjected to strict German control or replaced by new organisations under Nazi rule. It was questionable whether they still truly represented the national member stations as they no longer operated on the basis of licences granted by legitimised national governments.

The events of 1941, albeit justifiable with a policy of (neutral) 'objective operation', sealed the IBU's future. Members from 10 European countries – among them the pioneering British Broadcasting Corporation (BBC) – subsequently turned away from the IBU. The accusation of Nazi collaboration permanently damaged the organisation's reputation. Non-German member stations and governments considered the IBU as a union of axis powers (and occupied countries) protected by Swiss neutrality. The exile governments in London protested against the decisions taken by the IBU and even declared in BBC broadcasts that they felt no obligation to adhere to them. Balancing neutrality and maintaining objective operation proved to be increasingly difficult for the Swiss general secretariat. Nevertheless, Glogg and von Reding decided to continue all operations, including annual general assemblies and contacts with all broadcasting partners from the countries at war, simply to keep the IBU alive.

4. *From Wartime to Peacetime*

The Swiss general secretariat adhered to its 'line of action' even when the end of the war was in sight in 1944. It kept contact with both sides: for instance, the general secretariat offered the German heads of the Brussels Checking Centre the opportunity to put their technical equipment under the protection of the Swiss embassy in order to avoid damage as the Allied forces liberated Belgium in 1944. The occupying German forces again demonstrated their lack of interest in the IBU's aims and simply evacuated the equipment to Berlin for their own use. However, Glogg and von Reding also travelled to Brussels and Paris in December 1944, to discuss the IBU's upcoming activities. For the general secretariat, the logical next step after the hostilities ended in May 1945 was to convoke a general assembly in Lausanne, scheduled just one month later, in June 1945.

Broadcasting stations across Europe were appalled by the Swiss attempt to continue as if nothing had happened. They rejected the proposed general assembly, although there was an urgent need to discuss the allocation of frequencies as numerous interferences impacted the transmissions when the national broadcasters restarted their services in 1945. For the broadcasters, it was crucial to analyse their wartime experiences and to negotiate a new common agreement on broadcasting operations.

The Belgian radio broadcaster took the initiative to launch the necessary evaluation, with strong support from the BBC. Both were convinced that the IBU was the wrong setting and the secretary general the wrong person for this. The Belgian broadcasting organisation immediately rebuilt the Brussels Checking Centre and invited its foreign partner organisations to an informal meeting in Brussels in January 1946 – outside of the IBU, just 'entre amis' – to discuss the IBU's future. They not only approached all IBU members except for Germany and Spain, but also Radio Luxemburg and the Soviet Union's broadcasting organisation, both of which had not been members of the IBU before the war.

At the meeting in Brussels, the broadcaster's representatives had to answer difficult questions: What lessons could be learned from their wartime experiences? Should the IBU be replaced or reorganised? Should it be transformed into a global organisation within the UN? From the beginning, there was a consensus among participants that the IBU should not continue in its current form. The Soviets in particular demanded the dissolution of the IBU and a rollback of Swiss influence. Nevertheless, a compromise could not be found at the Brussels meeting as the Soviets blocked a majority vote for the continuation of the IBU under the condition of a comprehensive reorganisation. By this stage, the IBU no longer had any say in the matter. To mitigate the tensions, Glogg and the IBU staff refrained from any further action and put the IBU's fate in the member organisations' hands. Glogg took part in all the meetings, but only in his capacity as the director-general of the Swiss broadcasting organisation, and he abstained from influencing the discussion. According to Henrik Hahr, he "was fed up".

Additional meetings in March, May and June shifted the focus towards the creation of a new broadcasting organisation, with the intention to extend it from a European to a global body. For this purpose, the majority of broadcasting organisations in Europe set up the 'Organisation Internationale Radiodiffusion' (OIR) on 27/28 June 1946. However, the BBC was unwilling to join the new organisation as long as the UN and the ITU were still discussing a reorganisation of global telecommunication regulation.

By its refusal to join, the BBC indirectly prevented the IBU from being dissolved by its remaining members two days later.

In the following three years, the discussion about the future organisation of international broadcasting cooperation became increasingly entangled in Cold War politics. The telecommunication authorities of the 'big five' dropped the idea of founding a global broadcasting organisation (for long and medium wave broadcasting) as early as November 1946. Subsequently, both the IBU and the OIR unsuccessfully aspired to become expert organisations with voting rights at the World Radio Conference (WARC) in Atlantic City (1947) and the European Broadcasting Conference in Copenhagen (1948). They had to content themselves with an observer status. The competition between both organisations was overshadowed by a dispute about voting rights within the OIR. The Soviet broadcasting organisation in particular strove for an Eastern Bloc quorum and demanded voting rights for their individual Soviet republics. The political tensions of the Cold War hampered cooperation within the OIR and changed Western European broadcasting organisations' attitude. In 1949, they decided to leave the OIR, but were also not prepared to rejoin the IBU. The creation of the 'European Broadcasting Union' (EBU) in 1950 was the Western European compromise. The IBU (as a pan-European broadcasting organisation founded in the interwar period) became redundant and was dissolved when the EBU began its operations. The IBU's assets were transferred to the EBU, which in many respects stepped into the IBU's shoes: for example, it retained its seat in Geneva, its Checking Centre in Brussels and the committee structure.

5. Conclusion

The third (neutral) way to navigate political tensions in wartime in the end proved too difficult for the IBU and the Swiss general secretariat. While the organisation managed to maintain the institutional capacities to immediately restart the IBU's activities after the Second World War, the attempt to continue operations during wartime completely undermined the IBU's reputation. When the Swiss secretary general Alfred Glogg invited members to a general assembly in June 1945, he envisioned 'business as usual'. It became immediately obvious that this was impossible. The directors of the broadcasting organisations, particularly from formerly occupied countries did not share his view that "continued activities in Geneva during the war must be seen as a guarantee that the IBU was in a good shape to immediately solve the problem of broadcasting after the war". The IBU did not succeed in balancing objective operation and maintaining a pan-European approach to broadcasting cooperation. Therefore, its members demanded a thorough evaluation of the IBU's administration during the war, although there was a general consensus that the work carried out by the IBU in the interwar period had to be continued as soon as possible. The fact that the IBU was replaced by two new organisations rather than one was not a consequence of the 'third way', but rather of the looming Cold War. The IBU's interwar structure, vision and even the individual representatives survived the rupture during the war and continued their work within these new organisations.

6. References

Codding, George A.: *The International Telecommunication Union. An Experiment in International Cooperation*, Leiden 1952.

Degenhardt, Wolfgang / Strautz, Elisabeth: *Auf der Suche nach dem europäischen Programm: Die Eurovision 1954 – 1970*, Baden-Baden 1999.

Eugster, Ernest: *Television Broadcasting Across National Boundaries. The EBU and OIRT experience*, New York 1983.

Fickers, Andreas / Griset, Pascal: *Communicating Europe*, Basingstoke 2019.

Fickers, Andreas / Lommers, Suzanne: "Eventing Europe: Broadcasting and the mediated performance of Europe", in: Badenoch, Alexander / Fickers, Andreas (eds.): *Materializing Europe. Transnational Infrastructures and the Project of Europe*, New York 2010, pp. 225 – 251.

Lommers, Suzanne / Hahr, Henrik: *Europe – On Air*, Amsterdam 2013.

Tworek, Heidi: *News from Germany. The Competition to Control World Communications*, Cambridge 2019.

Wallenborn, Leo: "From IBU to EBU: The Great European Broadcasting Crisis", in: *EBU Review* 1 (1978), pp. 25 – 34 and 2 (1978), pp. 22 – 30.

Wormbs, Nina: "Technology-dependent commons: The example of frequency spectrum for broadcasting in Europe in the 1920s", in: *International Journal of the Commons* 1 (2011), pp. 92 – 109.

Giuseppe Gneme (1872 – 1958): The "Dean" of Telecommunications

Valentine Aldebert

At a tribute for the retirement of 85-year-old Giuseppe Gneme in 1957, the Chairman of the ITU Administrative Council stated:

> We are experiencing [...] an event in the life of our Union, one that is both remarkable and unusual: the retirement from active service of our dean, the Honourable Grand Officer Giuseppe Gneme, who is leaving us after fifty years of the most fruitful and impressive activity for the Union, and sixty-five years in the service of his country, Italy[1].

In our view, the secret of this extraordinary longevity resided in the Second World War, for it was during the founding congress of the European Postal and Telecommunication Union in 1942 that Giuseppe Gneme came out of retirement to serve as an Italian delegate.

Giuseppe Gneme was born on 26 May 1872. After studying physics and mathematics at the University of Rome, he entered the senior staff of the General Directorate of Telegraphs of Italy, and was assigned to the central telegraph office in Rome on 1 February 1892 after passing a competitive examination. In 1896, he joined the central administration of the Ministry of Posts and Telegraphs (the future Ministry of Communications), where he became familiar with more general issues in telegraph operations (domestic and international), pricing[2], and regulation.

His first contacts with the Central Office of the International Telegraph Union in Berne date back to the beginning of the new century, during preparations for the conferences on wireless telegraphy that were organised in Berlin in 1903 and 1906 to counter the monopoly of his compatriot Marconi. In 1908 he took part in a telegraph conference in Lisbon, where

---

1 *Journal des Télécommunications* 9 (1957), p. 197.

2 In 1916 he wrote *Le tariffe telegrafiche interne: tariffa dei telegrammi ordinari e della stampa - dei telegrammi lettera - per l'uso di indirizzi abbreviati e* convenuti, Recanati, Tip. R. Simboli, 1916.

he signed the International Telegraph Regulations for the first time as the head of Italy's delegation.

From that point on, Gneme continued to be part of the transnational community of experts in telegraphy and telephony, meeting at the international conferences of the ITU and other assemblies of its advisory committees[3]. Before the war, he served as laboratory director at the Military Radiotelegraphic Institute, which placed him in the crucial field of radio communications[4].

After the First World War, he was Italy's delegate to the telegraph meetings in Paris (1920) and Prague (1921) regarding the restoration of communications and services. His rise within the ministry continued. At the international telegraph conference in Paris in 1925, he chaired the Italian delegation as Director and Head of Division. Convinced of the need to separate their regulatory provisions for telephone service from other telegraph regulations, he contributed to a reform effort via international legislation, which led to a reorganisation of the Union at the next conference, held in Madrid in 1932. These two separate regulations allowed the United States to join the organisation. In Madrid there was also talk of wireless telegraphy, a subject to which Gneme was no stranger. As chairman of the Italian delegation and chairman of the tariff commission at the 1927 Washington International Conference, he was in favour of merging the St Petersburg International Telegraph Convention (1875) and the International Radiotelegraph Convention. Gneme introduced a proposal that the Spanish Government should organise both the telegraph and radio conferences, which had hitherto been held separately and concurrently. The proposal was adopted, and the name of the organisation was changed from the Telegraphic Union to the brand new International Telecommunications Union, which encompassed the three regulations of telegraphy, telephony and radiocommunications.

Gneme was a prominent figure in this world of telecommunications — undergoing international reorganisation at the time — and was present at almost every meeting. Following the decision to set up an International Committee on Agreed Language (Commit international du langage con-

---

3 CCIT, CCIF, CCIR. Created in the 1920s.

4 Gneme would later publish a synthesis on marine applications, *Uno sguardo al servizio delle radiocomunicazioni con le navi,* [EDITION] Roma: Ist. Poligr. dello Stato (1936).

venu) at the 1925 conference[5], he chaired its first meeting in Cortina d'Ampezzo in 1926[6]. Agreed language is a system that simplifies the letters and symbols of certain (mostly non-European[7]) languages in order to facilitate transmission between countries. In 1928, Gneme published a Regulation on the Agreed Language in International Telegrams[8]. His activity did not slow, as he served as the chairman of the Italian delegation and chairman of commissions at the European broadcasting conferences held in Lucerne (1933) and Montreux[9], which regulated the frequency spectrum, as well as at the telegraph-telephone and radiocommunication conferences in Cairo (1938)[10]. He also intervened in telegraph and telephone matters at the meetings of the International Chamber of Commerce (Paris in 1931, Berlin in 1937, Copenhagen in 1939) and the International Legal Committee (Rome in 1928 and Liège in 1935). His experience was praised by his peers, who recognized him as Dean at the Plenary Assembly of the International Telegraph Consultative Committee in Lisbon (1934). He retained this honorary office for twenty-three years!

It is unclear exactly when Giuseppe Gneme retired from the Italian PTT Administration, but it was in the early 1940s, before he was called back to office — "retired head of the (telegraphic) service recalled to duty" — as a February 1943 decree put it[11]. This probably happened in the context of

5 Amendments to the proposal of the Tariff Commission concerning the constitution of a study committee, in: *Procès-verbal de la quatrième séance plénière de la Conférence de télégraphique internationale*, Paris 1925, p. 417.

6 At the time Gneme held the title of Grand Officer of the Order of the Crown of Italy.

7 "The agreed language is used by most of the Countries in their relations with the non-European regime", in: *Procès-verbal*, Paris 1925, p. 418.

8 Gneme, Giuseppe: *Regolamentazione del linguaggio convenuto nei telegrammi internazionali,* Roma 1928.

9 Introduced as General Inspector of Telegraph and Radiotelegraphic Traffic at the Italian Ministry of Communications, Gneme headed the Italian delegation to the European Broadcasting Conference in Montreux in 1939. *Liste des participants à la Conférence européenne de radiodiffusion,* Montreux 1939, ITU website.

10 Gneme, Giuseppe: *Uno sgaurdo al telegrafo: Conferenza tenuta alle sedi di Roma e di Milano dell'Associazione Elettrotecnica italiana*, 1934.

11 *Capo servizio in pensione richiamato in servizio*, "Decreto Ministeriale 24 febbraio 1943-XXI. Instituzione e nomina dei componenti il Comitato esecutivo per la Conferenza europea postale e delle telecomunicazioni di Roma", in: *Gazzetta ufficiale del Regno d'Italia* 56 (1943.)

the founding congress of the European Postal and Telecommunications Union (EPTU), held in October 1942 (Vienna).

Gneme, who was 70 years old at the time, actively participated in the congress, although there is no sign of his participation in the preparatory meetings of 1941 and January 1942.[12] Why was he brought out of retirement? We can assume that his expertise was considered crucial for the proper implementation of the organisation; it is no coincidence that he was both a member of the commission preparing the Convention, as well as president of the commission on telegraph tariffs. Gneme brought his pre-war experience in cooperation to the new organisation. His expertise was once again sought out during the meeting of the second EPTU Standing Committee (Service) in Vienna. [13]

However, it should be noted that he was no longer appointed head of the Italian delegation during the Congress meetings of 1942 and 1943. Giuseppe Pession (born in 1881), who had served as Director General of Posts and Telegraphs since 1925 and was a specialist in radiotelegraphy, signed the agreement on October 1942. Could Gneme's relegation be explained by the context in which the EPTU was operating? It is important to emphasize the German administration's perspective on Gneme:

> About Gneme, it is well known that he is the man who led the international negotiations in the previous years. He staff does not hold him in high regard. He stands out from the others, and is neither loved nor appreciated by Pession[14].

This stands in such sharp contrast to Gneme's pre-war distinctions! Gneme's great experience clearly gave him a kind of independence, which was frowned upon by the Reich's PTT administration.

At the end of the Second World War, the esteem in which Gneme was held (and no doubt his relative "effacement" during the conflict) allowed

---

12 The previous year he published a report on the use of the frequency spectrum, under the title *Dieci anni di utilizzazione dello spettro delle frequenze*, Roma 1941.

13 The second meeting of the telecommunications committee: September 1 – 7, 1943. The Duce was no longer governing at that time. The Badoglio Government that was in power was still officially on the side of the Germans. This changed with the Badoglio armistice of 8 September 1943. However, the Germans arrived in Rome a few days later, and established the Repubblica Sociale Italiana on 23 September 1943, putting Mussolini back in power.

14 Working meeting of the Reichspostministerium from March 18 to 28, 1943, Berlin-Lichterfelde, R 4701/11248

him to return to the forefront of the Italian scene. He was chosen to lead the Italian delegation in the decisive conferences held in Atlantic City in 1947, which reorganised the ITU and placed it within the new United Nations Organisation. Giuseppe Pession also died in 1947 and was purged in December 1944 because of his fascism.[15] Gneme, a key expert for both Italy and the international community, became a founding member of the ITU Administrative[16], and even served as Chairman for the Council's tenth session in 1953.

His consecration was complete. In his own country, he was showered with honours before, during, and after the war. He had been a Grand Officer of the Order of the Crown of Italy since 1926 and was also made Grand Officer of the religious order of Saints Maurice and Lazarus in December 1941, before being elevated in 1952 to the status of Commander in the new Order of Merit of the Italian Republic instituted by the new regime, which merged the two previous orders. At the same time, he was involved in telegraph and telephone matters for the meetings of the International Chamber of Commerce in Paris in 1946, and then took part in the Maritime Radiocommunication Conference in Copenhagen on 7 September 1948. Gneme did not retire until 1957, at the age of 85; he died in Rome less than a year later, on 17 April 1958.

Gneme's incredible professional longevity is impressive: he served under successive political regimes (monarchy, fascism, Italian social republic), as well as two world wars. He is unquestionably a witness and key player of the great changes that occurred in the field of telecommunications during the twentieth century. He was particularly involved in international regulation and was a part of Europe's long history of technical cooperation. This spirit of cooperation was emphasized by Gneme himself in his speech at the opening of the ITU Administrative Council:

---

15 [30 December 1944] "Notizie da radio Bari [...] rilevo il sequestro dei beni mobili ed immobili di due gerarchi fascisti: l'ex academico Pession, direttore delle poste e telegrafiche e Lazzari ex direttore delle Belle Arti", in: Marchis, Riccardo (ed.): *Carlo Chevallard. Diario 1942-1945. Cronache del tempo di guerra*, 2005, p. 429.

16 Consisting of 18 member states, it is responsible for assisting the Members and Associate Members of the Union in applying the provisions of the Conventions, Regulations, Agreements and decisions of the Conferences and meetings of the Union. It also ensures effective coordination of its activities and good administration.

> Over the last fifty years, I have had the privilege of witnessing, in our field of international telecommunications, the development of a magnificent spirit of cooperation, which has allowed us to overcome difficulties that were considered insurmountable, and to provide sufficient solutions to the problems that arose.[17]

In 1957, the Administrative Council had his bust placed in the ITU entrance hall—his figure has been keeping a watchful eye on the international community of experts ever since[18].

References

"Notizie da radio Bari [...] rilevo il sequestro dei beni mobili ed immobili di due gerarchi fascisti: l'ex academico Pession, direttore delle poste e telegrafiche e Lazzari ex direttore delle Belle Arti", in: Marchis, Riccardo (ed.): *Carlo Chevallard. Diario 1942-1945. Cronache del tempo di guerra*, 2005.

Capo servizio in pensione richiamato in servizio, "Decreto Ministeriale 24 febbraio 1943-XXI. Instituzione e nomina dei componenti il Comitato esecutivo per la Conferenza europea postale e delle telecomunicazioni di Roma", in: *Gazzetta ufficiale del Regno d'Italia* (5) 1943.

Journal des Télécommunications 9 (1957).

---

17 *Journal des Télécommunications* 9 (1957), p. 198

18 "The President reminded the Council that two other proposals had been made. One, that the portrait of Mr. Gneme be included in the series of portraits of great men in telecommunications published by the General Secretariat; the other, that the Secretary-General be authorized to arrange for a bust of Mr. Gneme to be placed in the entrance hall of the future ITU building. Both proposals were adopted unanimously". Ibid., p. 200.

Pierre Marzin: Innovator and Techno-Patriot

Pascal Griset

Table of Content

1. Introduction

The attitude of European elites during the Second World War has been the subject of much historical research, which has increasingly adopted a broader European approach to the role that experts played in constructing political spaces.[1] This research has also considered the role of technology — in this case information and communication technologies as well — in the genesis and development of contemporary Europe.[2] From a methodological point of view, raising such questions calls for an extremely broad conceptual field.

The aim of this text on Pierre Marzin is more modest. He was a key figure in the history of French telecommunications and high technology

1 Kohlrausch, Martin / Trischler, Helmut: *Building Europe on Expertise: Innovators, Organizers, Networkers*, Basingstoke 2014.

2 Laborie, Léonard: *L'Europe mise en réseaux. La France et la coopération internationale dans les postes et les Télécommunications (années 1850-années 1950)*, Brussels 2010; Fickers, Andreas / Griset, Pascal: *Communicating Europe: Technologies, Information, Events (1850-2000)*, London 2019.

during the second half of the twentieth century,[3] and served as a member of the French delegation to the European Postal and Telecommunication Union in 1943.[4] Here the focus will be the impact that the Second World War had on his career, a topic that calls for a *longue durée* approach, as well consideration of the circumstantial constraints and objectives that emerged at the time.

2. *Senior Civil Servants Under Vichy: What Analytical Framework?*

To understand how senior civil servants managed, in accordance with highly contrasting personal choices, the many contradictions imposed on them by their responsibilities in the specific context of the Occupation, we have available to us a historiography deeply marked by the "Paxtonian revolution."[5] The work of Marc Olivier Baruch offers an operational key for doing so[6] by analyzing how an administration continued to function in a collective dynamic consisting of extremely varied individual trajectories. It is crucial to break with a history of "judgment." The analytical lens proposed by Philippe Burrin offers another element that inscribes these trajectories not in "models" — difficult to identify and impossible to use — but rather in a series of references that move beyond the specificities of multiple fates. The categorization of choices in terms of involvement with the enemy, in conjunction with the concept of *accommodation*, help avoid the binary history that emerged during the aftermath of the war, which identified actors through the binary lens of *"collabos"* (collaborators) and *"résistants*."[7] The historiography has also emphasized that the evolution of the conflict, the struggles within Pétain's l'Etat français (French State), the preservation of a "free" zone and its subsequent occupation, and the situation in the colonies reveal the multiple spatial and temporal variables that were behind changes to many stances.[8] The men who saw these dark times

3 Fridenson, Patrick / Griset, Pascal (dir): *Entreprises de haute technologie, État et souveraineté depuis 1945*, Paris 2013.

4 Internal reference to Valentine Aldebert's chapter in this book.

5 Paxton, Robert: *La France de Vichy*, Paris 1973.

6 Baruch, Marc-Olivier: *Servir l'État français: l'administration en France de 1940 à 1944,* Paris 1997.

7 Burrin, Philippe: *La France à l'heure allemande (1940-1944)*, Paris 1995.

8 Baruch, Marc-Olivier / Duclert, Vincent: *Serviteurs de l'État: une histoire politique de l'administration française, 1875 – 1945*, Paris 2000.

as a moment to advance projects preparing the country's future recovery stand out within the French administration[9]; they took their place in the "technocracy" that sought, already in the 1930s, to overcome the Great Depression and the country's structural problems through modernization. Without being the sole actors, engineers played a major role in this dynamic, especially *polytechniciens* (graduates of l'Ecole Polytechnique) due to their specific role in positions of power, as well as their modernist vision of France.[10]

Analyzing Marzin's career requires special consideration of the fact that he was an engineer from l'Ecole Polytechnique.[11] This approach focusing on *polytechniciens* under the Occupation, initiated by Marc Olivier Baruch and Vincent Guigueno, provides a first basis. However, studying graduates from "X" (nickname for l'Ecole Polytechnique) in positions of power leads, almost automatically, to an exclusive focus on the two most prestigious engineering "Corps."[12] Engineers from the Direction des Télécommunications (DT, Directorate for Telecommunications) were not highly considered at the time, even though this period marked the beginning of their increasing role between the 1960s and 1980s. This ascension was correlated with the growing presence of their field of expertise, which they succeeded in having recognized as a national priority.[13] Marzin led this objective, and combined it with a broader project of freeing French telecommunications from dependence on foreign industries. Only careful consideration of this transformation as it unfolded over the *longue durée* can provide a clear analysis of his career and decisions between 1939 and 1945.

---

9 Dard, Olivier: „Les élites technocratiques dans la Résistance française", in: Marcot, François / Musiedlak Didier (dir.): *Les Résistances, miroir des régimes d'oppression. Allemagne, France, Italie*, Presses universitaires de Franche-Comté 2006.

10 Baruch, Marc-Olivier / Guigueno, Vincent: *Le Choix des X: L'École Polytechnique et les polytechniciens, 1939 – 1945*, Paris 2000.

11 Joly, Hervé: *A Polytechnique. X 1901. Enquête sur une promotion de polytechniciens, de La Belle Époque aux Trente Glorieuses,* Paris 2021.

12 Graduates from the Mines and Ponts et chaussées schools held, as part of the traditional *cursus honorum*, the most important positions based on established dividing lines and evolving influence. While they were not absolutely frozen, they evolved slowly.

13 Griset, Pascal (dir): *Les ingénieurs des Télécommunications dans la France contemporaine: Réseaux, innovation et territoires, XIXe-XXe siècles*, Paris 2014.

3. From Agricultural Mechanics to Telecommunications

Engineers are ultimately humans: to understand them, one must grasp their background, personal culture, and values. Marc Olivier Baruch, himself a *polytechnicien*, has invited us to do just that by gathering the information traditionally included in a prosopography:

> Who exactly is Mister X, a bureau chief, an engineer at the Ponts et Chaussées (leading engineering *grande école*), a ministry director, an under-secretary? How old is he? Who are his parents? Where was he born? What kind of a marriage did he have? How many children did he have.[14]

There are many biographical questions involved, and I will begin with a few elements in this regard.

Marzin was born on October 24, 1905 in Lannion, in the Côtes du Nord department. His grandfather Guillaume had created an agricultural machine factory that was quickly recognized beyond Northern Brittany for its quality. With the support of a local investor, he produced a "gorse grinder" that was presented in Paris, and noticed as far as England. His father Charles took over and diversified its activity by opening a garage in 1910 to repair the first automobiles that ventured on the difficult roads of the Trégor, a region that still had poor infrastructure at the time. Pierre's older brother Yves-Marie opened his own agricultural machine company the following month. One year later, before an audience of three hundred farmers, he presented a flax gin invented by abbot Bonniec, a professor of agriculture at l'Institution Saint-Joseph. While it was not among the city's "notables," the Marzin family nevertheless left a mark on the city through its dynamism, which was essentially oriented toward the surrounding countryside. It extended its activities and took full advantage of the opportunities created by the state to grow flax, and more broadly by the economic recovery that had emerged since the beginning of the century. Marzin products were adapted to the needs of an agricultural clientele that was not wealthy. Le Trégor was a poor province of Brittany, far less prosperous than the neighboring Léon.

Pierre thus grew up in a family of entrepreneurs who were oriented toward technology, and used pragmatism and responsiveness to find com-

---

14 Baruch, Marc-Olivier: „Négocier la contrainte; Les „administrations polytechniciennes" face à l'occupant", in: Baruch, Marc-Olivier / Guigueno, Vincent: *Le Choix des X: L'École Polytechnique et les polytechniciens, 1939 – 1945*, Paris 2000, p. 112.

mercial outlets for their initiatives. While he was completing his secondary education at the *collège* (middle school) in Lannion, his father sent him, at the age of fifteen, to farms to repair his clientele's machines. The child's curiosity was not limited to mechanics. He played the violin, and quickly excelled at his studies. He distinguished himself in mathematics and physics, and supplemented his knowledge with sometimes dangerous chemistry experiments with his younger brother Ludovic. He was an adolescent drawn by the sciences, but also very familiar with everyday issues and constraints. He left his native city after obtaining his *baccalauréat* (high school degree).[15] Encouraged by his teacher Mr. Colvez, his parents sent him to Rennes to attend preparatory courses for engineering schools. As a boarding pupil, he passed the competitive exam for admittance to l'Ecole centrale, but preferred to be held back a year in order to join Polytechnique the following year. This was a highly remarkable success for the young man, in keeping with the upward mobility fostered by the French Third Republic. While his departure for Rennes was already a major break, his arrival in October 1925 at l'Ecole polytechnique, located on the Montagne Sainte-Geneviève in Paris, truly changed Pierre's world. He apparently adapted with little difficulty to this new environment, and met his wife Catherine during the school's prestigious ball. He also established a number of friendships that he would offer him loyal support throughout his career.

After completing his military duty in the engineering corps, the branch that was in charge of the French army's transmissions at the time, he decided on his specialization. He attended courses at Supélec (Graduate School for Electrical Engineering), and was admitted to l'Ecole nationale supérieure des Postes, Télégraphes et Téléphones (ENSPTT, National Posts and Telecommunication Engineering School), where he familiarized himself with radio communications, and received education provided by engineers from the Service des études et des recherches techniques (SERT, Technical Studies and Research Department). It was to this institution that the young "*ingénieur ordinaire*" was assigned upon graduating

15 For the elements relating to Marzin's personal life, see: Griset, Pascal: *Les réseaux de l'innovation: Pierre Marzin 1905 – 1994*, Paris 2005 and Demouron, Frédéric: „ Pierre Marzin, ingénieur des Télécommunications", Master's Thesis (Paris-Sorbonne), Griset, Pascal (dir.), 2004.
The sources used for these two texts include the local press, the Marzin family archives, and administrative archives, notably the Légion d'Honneur file for Pierre Marzin.

from l'Ecole. SERT was not a large laboratory. It was more of a technical support organization, tasked with ensuring that the PTT (Post, Telegraph, and Telephone) network functioned properly. As a result, Marzin chiefly worked to meet the needs of a network of poor quality, although this task did not prevent him from directing his talent toward more stimulating fields. In the 1930s he took an interest in television, a field full of promise, but still in its beginnings. His research was recognized by a number of publications, as well as by the granting of patents, which was more rare for a civil servant. Its diversity underscores the openness of a researcher who enjoyed solving concrete operational problems. It was to this end that he produced a device that markedly improved the acoustic performance of telephones. Under the name of the "Marzin capsule" — a device that was more ingenious and perfectly designed than truly revolutionary — met with great success, and brought him attention. However, his initiatives were not always appreciated by a hierarchy that expected its agents to firstly carry out their task of controlling the equipment being used. Nevertheless, the young engineer continued his research, which notably developed a system allowing multiple telephone conversations to pass through the same conductor. This technique, known as "*courants porteurs simplifiés*" (power line technology), earned him a real reputation as a researcher. PTT agents called the device the "Marzinette."

This first phase of his career underscores Marzin's pragmatism. He did not graduate from the most prestigious corps of l'Ecole polytechnique, namely the *corps des mines*, but he chose the field of telecommunications, which he sensed offered room for dynamic activity. He clearly expressed, from that time forward, a taste for innovation combined with unrelenting pragmatism, which prompted him to direct his activities toward higher but specific and feasible objectives.

4. War and the First Realization of an Extended Project

In 1938, Marzin, who was working on a prototype for an answering machine, was asked to develop a gas mask that could be worn while making telephone calls...The war was near. In September 1939, he was mobilized and assigned to the general staff as a signals captain. He had retreated to the Landes when the armistice was signed, and was demobilized in the fall of 1940, before taking up his position at SERT in Paris. The shortages under the occupation made his power line system, which could increase network flow rate at low cost, of particular interest. Its capabilities were quickly improved, and Marzin filed for a patent for the improvements made to his device, which could now handle six bilateral ways.[16]

He believed that France's defeat was due largely to its technological inferiority compared to Germany, thereby agreeing with the analysis made by General de Gaulle in his Appeal of June 18. This inferiority was in keeping with the underdevelopment of French telecommunications, whose manufacturing industries were dependent on patents held notably by International Telegraph and Telephone (ITT), an American company. Marzin for a long time pointed out that his technicians, who intervened on the long-distance lines of the PTT network, had to step aside so that staff from the LMT, an ITT subsidiary, could intervene on certain elements that remained under seal. His desire to marshal the means to give French telecommunications their full role in the country's recovery was supported by the may-june 1940 "débâcle", but also preceded it. He was among those civil servants, in the specific context of PTT, who saw France's modernization—and preparations for it despite the occupation of a large part of its territory by German troops—as the only conceivable way to prepare for the future and better days. Just as it was important to right the ship after a humiliating military defeat, telecommunications had to finally assume their appropriate role in a modern country. The submission of "*télécommunicants"* (telecommunications staff) to *postiers*, (postal staff) within the PTT administration was seen as one of the causes for this lateness.[17] Two quests thus had to converge: independence from *postiers* and independence from foreign companies. Marzin shared this ambition with the engineers on his teams. SERT engineers, along with those from the Service des lignes à longue distance (Department for Long-distance Lines), belonged to a highly autonomous elite within the PTT administration. They were not subject to the power of the "*marchands de timbres*" (stamp sellers).[18] They were united by a common technical culture, one that saw research as the only way to achieve this dual independence from *postiers* and the Americans. This research could not be conducted separately from the operation of the network. The culture of *ingénieurs-chercheurs* (engi-

16 Marzin, Pierre / Sueur, René: „ Système à courants porteurs à 6 voies pour lignes aériennes", in: *Étude no 394 de la Direction des Études et Recherches des PTT*, 1942.

17 Carré, P. / Griset, P.: „Innovation et construction d'une culture d'entreprise de la DGT à France Télécom", in: *Entreprise et Histoire*, 29 (2002), p. 31 – 34

18 Entretien de Carré, Patrice / Clavaud, Georges: *Les Cahiers Télécommunications Histoire et Société*, 1995, p. 108 – 123.

neer-researcher) was not the same as scientists, nor was it identical to that of researchers in private laboratories. French industry had, in the form of the Compagnie Générale de Telegraphie sans fil (General Wireless Telegraphy Company), a high-level technological company devoted to electronics. Marzin's profile was very different from that of Maurice Ponte, who was working at the time on the Magnétron and aerial detection systems at the CSF.[19] Marzin and his men had a culture of network operators, and believed that only ambitious public research, directly connected to the operation of a national network, could achieve success. Marzin supported the idea of preserving the link between research and operation, all while ending the former's dependence on the latter.

This vision was partially fulfilled in February 1941. The law relating to the organization of the secretariat for communications created a Direction des Télécommunications (DT, Directorate for Telecommunications) that was distinct from the Direction des Postes et Bâtiments (Directorate for Postal Service and Buildings).[20] This was a first step toward independence. The creation in August 1941 of the Direction de la recherche et du contrôle technique (DRCT, Directorate for Research and Technical Control) confirmed this trend, and clearly affirmed the central role of technology in this process. This organization, with an augmented status and means at its disposal, was designed to promote a faster pace of research than that adopted by SERT. The DRCT brought together, in a single organization, both research and technical control. "A telecommunications researcher can conduct good research only when touching existing equipment, and being concretely aware of its imperfections and deficiencies," wrote its director Jean Dauvin.[21] In 1942, Marzin was appointed head engineer, and became Dauvin's deputy. This position allowed him to be associated, from its very conception, with the project for a major interministerial telecommunications laboratory, whose driving force would be the DRCT. Dauvin took as his example Great Britain, where the

> government had gained the benefit of moral influence over its manufacturers, and the limitation of their enslavement to foreign technology. It was similar results

19 Griset, Pascal: „ La Société Radio-France dans l'entre-deux-guerres", in: *Histoire, économie et société, Le changement technique contemporain: approches historiques* 1 (1983), p. 83 – 110.

20 Décret du 9 février 1941 (Decree from February 9, 1941), Journal Officiel, February 17, 1941.

21 Décret du 23 août 1941 (Decree from August 23, 1941). Jean Dauvin's role in this evolution was crucial.

> that led Germany and England to develop, over the last twenty years, research departments in the field of telecommunications and radioelectricity, amid conditions that strike us as being titanic in scale.[22]

The project was thus in keeping with a perspective of national independence within a European frame of reference. This would take place through the establishment of technology conceived in France, driven by companies controlled by national industry. Dauvin's sentiments reflected opinions shared by all of the engineers on his teams, in which his deputy Marzin already played an undeniable role as a leader.

These principles were once again present—and their fulfillment amplified—with the creation of the Centre National d'Etude des Télécommunications (CNET, National Center for Telecommunication Studies) by the law of May 4, 1944.[23] The center's mission was defined by a modern sense of the term "telecommunications":

> Electrical communications with or without wires — telecommunications — have developed considerably in recent years. Taking various forms and with an increasing number of users, they have extended their domain not only to the telephone and the telegraph, but also to radio broadcasting, television, acoustics, signaling, beacons, and security. This broad range of "telecommunications" has assumed an increasingly important role in the life of the Nation and its relations with the rest of the world.[24]

While the DRCT was an organization that reported solely to the Ministry for PTT, the CNET emerged as an interministerial organization that had to "conduct, or have conducted, the research requested by various ministerial departments and public services." From this intention there grew a somewhat heterogeneous structure, with the laboratories affiliated with the center being answerable to five different ministries:

- Direction des recherches et du contrôle technique, Laboratoire national de radioélectricité (Directorate for Research and Technical Control, National Laboratory for Radioelectricity) (Ministry for PTT);
- Section d'études du matériel de transmission (Department for the Study of Transmission Equipment) (Ministry for War);
- Laboratoire des Télécommunications (Laboratory for Telecommunications) (Ministry of the Navy);

22 Rapport DRCT 1942, cited by Atten, Michel: „La construction du CNET (1940-1945)", in: *Réseaux*, vol. 14, 1 (1996), p. 51.
23 Loi n° 102 du 4 mai 1944 (Law No. 102 from May 4, 1944).
24 Validation order issued by the provisional government on January 29, 1945.

- Laboratoire du ministère de l'Air (Laboratory of the Ministry of Air);
- Laboratoire de radiodiffusion du ministère de l'Information (Radio Broadcasting Laboratory of the Ministry of Information).

This project was therefore not limited to the general context of PTT, as argued by François Rouquet.[25] It went beyond a "desire to implement a technocratic ideal driven by earlier corporatist conflicts."[26] The model that would take hold in the 1960s began to emerge, and saw the development of research on a global scale conducted under the auspices of the DT, and industrialized by "national" companies.

5. *Marzin and the Resistance*

PTT staff[27] had an important role in the Resistance's fight against German occupation.[28] The most symbolic figure of the sacrifice is of course that of Simone Michel-Lévy, Compagnon de la Libération (Companion of the Liberation), who was deported and then hung on April 13, 1945 at the Flossenburg camp.[29] While many of these actions were conducted by resistance groups led by members of the military, the diverse trajectories involved and forms of action were particularly striking.[30] As his Senate biography points out, "Pierre Marzin took part in the Resistance."[31] From 1940 onward he directed a technical operation that allowed PTT engineers to prepare, through secret research, the reconstruction of transmissions af-

25 Rouquet, François: *Une Administration française face à la seconde guerre mondiale: les P.T.T.*, Ph.D. diss., Université de Toulouse 2, 1988, p. 290 – 300.

26 Rouquet, François, cited by Atten, Michel: „La construction du CNET (1940 – 1945)", p. 49.

27 Which included both *postiers* and telecommunications staff. *L'œil et l'oreille de la Résistance, action et rôle des agents des P. T. T. dans la clandestinité au cours du second conflit mondial.* Proceedings of the conference held in Paris on November 21 – 23, 1984, Toulouse, Comité d'Histoire des Postes et Télécommunications, Institut d'Histoire du Temps Présent (CNRS), 1986.

28 http://beaucoudray.free.fr/RPTT2.htm.

29 https://www.ordredelaliberation.fr/fr/compagnons/simone-michel-levy.

30 http://museedelaresistanceenligne.org/musee/doc/pdf/358.pdf.

31 Almost a homonym, Pierre Francis Marzin was a very active communist Resistance member whose activity was described in Maitron. https://maitron.fr-/spip.php?article120796, entry for MARZIN Pierre [MARZIN Francis, Pierre] by Yann Le Floc'h, Alain Prigent, François Prigent, version published online on November 30, 2010, last updated on March 13, 2019.

ter the German occupation."[32] Marzin did not go into hiding, and did not, strictly speaking, conduct any directly operational resistance activities that physically engaged him with the enemy. However, he provided support, means, and protection for many of his colleagues or subordinates who were directly engaged in action. This was especially true for what was known as the "Keller Network,"[33] whose activity reveals the cooperation between Marzin's DRCT research team and the engineers and technicians from the Lignes à longue distance. The idea of listening to the German army's communications was formulated by Captain Combaux, a member of the Services de renseignement français (French Intelligence Service), who was hidden within the PTT. As Georges Clavaud bore witness, when he confided in

> Misters Sueur and Marzin, the former believed that he could develop a technical solution, while the second would provide cover for the operation. The most sensitive part would be 'nabbing' the cable without alerting the Germans. Mr. Sueur proposed Robert Keller for this daring mission.[34]

Robert Keller, a mechanic and later a junior engineer in the Lignes à longue distance, had been mobilized as part of military telegraphy in 1939. His deeds earned him the Croix de Guerre. Once demobilized, he joined his center in Paris and engaged in the struggle against the occupier, despite being the father of four children. He was the only trustable and willing PTT technician who possessed all of the required skills and qualities to carry out the plan conceived by Combaux. When Combaux contacted him, "he accepted the mission immediately, and vouched for the PTT technicians he wanted to involve in carrying it out."[35] In 1942 Combaux rented a detached house in Noisy-le-Grand, located on the route travelled by the Paris-Metz (and then Berlin) cable used by the Germans.[36] "After a six-

32 https://www.senat.fr/senateur/marzin_pierre000136.html

33 Source K, https://unatrans.fr/documents/sourcek.pdf.

34 Mr. Georges Clavaud, who became head engineer and head of human resources at the DT, was Keller's comrade in arms, and a firsthand witness to his activity. "Robert Keller et la source K," account by Georges Clavaud, collected by Maurice Bruzeau, Revue T, 12 (1974), http://memoiredeguerre.free.fr/biogr/guillou-pierre.htm.

35 Romon, François: „La lettre de la fondation de la Résistance" 94 (2018), p. 7.

36 Combaux, Edmond: „Ce que fut la Source K". Speech given at the inauguration of the Centre téléphonique Robert Keller, December 1948, in: *La source K. Un des mystères de la dernière guerre. Un épisode extraordinaire de la Résistance dans l'administration des PTT au service des lignes souterraines à grande distance,* Paris 1949.

month preparatory period (...) Keller and his team diverted the cable under the Noisy-le-Grand house without raising the suspicion of the German technicians at supervisory measurement stations."[37] After five months of wiretapping, the operation had to be stopped due to indiscretions. A similar operation was successfully completed in Livry-Gargan on the Paris-Strasbourg cable. "We listened to and recorded the Führer himself, Goering, Keitel, von Rundstedt, Jodl...".[38] These two diversions:

> ...provided a considerable amount of intelligence regarding the German high command's projects. They were transmitted to the British Intelligence Service via the French intelligence service's Olga contacts, or through radio transmission from the secret PC Cadix intelligence center run by Gustave Bertrand, or by the French diplomatic posts in Bern and Lisbon.[39]

A denunciation brought an end to the network's activity, almost all of whose members were arrested. Keller, Georges Lobreau, Pierre Guillou, Laurent Matheron, and Gérard Grimpel were deported. Only Lobreau returned in 1945, having survived the death camps. Keller's silence under torture ensured that neither Combaux nor René Sueur were involved. Marzin's closest collaborators had acted with his agreement and under his protection. When Combaux, who was in Lyon when the first arrests were made, returned to Paris, it was Marzin he sought out.

> I had to know at all costs the reason for the arrest, and to go to Livry-Gargan to warn my operators, if there was still time to do so. I contacted Marzin [Inspector General, Director of Research and Technical Control for the PTT, the service to which Sueur belonged] in Montparnasse. He could only inform me of one thing, the arrest of a controller. It turned out to be, as I learned later on, Mr. Lobreau. I asked Mr. Marzin to clean out my office in the rue Bertrand.[40]

Marzin did so, accompanied by his son Guillaume and R. Sueur.[41] "They destroyed the reserve equipment, the subassemblies, and the technical

---

37 „Robert Keller et la source K", account by G. Clavaud, collected by Maurice Bruzeau, Revue T, 12 (1974).

38 Navarre, Henri: *Le service de renseignements, 1871-1944*, Paris 1978.

39 Ruffin, Raymond: *Résistance PTT*, Paris 1983, p. 51.

40 Account by colonel Combeaux in: „Les Ecoutes, la Source K, le SSC. Ce qu'il faut en savoir." https://www.aassdn.org/ECOUTES.pdf.

41 According to the family's memory, as gathered by Frédéric Demouron. Demouron, Frédéric: „Pierre Marzin, ingénieur des Télécommunications", Master's Thesis (Paris-Sorbonne), supervised by Pascal Griset, 2004, p. 50.

documents hidden in the cellar. Everything that was not burned or completely dismantled was thrown in the night into nearby sewers."[42]

Another account, written by the Resistance member and deportee Georges Raynaud,[43] allows us to better identify Marzin's position at the time.

> Resistance activity was dangerous, and required great secrecy. I will therefore speak in the conditional. I am almost certain that Marzin directly or indirectly was in relation with those who led the secret wiretapping of German circuits on the Paris-Strasbourg cable. R. Sueur, his faithful deputy, was close to G. Clavaud at the management for Lignes à Grande Distance, and no doubt with the works engineer Robert Keller. One thing is absolutely certain: the high input impedance amplifiers that made it possible to secretly listen to German circuits were studied and tested at the Transmission department's laboratory. This study was conducted by François Job, a young DT engineer that Marzin had ordered not to wear the yellow star…I was engaged in Resistance activity, which resulted in my arrest by the Gestapo at my home during the night of June 18, 1944. My mother informed lead research engineer G. Perinet of my arrest. When the Gestapo agents came to look through my personal things at the lab in rue Bertrand, and to arrest three colleagues who were similarly engaged (A. Peyrat, R. Carpentier and Y. Vincent), Marzin retained them in his office as long as he could, which allowed my three colleagues to deceive the Gestapo agents monitoring the rue Bertrand entrance, and to escape by the other exit on l'avenue de Saxe. To the credit of Marzin and his team, throughout my period of deportation my salary was, against all rules, paid to my mother.[44]

Georges Clavaud, a member of the Jade-Fitzroy network since 1943, who had previously helped the Keller group, explained that this practice was forbidden by administrative services, and that the spouses of deportees were financially supported by secret fund-raising efforts to which many agents of all ranks contributed, and then by funds transferred from London.

> There were many who played the game. In the Jade-Fitzeroy network there were about fifty men from the long-distance lines department who provided information. This activity was not very dangerous, but still: we asked them to give us the cable notebooks for a particular day. That way we had cable notebooks for all

42 Bata, Philippe / Bloch, Jean-Paul (eds.): *Le Centre National D'Etudes des Télécommunications 1944 –1974, Genèse et croissance d'un centre public de recherche*, Paris 1990, p. 33.

43 Written account sent to Georges Raynaud in 2003 and reproduced in his thesis, „ Pierre Marzin, ingénieur des Télécommunications", Griset, Pascal (dir.), 2004, p. 199 – 206.

44 Idem.

> stations. We transmitted to London, and London was able to precisely locate Germans CPs [Command Posts].[45]

The activities of Resistance networks also proved decisive in implementing Plan Violet, which cut almost all of the telecommunications lines used by the Germans during the D-Day landings on June 6, 1944.

We have seen the role played by Marzin, who relied on his high level hierarchical position to cover for his troops and produce equipment for their activities, without compromising himself directly with the Germans. This action materialized in very specific and personal form when Marzin hid Job, even when both of his parents had been deported as Jews and he was being actively sought. Job was "cloistered" in Marzin's apartment, "playing ping-pong with Pierre Camille and Charles, the couple's eldest sons."[46]

6. Liberation and Reconstruction

The entry of troops from the 2nd Armored Division in Paris on August 24, 1944 was a major stage in the Liberation of France. The sacrifice of PTT civil servants involved in the Resistance contributed to this victory. Yet as the German enemy was pulling away, a new but different kind of opponent, for the *télécommunicants* appeared alongside the liberating troops. On August 25, Sosthenes Behn, the founder of ITT, arrived in Paris wearing the uniform of the US Army, in which he served as a Lieutenant-Colonel. He took direct control of Le Matériel Téléphonique (LMT, Telephone Equipment),[47] and quickly established coordination between the Allies and French telecommunications services. On August 26, Georges Clavaud, who was highly involved in sabotage operations, was appointed by his superior

> as an advisor for long-distance cables with the First US Army's Strategic Command (…). I was summoned to avenue de Breteuil, to the LMT laboratory, and found myself before a colonel, a big guy: it was Behn...In perfect French he in-

45 Carré, Patrice, Interview with Georges Clavaud, transcription.

46 Interview with Pierre Camille Marzin, January 31, 2004. Demouron, Frédéric: „Pierre Marzin, ingénieur des Télécommunications", Master's Thesis (Paris-Sorbonne), supervised by Pascal Griset, 2004, p. 51/52.

47 http://siteedc.edechambost.net/CSF/ITT_Seconde_Guerre_mondiale.html This site compiles many sources and references on the history of French telecommunications companies.

> formed me that I had been assigned to the First Army to reestablish telephonic communications. I was thus tasked, under the orders of Colonel Williams, Chief of Signal for the First US Army, with putting my knowledge of the network at the service of the Allies. Beginning on the morning of the 28th, I shared life in the field with officers of the Signal Corps.[48]

The administration quickly provided means, but did so in connection with private companies.[49] Behn was soon joined by Maurice Deloraine, who was also in American uniform. The Paris laboratory director for LMT—the subsidiary of the powerful American company—had left France in October 1940, along with two engineers from his laboratory. He traveled to the United States via Portugal and North Africa, and transmitted the plans for a highly innovative electronic system called "Huff Duff," which played a major role in detecting enemy submarines throughout the conflict.[50] The political activity of ITT, from its creation in the mid-1920s until the 1970s, has led to protracted debates.[51] While the relations of its German subsidiary with Nazi authorities led to specific questions in this regard,[52] the investigations conducted into LMT directors upon Liberation did not lead anywhere.

While the brotherhood of arms was of course fully genuine, a new telecommunications "geopolitics" had emerged, and with it the reality of subordination to American interests, which was imposed even before the last Germans had left Paris. Later, the memory of Behn's arrival would be equally ambivalent. While the two forms of dependence were of course radically different, the key to escaping both was the same: the technological independence of French telecommunications. The continuity of this struggle was quickly superimposed on the decisive break represented by the Liberation. The other priority, which was indissolubly connected to the first, was still relevant: *télécommunicants* had to be freed from the administrative supervision of *postiers*. This objective could also be met only through control over the technologies of the future. The technical culture

48 Interview with de Carré, Patrice / Clavaud, Georges: *Les Cahiers Télécommunications Histoire et Société*, 1995, p. 108 – 123.

49 Carré, Patrice: „ Etre informé, faire parvenir les ordres, s'assurer de leur exécution. Les Télécommunications en France 1944 – 1946", in: *Le rétablissement de la Légalité Républicaine 1944,* Editions Complexe, 1996 p. 599 – 622.

50 Chapuis, Robert / Joel, Amos: *100 Years of Telephone Switching: Manual and Electromechanical Switching, 1878 – 1960's*, Ios Pr Inc, 2003, p. 306.

51 Sobel, Robert: *The Management of Opportunity,* New York 1982.

52 Sampson, Anthony: *The Sovereign State, The Secret History of ITT,* Holder and Soughton, 1973.

of telecommunications engineers eventually won out, Marzin believed, over the administrative culture on which the postal supremacy was based.

The continuity of these objectives, and their integration within a project of national recovery, clearly emerged when the Provisional Government of the French Republic confirmed in January 1945 the creation of CNET, especially in light of its organization and remit.[53] In the context of compromise between Gaullists and communists, its leadership was entrusted to Henri Jannès. Jean Dauvin, who was "…too close to the Vichy regime, and [was] thought to have worn the Francisque [honorary order under Vichy France] a little too conspicuously," was passed over in October 1944.[54] His deputy Marzin, "whose attitude during the war (…) was considered irreproachable," and whose research and patents had demonstrated his technical leadership, was the logical successor.[55] Marzin, who was appointed as director of CNET's Section particulière des PTT (Special PTT Department), soon found himself in opposition with its director. While he defended the notion of a powerful French industry, to be developed through a genuine partnership with public research, Jannès, who was very close to the communists, imposed an authoritarian policy and intrusive price controls that were very poorly received by industrial actors. This fundamental disagreement, combined with the conviction that his teams would have real means at their disposal only if reporting to the Ministry for PTT, prompted Marzin to request a revision of this organizational arrangement. This is precisely what he secured in 1946, when the Section particulière des PTT officially regained its independence.

7. *A Leadership Not Without Its Rough Patches*

This was a sea change in Marzin's career. Between 1944 and 1946, he had to assert himself in an environment in which political aspects often prevailed over scientific and technical expertise in determining an individual's career or the successful outcome of a project. To understand Marzin at this time, we can once again turn to Baruch, in an effort to move beyond strictly personal characters toward "a kind of intellectual history." Let us

53 The law from May 1944 was confirmed on January 29, 1945 via the order of validation issued by the provisional government.

54 Atten: " La construction du CNET (1940-1945)" p. 55.

55 Idem.

try to answer a few of Baruch's questions: "with what kind of knowledge did our civil servant begin an administrative career, after what career path…what god did he believe in, if he believed? How did he vote? What newspapers did he read?"[56] In terms of religion, the children of notables from Lannion studied during the postwar period at the new Collège Saint-Joseph (Saint Joseph middle school); Pierre was enrolled at the smaller and secular Collège de Lannion. Politically, he was clearly Gaullist in sensibility. However, to our knowledge he did not demonstrate any political engagement upon Liberation. His ideas, which were those of a moderate, were revealed when he was elected to the Senate in 1971 as part of the Gauche Démocratique ticket. His connection to the left was "minimal"— somewhat opportunist and driven by his Breton friends — for it was necessary to be elected in the left-leaning Côtes du Nord. He incidentally would be "outflanked" on his left, and beaten during the 1977 elections by a socialist slate. Professionally, he worked with the communists, including the *polytechnicien*, Christian activist, and Resistance member François du Castel,[57] who joined the 2nd Armored Division in 1944, fighting until Strasbourg. He joined the Parti Communiste[58] after the war and served as an activist — at CNET where he spent most of his career—with the Confédération Générale du Travail des PTT trade union (CGT/PTT). As a result, his opinion of Marzin cannot be suspected of deference. When questioned regarding his boss, he referred to the successive nominations that led Marzin to the head of the DT in 1967 with the following words: "I think Pierre Marzin's role in the Resistance and his involvement with the Freemasons, which was powerful at the PTT at the time, had an impact. But was there a better candidate…?"[59] Du Castel's account also reveals a personality that did not leave people indifferent.

> Pierre Marzin had a strong personality that enabled him to complete major tasks. He successfully invented an organization that simultaneously conducted highly scientific research and highly technical studies. This same personality sometimes

---

56 Baruch: „Négocier la contrainte; Les „administrations polytechniciennes" face à l'occupant", p. 113.

57 Two accounts on the same action within l'Ecole Polytechnique are available: https://journals.openedition.org/sabix/653

58 https://maitron.fr/spip.php?article145045, entry for DU CASTEL François, known as DUCASTEL François, version published online on February 18, 2013, last updated on February 18, 2013.

59 Interview with François du Castel. Demouron: „Pierre Marzin, ingénieur des Télécommunications", p. 236.

> led him into major conflicts (…). It sometimes expressed itself in outrageous language and very rude manners. But Marzin also knew how to trust researchers when it came to research that did not have a direct or immediate impact.

Georges Raynaud's account refines this point of view: "How to characterize Marzin? Very lively, I would say even virile, which did not exclude a certain timidity, he was a man who made sweeping decisions."[60] The energy, will, and capacity to free oneself from certain administrative rules were part of the Marzin "style." More than just an administration director, he was a leader, and could create and preserve genuine loyalty over the long-term. This loyalty was built over time through a bond with the man and a shared project. The men he knew between 1940 and 1944, those with whom he was involved in the Resistance, would remain with him throughout his career, creating bonds of friendship, solidarity, and especially trust. There was a real camaraderie that grew out of bonds forged in combat, but one that adhered to a hierarchy that none ignored. Years later, when presenting Edmond Combaux to a young historian, Marzin explained with a sly grin: "he is neither one nor the other." The bonds that were created were unbreakable.[61] His subordinates followed him without hesitation in the sometimes-bold decisions he subsequently had to make. This leadership hardly followed procedures, and was not really particularly with transparency. Du Castel, who was loyal to his union commitment, found fault with his boss's informal way of managing his teams. While he recognized his ability to "secure funds and better compensate his researchers," he also underscored Marzin's "highly personal management," as well as bonuses distributed "to the researcher according to his own discretion (…) attributed without controls."[62] These were clear instances of pragmatism, of a sense of "mission." Du Castel pointed out, not without respect: "Pierre Marzin had a high ideal of the PTT's public service, because he had a great sense of the state."[63]

60 Account transmitted by Georges Raynaud to François Demouron. Demouron: Pierre Marzin, ingénieur des Télécommunications, p. 206.

61 Personal memory of the author.

62 Interview with François du Castel, Demouron: „ Pierre Marzin, ingénieur des Télécommunications", p. 235.

63 Idem, p. 236.

8. Conclusion

During these ten years, Marzin affirmed his ideas and strong personality, which were rooted in his rural youth in Brittany. He used institutions to complete his own projects, in the service of a vision that looked past the overly rigid structures of the present. His pragmatism was that of an ambitious man, but one who was also modest. He knew how to assemble means, which were almost always lacking, and how to seek out opportunities, even if it meant waiting and accepting less favorable situations. His management of people was partly based on affection. He fostered rapid initiative and decision-making, and relied on trust in an essentially oral form of communication. Marzin wrote little. He accepted the rules in order to better circumvent them for a project he deemed to be of great interest. In the 1950s and 1960s, he laid the foundation for the renewal of French telecommunications.[64] Marzin served France and the state. Yet he can be defined as a patriot not for the nationalist vision of his action, for his mode of operation was more broadly that of a man of proximity and loyalty. He was thus able, not without opportunism, to ensure that Lannion was the site selected for the CNET's partial decentralization in the early 1960s. Asked a few years later regarding the origin of this crucial decision, which had rejected Grenoble in favor of his native region, he explained, not without guile, that he had little to do with it: "It was the staff who decided. I simply asked them if they preferred the sea or the mountains...And they answered the sea."[65]

9. References

Baruch, Marc-Olivier / Duclert, Vincent: *Serviteurs de l'État: une histoire politique de l'administration française, 1875 – 1945,* Paris 2000.

Baruch, Marc-Olivier / Guigueno, Vincent: *Le Choix des X: L'École Polytechnique et les polytechniciens, 1939 – 1945,* Paris 2000.

Baruch, Marc-Olivier: „Négocier la contrainte; Les „administrations polytechniciennes" face à l'occupant", in: Baruch, Marc-Olivier / Guigueno, Vincent: *Le*

64 Griset, Pascal: „Le développement du Téléphone en France depuis les années 1950. Politique de recherche et recherche d'une politique", in: *Vingtième Siècle, revue d'histoire*, 24 (1989), p. 41 – 54.

65 Memory of a conversation with the author.

Choix des X: L'École Polytechnique et les polytechniciens, 1939 – 1945, Paris 2000.

Baruch, Marc-Olivier: *Servir l'État français: l'administration en France de 1940 à 1944,* Paris 1997.

Bata, Philippe / Bloch, Jean-Paul (eds.): *Le Centre National D'Etudes des Télécommunications 1944 – 1974, Genèse et croissance d'un centre public de recherche*, Paris 1990.

Burrin, Philippe: *La France à l'heure allemande (1940 – 1944)*, Paris 1995.

Carré, P. / Griset, P.: „Innovation et construction d'une culture d'entreprise de la DGT à France Télécom", in: *Entreprise et Histoire* 29 (2002), p. 31 – 34.

Carré, Patrice: „Etre informé, faire parvenir les ordres, s'assurer de leur exécution. Les Télécommunications en France 1944 – 1946", in: *Le rétablissement de la Légalité Républicaine 1944, Editions Complexe*, 1996, p. 599 – 622.

Chapuis, Robert / Joel, Amos: *100 Years of Telephone Switching: Manual and Electromechanical Switching, 1878 – 1960's*, Ios Pr Inc, 2003.

Combaux, Edmond: „Ce que fut la Source K". Speech given at the inauguration of the Centre téléphonique Robert Keller, December 12, 1948, in: *La source K. Un des mystères de la dernière guerre. Un épisode extraordinaire de la Résistance dans l'administration des PTT au service des lignes souterraines à grande distance*, Paris 1949.

Dard, Olivier: "Les élites technocratiques dans la Résistance française", in: Marcot, François / Musiedlak Didier (dir.): *Les Résistances, miroir des régimes d'oppression. Allemagne, France, Italie, Presses universitaires de Franche-Comté*, 2006.

Demouron, Frédéric: „Pierre Marzin, ingénieur des Télécommunications", Master's Thesis (Paris-Sorbonne), supervised by Pascal Griset, 2004.

Fickers, Andreas / Griset, Pascal: "Communicating Europe: Technologies, Information, Events (1850 – 2000)", London 2019.

Fridenson, Patrick / Griset. P. (dir): *Entreprises de haute technologie, État et souveraineté depuis 1945*, Paris 2013.

Griset, Pascal: „La Société Radio-France dans l'entre-deux-guerres", in: *Histoire, économie et société, Le changement technique contemporain: approches historiques*, n°1 (1983), p. 83 – 110.

Griset, Pascal: „Le développement du Téléphone en France depuis les années 1950. Politique de recherche et recherche d'une politique", in: *Vingtième Siècle, revue d'histoire*, 24 (1989), p. 41 – 54.

Griset, Pascal: *Les réseaux de l'innovation: Pierre Marzin 1905 – 1994,* Paris 2005.

Griset, Pascal, (dir): *Les ingénieurs des Télécommunications dans la France contemporaine: Réseaux, innovation et territoires, XIXe-XXe siècles*, Paris 2014.

Joly, Hervé: *A Polytechnique. X 1901. Enquête sur une promotion de polytechniciens, de La Belle Époque aux Trente Glorieuses*, Paris 2021.

Kohlrausch, Martin / Trischler, Helmut: *Building Europe on Expertise: Innovators, Organizers, Networkers,* Basingstoke 2014.

Laborie, Léonard: *L'Europe mise en réseaux. La France et la coopération internationale dans les postes et les Télécommunications (années 1850-années 1950),* Brussels 2010.

Marzin, Pierre / Sueur, René: „Système à courants porteurs à 6 voies pour lignes aériennes", in: *Étude no 394 de la Direction des Études et Recherches des PTT*, 1942.

Navarre, Henri: *Le service de renseignements, 1871-1944*, Paris 1978.

Paxton, Robert: *La France de Vichy*, Paris 1973.

Romon, François: „La lettre de la fondation de la Résistance" 94 (2018).

Rouquet, François: *Une Administration française face à la seconde guerre mondiale: les P.T.T.*, Ph.D. diss., Université de Toulouse 2, 1988.

Ruffin, Raymond: *Résistance PTT*, Paris 1983.

Sampson, Anthony: *The Sovereign State, The Secret History of ITT, Holder and Soughton,* 1973.

Sobel, Robert: *The Management of Opportunity*, New York 1982.

German Careers within the European Postal and Telecommunications Union (EPTU) – Continuities and Discontinuities

Christian Henrich-Franke, Sabrina Proschmann

Table of Content

1. Introduction

The creation of the European Postal and Telecommunications Union (EPTU) – the first European body for these two sectors – in 1942 involved multiple actors from different countries. To trace continuities and discontinuities and to understand the individual motivations of the actors involved, we need to shine a light on their backgrounds and career paths.

To this end, we have chosen to focus in detail on the careers of two high-ranking German officials who promoted cooperation in the postal and telecommunications sectors during the Second World War: Helmut Bornemann (1902-1991) and Friedrich Risch (1895-1965).

Both are representative for careers of actors within the German postal and telecommunications services involved in the creation of the EPTU. Helmut Bornemann was a telecommunications engineer working within the *Reichspostzentralamt* (the German postal service's technical department and centre for technical research) during the war. Friedrich Risch was head of the international department within the *Reichpostministerium* – the ministry in charge of the German postal and telecommunications services and tasked with the creation of the EPTU. Both also reflect the spectrum of actors involved – from higher ministerial levels to renowned experts within the administrations, from very little to vast experience in international relations and from a responsibility for settling the general and/or legal aspects of international cooperation to negotiating technical standards.

Both men's careers share similarities with other actors in the sector: hence, Bornemann's career, that culminated in his appointment as secretary of state in the *Bundespostministerium* in the 1960s, resembled that of Paul Jäger and Friedrich Gladenbeck. Risch shared a similar career path to Willi Köhn: a high-ranking member of the SS, Köhn became a ministerial director and head of the department "East" (*Abteilung Ost*), which was responsible for the occupied territories in Eastern Europe. He had no specific knowledge of or experience with national or international postal affairs. The vast majority of the *Reichspost*'s appointees abroad, such as Wilhelm Engelhardt, Heinrich Habig, and Fritz Harder, charged with liaising with the other postal and telecommunications administrations also rose quickly through the ranks of the international scene. After having been promoted quickly after 1933, Risch's career in the postal services ended abruptly after the war – as did for instance Kurt Timm's.[1]

We assume that, alongside institutional and organisational structures, individual actors are also important vectors of continuity and discontinuity. Due to the war, they acted within contested institutional and organisational structures, and they made practices of cooperation visible. In this article, we examine how these two career paths developed and how they were influenced by their involvement in the EPTU. As a conclusion, we will outline some explanations for the differences between Bornemann and Risch's careers.

2. Helmut Bornemann: A Linear Career – Before, During and After the War

Helmut Bornemann was among the most prominent driving forces behind international telecommunications cooperation within the European Postal

---

1 Ueberschär, Gerd R.: *Die Deutsche Reichspost 1933 – 1945. Eine politische Verwaltungsgeschichte* (Vol. 2), Berlin 1999, S. 30.; Bundesarchiv, Berlin-Lichterfelde, R4701/39795, Haupt-Kartei Habig; R4701/39830 Haupt-Kartei Engelhardt; R4701/39829, Haupt-Kartei Harder; Landesarchiv Schleswig-Holstein, Abt. 460.13 Nr. 436 Timm, Kurt; Staatsarchiv, Hamburg, 221-11 C(P)774, Erwin Jacobi, Fr. Gienapp, Walter Donandt an Zentralstelle für Berufungsausschüsse zur Ausschaltung Nationalsozialisten, 30.07.1947.

and Telecommunications Union (EPTU) during the Second World War.[2] Convinced that the regulation and standardisation of telecommunications was a purely technical issue, Bornemann saw no reason to cease the activities of the International Telecommunication Union (ITU) during wartime, which included the meetings of the International Consultative Committees for Telegraph, Telephone and Radio (CCIT, CCIF and CCIR). After the ITU had postponed all conferences, in the autumn of 1940 Bornemann joined forces with Giuseppe Gneme, an Italian engineer and CCIF pioneer in the years preceding the war, and proposed to continue the committees' activities with some minor changes, e.g. standard setting for broadcasting and television by the CCIR. Bornemann and Gneme envisioned a working group as a temporary solution during the war, but the format was adopted by the EPTU. Bornemann therefore became a key player in EPTU meetings and modelled its institutional design on the ITU. Throughout the war, he even managed to maintain a connection to the few engineers from foreign telecommunication administrations such as the Swiss, who did not participate in the EPTU, and to indirectly involve them in technology-related discussions.

His involvement in the EPTU did not prevent Bornemann from returning to the international organisations, committees and networks responsible for the regulation and standardisation of international telecommunication and radio networks and equipment after the war. When Germany officially rejoined the ITU in 1949, Bornemann saw himself appointed to leadership positions as a chairman within the CCIs or as a head and vice-head of the German delegations to the plenipotentiary conferences in 1952 (Montreux), 1959 (Geneva) and 1965 (Buenos Aires). He even served as a member of the ITU's administrative council between 1959 and 1963. As a leading expert for international telecommunication issues, Bornemann was appointed as the German representative to the Spaak Committee, set up to discuss the creation of the European Economic Community (EEC) in 1955/56. In 1959, he became the chair of the European Conference of Postal and Telecommunication Administration's (CEPT) working group for telephony, and he

2 Henrich-Franke, Christian / Laborie, Léonard: "European Union for and by communication networks: continuities and discontinuities during the Second World War", in: *Comparativ* 1 (2018), p. 82 – 100; Henrich-Franke, Christian: "Engineering Expertise and the Regulation of International Telecommunications in Europe from the 1950s to the 1970s", in: Schneiker, Andrea / Henrich-Franke, Christian / Kaiser, Robert / Lahusen, Christian (eds.): *Transnational Expertise*, Baden-Baden 2018, pp. 75 – 100.

headed the establishment of intercontinental direct dialling. He was internationally well-known and well-respected in the telecommunication sector by the time he retired from the international arena in 1967.

Bornemann was able to pursue this linear career because engineers were bound together in specific expert communities that transcended political tensions and pressures. These engineers enjoyed a high degree of independence on the international stage, protected by a 'tacit political agreement' with the political authorities. They were given considerable leeway, provided that they enabled international connections and national equipment producers were protected from international competition. This 'tacit political agreement' existed before, during and after the war. Of course, their expertise also played an important role as technical staff with a unique and indispensible knowledge could not be easily replaced.

Bornemann entered the expert community in the interwar period. He studied engineering at the Technical Universities of Berlin and Darmstadt between 1921 and 1925. He attended lectures given by famous German physicists such as Albert Einstein, Max Planck and Max von Laue, forming part of a new generation of engineers trained in experimental research rather than in the traditional style of theoretical education. At that time, the amalgamation of mathematical, theoretical and experimental research resulted in a new type of (telecommunication) engineer with a distinctive self-image, setting them apart from other types of engineers. Bornemann, who was an expert for both undersea cables and radio technologies, began his professional career at the *Reichspostzentralamt* and became a CCIF member in the late 1920s. He was a pioneer in the field of international telephone connections in Europe and belonged to a generation of engineers, who transformed the three CCIs into important transnational forums for the standardisation of international telecommunications and radio in the 1930s. Joining the CCIF as a national engineer for Germany, Bornemann was equipped with a transnational approach to technological efficiency. Throughout the 1930s, Bornemann represented the German telecommunication administration at all Administrative Telephone Conferences and CCIF meetings. He became chair of the CCIF's study group IX, where he was responsible for reaching reasonable compromises that satisfied national needs across Europe. After the Second World War, the CCIF resumed its activities with a plenary assembly in London as early as August 1945, followed by a second one in Montreux just a year later. Germany was not invited and, as a result, Bornemann was not present at the meetings. He was, however, informally kept up to date about the CCIF's activities and encountered few difficulties being readmitted to the CCIF officially in 1949.

Subsequently, Bornemann rose up through the German administration's internal hierarchy and was in a position to shape international cooperation in the telecommunication sector. In the Spaak Committee, Bornemann and some of his international engineer colleagues, who were also appointed as their governments' representatives, were in a key position to influence decisions about a supranational European policy on telecommunications. There, they tried their utmost to prevent the supranational EEC from entering the telecommunication sector, which they perceived as a potential threat to the independency of engineers. Technical experts such as Bornemann rejected everything they deemed incompatible with the established forms of regulation and cooperation.[3] It is possible that Bornemann's motivation came from his experiences during the war, when the idea of an expert working group was superseded by a (political) project like the EPTU.

In 1963 Bornemann finally crowned his career with the appointment as secretary of state in the German Ministry for Post and Telecommunications, with responsibility for the entire area of telecommunications, reporting directly to the federal ministers Richard Stücklen and Werner Dollinger until his retirement in 1968.

3. Friedrich Risch – A Wartime Career

As the head of the international department within the German *Reichspostministerium*, ministerial director Dr Friedrich Risch was instrumental for the creation of the EPTU. His department was also key for international postal relations, as Germany had formally left the Universal Postal Union (UPU) in 1939. After the Postal Union Congress in Buenos Aires the German administration refused to sign the final agreement because Czechoslovakia was still mentioned as a signatory.[4] However, the UPU's German vice-director Wilhelm Triest stayed in his position after 1939.[5]

The *Reichpostministerium*'s international department was founded by *Reichsminister* Wilhelm Ohnesorge in late 1940, with the primary aim of shaping the EPTU. Risch, however, stated that he had travelled to Russia as early as in the spring of the same year to discuss the idea of a European

---

3 Franke, Christian: "Das Post- und Fernmeldewesen im europäischen Integrationsprozess der 1950/60er Jahre", in: *Journal of European Integration History* 2 (2004), pp. 95 – 117.

4 Ueberschär: Die Deutsche Reichspost, pp. 281 – 284.

5 Politisches Archiv, Berlin, RAV Bern 2582, Durchdruck Deutsche Gesandtschaft Nr. 183, 13.01.1941.

Postal Union.[6] From the end of 1940, Risch worked both with actors within Germany – including the staff of the *Reichpostministerium*, the *Reichspost* and the Foreign Ministry – and colleagues from other countries towards the creation of the EPTU in October 1942. From an organisational point of view, Risch was at the core of the EPTU project. In the area of postal services, he was the key figure in drafting and implementing the German European postal agenda in the following years. Present at all the preparatory meetings and committee sessions, his aim was to implement the goals that the *Reichspostministerium* had set for the EPTU in September 1940[7], most importantly abolishing the transit fee and harmonising the fee schedules based on the domestic German postal system.

Friedrich Risch was a lawyer before he joined the *Reichspost* aged 29 in 1924. He first worked in Regensburg, where he stayed for ten years before being promoted to the *Reichpostdirektion* in Berlin in 1934. In 1938, he became part of the ministerial staff and was promoted to ministerial director a year later. His promotion meant a career advancement from the administrative to the higher ministerial level.[8] After the war, he made no attempt to regain a position in the *Reichspost* or the ministry. Instead, he chose to work again as a lawyer within the administration of the Evangelical Regional Church in Hamburg. This confines his rather short-lived career to the National Socialist regime and the war years.[9] Despite his post-war career change, in 1948 Risch published a book about Heinrich von Stephan, the driving force behind the creation of the Universal Postal Union in 1874. Notably, the book only focused on von Stephan and makes no reference to the political situation at the time.[10]

While Risch's career within the postal services followed a typical path – first employed locally, then promoted through the *Reichspostdirektion* to the ministry – it was unusual in that careers within the international postal

6 Staatsarchiv, Hamburg, 221-11 C(P)774, Erwin Jacobi, Fr. Gienapp, Walter Donandt an Zentralstelle für Berufungsausschüsse zur Ausschaltung Nationalsozialisten, 30.07.1947, p. 3.

7 Bundesarchiv, Berlin-Lichterfelde, R4701/11248, Vortrag auf der Gesamtsitzung des RPM von Oberpostrat Dr. Timm.

8 Bundesarchiv, Berlin-Lichterfelde, R4701/39833, Haupt-Kartei Risch.

9 Staatsarchiv, Hamburg, 221-11 C(P)774, Erwin Jacobi, Fr. Gienapp, Walter Donandt an Zentralstelle für Berufungsausschüsse zur Ausschaltung Nationalsozialisten, 30.07.1947.

10 Risch, Friedrich Adolf: *Heinrich von Stephan: Die Idee der Weltpost*, Hamburg 1948.

services were generally quite long.[11] He had not been trained in the postal services before 1924, and on becoming head of the international department in 1940, he had never participated in an international postal congress. Under his authority, the *Reichspost*'s representatives abroad created a new system of international connections that compensated the lack of an established network.[12] His rise within the ministerial structures in 1938 is surely also due to the staff policies of Reichspostminister Wilhelm Ohnesorge. Before becoming minister, Ohnesorge had already been state secretary, but his new position gave him the power to implement staff policies strongly influenced by National Socialist thinking. Officials close to him, including Risch in his early days at the ministry, benefitted from this, which also explains his promotions. Risch's relationship with the minister worsened as he refused to renounce his religious beliefs.[13] His career was also limited to Ohnesorge's tenure and therefore cut short by the end of the war. After 1945, Risch claimed that the EPTU was nothing short of a resistance movement, as it attempted to connect people in times of great division, and that it had been counteracting the general direction of the *Reichspostministerium*. He insisted that this difficult "game against all rules of diplomacy"[14] had only been possible because the Reich's leading figures, including Reichpostminister Ohnesorge, lacked understanding of the EPTU project. Risch attempted to prove his point by highlighting that his article on the possibilities of a European postal union had been published by the Universal Postal Union and that he had even received praise by an English telecommunications expert.[15] The expert referenced was General Mance, but his alleged praise of the EPTU could neither be verified in the German nor in the English version of his book.[16] It is also debatable whether the higher-ranking ministerial officials, including the minister Ohnesorge, did not understand the EPTU. He had ample experience in the postal services – having started his

---

11 Laborie, Léonard: L'Europe mise en réseaux. La France et la coopération internationale dans les postes et les télécommunications (années 1850-années 1950), Bruxelles 2011, pp. 115 – 122.

12 Politisches Archiv, Berlin, RAV Zagreb 147, Aufgaben der ins Ausland entsandten Beauftragten der DRP, undatiert.

13 Ueberschär: Die Deutsche Reichspost, pp. 25/26.

14 Own translation: "ein Spiel gegen alle Regeln der Diplomatie", Staatsarchiv, Hamburg, 221-11 C(P)774, Erwin Jacobi, Fr. Gienapp, Walter Donandt an Zentralstelle für Berufungsausschüsse zur Ausschaltung Nationalsozialisten, 30.07.1947.

15 Ibidem.

16 cf. Bridg.-Gen. Sir Mance, Osborne (1944): International Telecommunications, London, p. 7; German edition: p. 8.

career in 1890.[17] The idea that the EPTU was a peace project connecting peoples was also promoted overtly by the minister and the *Reichspostministerium*.[18]

4. Comparison

As mentioned above, the two careers are strikingly different, which partly can be explained by the positions Bornemann and Risch held within the ministry and the *Reichspostzentralamt*. We will base our comparison on a variety of criteria: from their training to the length of their career, their role within the EPTU and their post-war careers.

- Bornemann was a highly trained expert in his field. He had an expertise that was difficult to acquire and therefore it was difficult to replace him. He was a key member of the transnational expert community within the CCIs. Risch was a trained lawyer with a broad rather than specific knowledge of the postal services and the international postal communities.
- Bornemann had a career of just under 40 years in the telecommunications field – with more than 30 years at the top tier of international cooperation. Risch worked for the *Reichspost* for 21 years, with 5 of these years spent as the head of the international department. This was certainly the height of his international career in the postal services.
- Bornemann was primarily involved in the committees that focussed on technical standardisation and regulation due to his participation in the initiative to create a working group for telecommunications late in 1940. Risch was appointed as head of the international department with the task of creating a European Postal Union. He was therefore involved in the committees regulating international postal services and the EPTU's organisational aspects. In his position, he was the leading figure on the German side. He was also responsible for the political and/or diplomatic negotiations with the German Foreign Ministry.
- Bornemann's position during the Third Reich did not damage his postwar career. He quickly rose through the ranks in the *Bundespost* and reached an even higher ministerial level than Risch when he had be-

17 Bundesarchiv, Koblenz, R4701/25644.
18 Europäischer Postkongress, pp. 12 – 16.

come head of the international department within the *Reichspostministerium* in 1938. Risch left the postal services to work for the Evangelical Church in Hamburg. His undersecretary Dr Friedrich Reiss would later be responsible for the foreign relations within the *Bundespost*, which made Risch's publication about the EPTU resurface in the files in 1951.

How can we explain the differences in these two careers?

- There is a difference in infrastructure systems that may have a decisive influence on careers in these sectors: the postal services depend on other infrastructures' physical communication and transportation networks such as roads, railways or airlines. The technical standards of these networks are predominantly defined outside the postal administrations' sphere of competence. They are by their nature less technical. Negotiations on international postal networks focus on tariffs and legal standards as well as revenue, while telecommunications have their own physical networks that require technical standardisation.
- The more technical an infrastructure system is, the more indispensable the experts become, as a high degree of specialist expertise is required. The case of Bornemann illustrates this quite well: he developed a very specific knowledge that made him difficult to replace – not just from a German, but also from an international perspective. The postal services on the other hand are only technical in terms of transportation and the knowledge required seems easier to transfer as it is less specific. The actors in the postal services are therefore more interchangeable.
- Telecommunication and in particular telephony saw a period of rapid technical development during the 1930s and 1940s. It spread across European societies in the interwar period and turned out to be a transnational technology. It was planned and built by an enthusiastic, transnational community of engineers, which transcended the political tensions between the wars. In the postal services (with the exception of airmail) no such bonds between experts formed on an international level.

In conclusion, both Bornemann and Risch's careers were fairly typical for German officials within the EPTU, although with very different outcomes in terms of continuity. Tracing these individual careers sheds new light on reasons and mechanisms behind continuities and discontinuities surrounding the European postal and telecommunications services.

5. References

Europäischer Postkongress. Wien 1942; Original-Nachdruck zur postgeschichtlichen Forschung in deutscher (ohne italienische) Sprache = Congresso Postale Europeo, 2013. Licensed ed., [Reprint] of the ed. Berlin, Reichsdr., 1942. Berlin-Schönefeld: Morgana-Ed (Moderne Postgeschichte, GG 77).

Franke, Christian: "Das Post- und Fernmeldewesen im europäischen Integrationsprozess der 1950/60er Jahre", in: *Journal of European Integration History* 2 (2004), pp. 95 – 117.

Henrich-Franke, Christian: "Engineering Expertise and the Regulation of International Telecommunications in Europe from the 1950s to the 1970s", in: Schneiker, Andrea / Henrich-Franke, Christian / Kaiser, Robert / Lahusen, Christian (eds.): *Transnational Expertise*, Baden-Baden 2018, pp. 75 – 100.

Henrich-Franke, Christian / Laborie, Léonard: "European Union for and by communication networks: continuities and discontinuities during the Second World War", in: *Comparativ* 1 (2018), pp. 82 – 100.

Laborie, Léonard: *L'Europe mise en réseaux. La France et la coopération internationale dans les postes et les télécommunications (années 1850-années 1950)*, Bruxelles 2011.

Risch, Friedrich Adolf: *Heinrich von Stephan: Die Idee der Weltpost*, Hamburg 1948.

Ueberschär, Gerd R.: *Die Deutsche Reichspost 1933-1945. Eine politische Verwaltungsgeschichte* (Vol. 2), Berlin 1999.

Representing the EPTU to a Wider Public – Stamps Commemorating the Union's Foundation

Sabrina Proschmann

The European Postal and Telecommunications Union could not only be experienced by users through sending mail but also by buying stamps. At least in four countries, Germany, Norway, Slovakia and the Netherlands, this was possible. Not all of the participating administrations commemorated the occasion by emitting a stamp. This might not only be due to lacking will but to missing available funds. Special stamps cost money and all of administrations were on a tight budget because of the ongoing war.

The German postal administration emitted three different stamps – two of them depicted the postman on horseback that was also the symbol of the congress. One stamp also had light coming from above while on the other one the postman was above a globe. The third stamp showed a postman blowing his horn in front of a map of Europe. The motifs of the stamps contained the lettering: European postal congress.[1] These stamps all reflect some form of hegemony – the postmen are bigger than Europe and the globe respectively. They also bear witness to the new start for European postal relations that the EPTU was supposed to bring according to its founders. This can be seen by the light from above on one of the stamps. The connection to postal services was made clear through the postman and the horn –very common and more importantly neutral symbols. The aim of the stamp was not to celebrate German hegemony in the new postal Europe.

The Norwegian postal administration published one stamp in two different colours on the same day the German administration did: 12th of October 1942 – which was the starting date of the congress. This means that it was not the congress but rather than the newly founded European postal union that was supposed to be commemorated. The motif of the stamp was

1 Michel® Deutschland 2019/2020 2019, p. 167.

divided into two sections: one that showed the head of Vidkun Quisling[2], the other one showed a lion with a double-paw. The first one was the exact motif of the last stamp emitted in Norway and the other one was a replica of the first ever Norwegian stamp (however, a mistake was made and the replica was not exact which cause great discussions among philatelists). The frame around the two sections read "12th October – European Postal Union Vienna 1942".[3] Given the fact that the agreements to create the union were not yet signed at this date, it can be said that the Norwegian administration appeared to have been very sure that they would be. Apart from the lettering, this motif has little to do with Europe or a postal union and has to be interpreted before the national background and Quisling's attempt to legitimate himself as the leader of Norway. The bringing together of the first and the last Norwegian stamp emitted was probably supposed to signify continuity. Vidkun Quisling was the one politician that would give Norway a new place in the "New Europe".

The stamp that the Slovakian administration emitted in three colours to commemorate the foundation of the EPTU combined "international" elements in the form of a series of coat of armours starting in the left bottom corner with flags of the Germany and Italy at the beginning. Not all flags are visible, thus one has to assume that the other countries' flags follow. The date of the congress, the Stephan's Dome in Vienna and carrier pigeon with a petal of linden in its beak in the forefront of the stamp completed the motif[4]. A "normal" user of the stamp would have to draw the connection to the EPTU with the help of the indications date, place, pigeon for postal services and the flags of the countries of the member administrations – which appears quite challenging. In contrast to the other administrations, the Slovakian administration chose to use a very political symbol, namely the flag, for the stamp. The connection to postal services appears to be rather weak compared to the stamps from Germany and the Netherlands. As it was the case regarding the Norwegian stamp, it seems as though the stamp rather puts Slovakia in the context of a "New Europe" at the side of Germany and Italy.

The Dutch administration only released its stamp in January of 1943. The stamp's motif consisted of the lettering "European PTT union – 19th

---

2 National-Socialist Minister President of Norway at the time.

3 Riksarkivet, Oslo, Postens sentralledelse, Fa-008, 309-310 Postforening.

4 Michel® Europa 2018. Band 1 2018, pp. 555 – 556.

October 1942" and a post horn in the background as well as the words "Netherlands".[5] This stamp is relatively simple and makes a clear connection to postal services. The fact that the post horn is only seen in the background actually leads to a focus on the lettering that announces the union.

The four administrations emitted stamps that are quite different – the motifs were not coordinated between them and thus highlight other aspects, most probably due to the national audience that needed to be served. In the 1920s and 1930s, the wish for a European postal union had often been connected to a common stamp that would give the peoples of Europe a feeling of belonging together[6]. It is thus noteworthy that the member administrations of the EPTU did not emit one common stamp and that the creation of one postal area within Europe was not also used to create one common stamp or to publish one collection at the same date in order to establish some sort of transnational audience. In fact, the idea to have one common stamp was discussed within the German *Reichspostministerium* but rejected due to financial and technical difficulties.[7] This points to the fact that one common stamp would have maybe been too symbolic. It would have attested a deeper unification than the administrations intended. The question of one common European stamp reappeared very quickly after the war and was answered with the so called "Europe stamps": Here, a same motif was emitted from 1958 until 1973 by the participating administrations. However, they were only valid nationally.[8]

References

Laborie, Léonard: "Enveloping Europe. Plans and Practices in Postal Governance, 1929 – 1959", in: *Contemporary European History* 27 (2) (2018), pp. 301 – 325. DOI: 10.1017/S0960777318000085.

---

5 Michel® Europa 2017/2018. Band 6 2017, p. 1228.

6 Laborie, Léonard: "Enveloping Europe. Plans and Practices in Postal Governance, 1929 – 1959", in *Contemporary European History* 27 (2) (2018), pp. 301 – 325. DOI: 10.1017/S0960777318000085, p. 305.

7 Bundesarchiv, Berlin-Lichterfelde, R4701/11448, Schulze an Rittmeister, 18.01.1943.

8 Rötzel, Werner: „Europamarken Gemeinschaftsausgaben", in: *Archiv für deutsche Postgeschichte* 1 (1979), S. 58 – 65.

Michel® Deutschland 2019/2020 (2019). 106. Auflage. Germering: Schwaneberger Verlag GmbH (Michel® Deutschland).

Michel® Europa 2017/2018. Band 6. *Westeuropa* (2017). 102. Auflage. Unterschlei[beta]heim: Schwaneberger Verlag GmbH (Michel Europa-Katalog. Westeuropa).

Michel® Europa 2018. Band 1. *Mitteleuropa* (2018). 103. Auflage. Unterschleißheim: Schwaneberger Verlag GmbH (Michel Europa-Katalog Mitteleuropa).

Rötzel, Werner: „Europamarken Gemeinschaftsausgaben“, in: *Archiv für deutsche Postgeschichte* 1 (1979), S. 58 – 65.

Chapter II: Comparison With Inland Transport Infrastructures

Inland Navigation Infrastructures and the Second World War: The Example of the Rhine Region

Guido Thiemeyer

Table of Content

1. Introduction

The period from 1914 to 1945 has long been considered a hiatus in the history of European integration. Recent research, however, has highlighted the importance of this period for the integration of infrastructures in Europe.[1] 1945 was by no means a „Stunde Null" or „Hour Zero" for European integration history: the Council of Europe, the European Coal and Steel Community and the European Economic Community formed part of a continuity of European integration that can be traced back to the 19th century. In this context, the period framed by the two world wars plays a major role.

Between 1914 and 1945, the integration of Europe was subject to intensive public debates. Well-known European integration projects such as those promoted by Richard Coudenhove-Kalergi[2] and Aristide Briand[3]

1 Kaiser, Wolfram / Schot, Johan: *Writing the Rules for Europe. Experts, Cartels, and International Organisations*, New York 2014, p. 179 – 218.

2 Conze, Vanessa: *Richard Coudenhove-Kalergi. Umstrittener Visionär Europas*, Gleichen/Zürich 2004; Ziegerhofer-Prettenthaler, Anita: *Botschafter Europas.*

were only two of many that fuelled the debate. During the Second World War, both sides discussed various ideas for the integration of Europe. While Adolf Hitler strongly opposed any commitment to integration, some National Socialists and Italian fascists drafted plans for post-war European integration.[4] Various resistance movements also developed their own projects for the unification of Europe.[5] In addition to these political concepts, technical internationalism was a major driver of integration during the entire period. Wolfram Kaiser and Johan Schot have argued that the First World War created early building blocks for European integration, as it led to a combination of technocratic internationalism with a European rhetoric.[6] From 1916, the United States, the United Kingdom, France and Italy established several international committees of experts in order to improve the cooperation of the *Entente* under the conditions of the war economy. The most famous was the Allied Maritime Transport Committee based in London under the leadership of Arthur Salter and Jean Monnet. Its main task was to pool the member countries' resources to ensure maximum efficiency of maritime transport. Important elements of the organisation became the blueprint for the European Coal and Steel Community established in 1952. After the First World War, technocratic cooperation at an international level continued in the sectors of rail, post and telecommunication. Even in the middle of the Second World War, in 1942, Italy and Germany created the *Europäischer Post- und Fernmeldeverein* (European Postal and Telecommunication Union) to facilitate trans-border communication.

Richard Nikolaus Coudenhove-Kalergi und die Paneuropa-Bewegung in den zwanziger und dreißiger Jahren, Vienna 2004.

3 Kießling, Friedrich: *Der Briand-Plan von 1929/30. Europa als Ordnungsvorstellung in den internationalen Beziehungen im 19. und frühen 20. Jahrhundert, in: Themenportal Europäische Geschichte*, 2008, www.europa.clio-online.de/essay/id/fdae-1457; Fleury, Antoine (ed.): *Der Briand-Plan eines europäischen Bündnissystems. Nationale und transnationale Perspektiven, mit Dokumenten*, Bern 1998.

4 Neulen, Werner: *Europa und das 3. Reich. Einigungsbestrebungen im deutschen Machtbereich 1939 – 1945*, Munich 1987; Bloch, Charles: *Le IIIe Reich et le monde*, nouvelle édition revue et augmentée d'une préface, Paris 2015; Freymond, Jean: *Le Troisième Reich et la réorganisation de l'Europe 1940 – 1942. Origines et projets*, Leiden 1974.

5 Dumoulin, Michel (ed.): *Plans Des Temps De Guerre Pour L'Europe D'aprèsguerre*, Bruxelles 1995.

6 Kaiser / Schot: Writing the Rules of Europe, p. 59/60.

In this article, I will focus on transnational internationalism in relation to the river Rhine during the Second World War. The Rhine was – and still is – the backbone of western European inland navigation and therefore an important part of the transport infrastructure. In recent years, historians have begun to research in more depth how the political organisation of the navigation on the Rhine developed over time.[7] The most important body, founded in 1815 and still existing today, was the Central Commission for the Navigation on the Rhine (CCNR). Two remarkable aspects of this organisation stand out: the CCNR was the world's first ever international organisation with elements of supranationality – i. e. the transfer of national sovereignty to an international body. It was also the institutional framework for legal, administrative and technical standardisation that became the blueprint for other river commissions worldwide. Economic historians have focused on the Rhine in the 19th and 20th centuries. Their approaches aim to explore the long-term transnational developments in the Rhine region from Rotterdam to Basel. Today, the Rhineland is one of the leading economic centres of Western Europe. This is without doubt due to the economic significance of the river as a transport infrastructure.[8]

In this contribution, I will examine the transnational administration of the Rhine as a waterway during the Second World War. How did the military and political conflicts during the 1930s and 1940s impact on inland navigation? What was the role of national governments, international organisations and private shipping companies? To what extent was the war a hiatus in the history of transnational cooperation on the Rhine, or was there also some continuity? To answer these questions, I will first concen-

---

7 Woerling, Jean Marie / Schirmann, Sylvain / Libera, Martial (eds.): *Commission Centrale pour la Navigation du Rhin. 200 ans d'histoire 1815 – 2015*, Strasbourg 2015; Tölle, Isabel: *Europäische Integration der Rheinschifffahrt Mitte des 19. und Mitte des 20. Jahrhunderts im Vergleich*, Baden-Baden 2016; Thiemeyer, Guido / Tölle, Isabel: „Supranationalität im 19. Jahrhundert? Die Beispiele der Zentralkommission für die Rheinschifffahrt und des Octroivertrages 1804 – 1832", in: *Journal of European Integration History* 17 (2011), p. 177 – 196.

8 Boon, Marten / Klemann, Hein / Wubs, Ben (eds.): *Transnational Regions in Historical Perspective*, London/New York 2020; Banken, Ralf / Wubs, Ben (eds.): *The Rhine. A Transnational Economic History*, Baden-Baden 2017; Klemann, Hein / Wubs, Ben: „River Dependence. Creating a transnational Rhine Economy, 1850 – 2000", in: Hesse, Jan Otmar / Kleinschmidt, Christian / Reckendrees, Alfred / Stokes, Ray (eds.): *Perspectives on European Economic and Social History*, Baden-Baden 2014, p. 219 – 245.

trate on the political cooperation in the Rhine region between 1936 and 1940. This period is of particular importance, because the political confrontation surrounding the Rhine navigation was triggered as early as 1936, when Nazi Germany decided to leave the Central Commission for the Navigation on the Rhine. Then I will move on to the war years: when the Franco-German *Phoney War* started in September 1939, the Upper Rhine was blocked by mines, and bridges were destroyed to prevent both armies from attacking. After the first battles had been fought in the spring of 1940, the infrastructure of the inland navigation in the Rhine area was quickly rebuilt and served again as an important transport artery. Between 1940 and 1945, the Rhine region was governed by the German leadership. Late in 1944, during the advance of the Allied forces in Western Europe, the frontline moved back to the Rhine and the infrastructure was severely hit by the fighting. Finally, I will discuss the organisation of the navigation on the Rhine after the Second World War.

In my considerations, I will look beyond the river to the entire Rhine region and its network of rivers and canals created with the Rhine as its backbone. Any technical and administrative standards produced for the Rhine applied to the whole system. The ports of Rotterdam, Antwerp, Duisburg and to a certain extent also Strasbourg and Basel were the most important intermodal junctions of the network.

2. *Dissolution of the CCNR and Cartelization in the 1930s*

The Treaty of Versailles had a major impact on the navigation in the Rhine region, first and foremost due to the fundamental political changes in the CCNR.[9] The first major change was that Switzerland, the United Kingdom, Belgium and Italy all joined the CCNR. Until then, membership had been restricted to riparian states. The addition of the new members now led to a Europeanization of the Rhine. Second, the presidency that until 1919 had been assigned by lot to a member state was now permanently given to the French delegation. Third, the CCNR headquarters were

---

9 Thiemeyer, Guido: „Die Zentralkommission für die Rheinschifffahrt und der Vertrag von Versailles“, in: Schirmann, Sylvain / Libera, Martial (eds.): *La Commission centrale pour la navigation du Rhin. Histoire d'une organisation internationale*, Paris 2017, pp. 103 – 119.

transferred from Mannheim in Germany to the French city of Strasbourg. These changes were enforced by the Treaty of Versailles, which was heavily influenced by the French desire to control Germany. Both the German and the Dutch governments were highly critical of these changes. The Germans were enraged by the French dominance in inland navigation on the Rhine. The Dutch, who had not been involved in the negotiations in Paris, rejected the changes because they feared a politicisation of inland navigation in Europe in general and on the Rhine in particular.[10]

However, the changes concerning the CCNR introduced by the Treaty of Versailles were only provisional arrangements. Art. 354 stipulated that „within a maximum period of six months from the coming into force of the present Treaty, the Central Commission [...] shall meet to draw up a project of revision of the Convention of Mannheim". The revision of the Convention of Mannheim turned out to be highly complicated. Deliberations started in February 1921 and soon were hampered by the political turmoil of the Ruhr occupation in 1923. While some progress was made between 1924 and 1928, a new convention for the navigation on the Rhine was difficult to reach. The French intended to strengthen the supranational authority of the CCNR, whereas the Netherlands and Germany attempted to make it an intergovernmental organisation. From 1929, the German delegation refused to accept any compromise in this respect. Another major problem was the rivalry between the Belgian port of Antwerp, supported by the French government, and the Dutch port of Rotterdam. In the context of the appeasement policy in the mid-1930s, the French government accepted the German demands to weaken the CCNR's supranational competencies (in particular concerning jurisdiction) and both governments agreed a *modus vivendi* that would serve as the basis for the navigation on the Rhine. The agreement of the *modus vivendi* was a diplomatic success for the German Reich, because most of the provisional regulations stipulated by the Treaty of Versailles were now revised.

To the surprise of all member countries, the German government resigned from the treaty in November 1936. Files from German archives reveal the background of this decision.[11] On 13th October 1936, the German

---

10 Woehrling, Jean-Marie / Schirmann, Sylvain / Libera, Martial (eds.): *Central commission for the navigation of the Rhine 1815 – 2015. 200 years of history*, Strasbourg 2015.

11 Politisches Archiv des Auswärtigen Amtes (PAAA), Berlin, R124077, German note dated 14.11.1936.

delegate to the CCNR, Georg Martius, informed the administrative leader of the Reich Chancellery, Heinrich Lammers, about the *modus vivendi* agreement to have it signed by Adolf Hitler. The „Führer" was not interested in inland navigation, but he rejected the CCNR as a symbol of French hegemony and the system of Versailles. Hitler therefore instructed his Minister of Foreign Affairs, Konstantin von Neurath, to leave the international organisation. Experts from the *Auswärtiges Amt* (Ministry of Foreign Affairs) and the *Reichsverkehrsministerium* (Reich Ministry of Transport) attempted to convince Hitler that leaving the CCNR was not in the interest of German inland navigation. However, Hitler was obviously not interested in economic cooperation in inland navigation and insisted on his decision to leave. Germany's exit (followed by Italy a few weeks later) was a purely political decision and an affront to the international legal system of the interwar period. From today's perspective, it can be seen as a step towards preparation for war.

Despite Nazi Germany's political blockade of inland navigation on the Rhine, the transnational administration of the waterway continued. One example of this are the traffic regulations agreed in the summer of 1938. Negotiations on these regulations had been launched in 1932 following a German initiative.[12] The German government's original aim was a common standard for traffic rules on all European inland waterways. The negotiations were held within the CCNR and, in September 1936, the delegates agreed a first draft of the common traffic regulations. This draft, however, was called into question when the Nazi government withdrew from the CCNR in November 1936. Only minor debates about some details still needed resolving. German shipping companies urged the government in Berlin to find a solution, because German industries depended on the transport infrastructure of the Rhine. In July 1937, the German government took the initiative again by sending a diplomatic memorandum to the CCNR's member states, inviting the respective governments to negotiations on common traffic regulations.[13] All governments accepted and, in September 1937, new negotiations started in Düsseldorf. Each state was represented by its commissioner to the CCNR, except for Germany.

---

12 Bundesarchiv Berlin-Lichterfelde (BA), R5/430 Revision der Rheinschiffahrtspolizeiordnung.

13 BA R5/436 Reichsverkehrsministerium, Akten betreffend Revision der Rheinschiffahrtspolizeiordnung, Auswärtiges Amt to the embassies in Paris, Bern, Brussels, The Hague, 30.7.1937.

Georg Martius, the former delegate of the Ministry of Foreign Affairs to the CCNR, had been replaced by Galinsky, head of the Rheinstrombauverwaltung in Koblenz. The delegates of France, Switzerland and Belgium began their speeches with a protest against the German withdrawal from the Commission. The Swiss delegate Herold stressed that his government accepted the invitation, but insisted the final decision on the common traffic rules must be made by the CCNR. An agreement on common rules for the navigation on the Rhine was in the interest of the Swiss economy, and this was the only reason why Switzerland participated in the deliberations. Herold stressed the fundamental conflict between his country and Germany concerning the CCNR's position. From his point of view, the results of the deliberations in Düsseldorf should only have provisional character. This position was supported by the French and Belgian delegations, both represented by their commissioners to the CCNR. In a second meeting that took place in Cologne in January 1938, the riparian countries' delegates finally agreed common traffic rules on the Rhine and the other European waterways.

According to the Swiss, French and Dutch governments, the agreement had to be approved by the CCNR. To this end, the CCNR scheduled a special meeting in Paris in August 1938.[14] In his opening remarks, the CCNR's French President, Gout, stressed that the provisions agreed in Cologne corresponded to the draft from 1936, with only minor changes. Therefore, in his view, the CCNR could accept the agreement without any reservations. This was true, but Schlingemann, the Dutch commissioner, pointed out an important legal difference: for the CCNR, the rules were common rules legally established by its own authority. Nazi Germany, by contrast, insisted that these were German rules that had been accepted by the other riparian states of the Rhine. In a diplomatic note on 3rd August 1938 the German government therefore stated that the regulations agreed in Cologne would come into force for the German part of the Rhine on 1st January 1939.

The close German-Dutch cooperation in the political sector was continued in the economic field. Working closely together, the Dutch and German Shipping companies and their lobby organisations complemented the cooperation in the administrative sector. In October 1937, two shipping

14 Commission Centrale pour la navigation du Rhin. 1938 Session extraordinaire, Protocole 2, Paris 24.8.1938, p. 3/4.

associations – the German "Schifferbetriebsverband für den Rhein" and its Dutch counterpart, the "Nederlandse Particuliere-Rijnvaart Centrale" – signed an agreement on close cooperation in the distribution of transportation charges.[15] Members of both organisations were now obliged to record all requests for transport on the Rhine in registration offices. All transport was to be distributed equally and appropriately among the organisation's members. In fact, this was a transnational cartel organising the bilateral transport in inland navigation. The Dutch-German cooperation was driven by two underlying motives: the first was that the treaty was the result of a growing interdependence between the Netherlands and the two German regions of the Rhineland and Westphalia. Despite Germany's withdrawal from the CCNR and the lack of any other political agreements, the chambers of commerce in the Rhineland and in Rotterdam were closely connected. On the occasion of the third international Port Day in Rotterdam in September 1937, the port administration invited the mayor of Cologne, Karl Georg Schmidt, to give a speech. Schmidt emphasised the close transnational cooperation between both regions. For the Rhine-Ruhr region, the industrial heartland of the German Reich, the Rhine was the most important infrastructure and connection to the international port of Rotterdam. From a Dutch perspective, the Rhine was the main artery for the export of agricultural products from the Netherlands to Germany. The second motive was that, in the 1930s, inland navigation was in deep crisis. In the wake of the world economic depression, the demand for transport had slumped at the beginning of the decade. Shipping companies suffered from an oversupply of transport in navigation. This situation was made worse by the growing competition from railways in the Rhine region. However, while inland navigation was dominated by (small) privately owned enterprises, railway companies (national monopolies) were run by the state, which gave them a major competitive advantage. Private shipping companies attempted to overcome this disadvantage by creating cartels, first on a national level and later with international agreements.

This example highlights two different aspects: on the one hand, diplomatic relations in the Rhine area deteriorated in 1936, partly due to the Wehrmacht's illegal occupation of the Rhineland. For European inland navigation, however, the Reich's withdrawal from the CCNR had even

15 „Engere Zusammenarbeit zwischen holländischer und deutscher Partikulierschiffahrt", in: *Deutsche Bergwerkszeitung*, Düsseldorf, 6.10.1939.

more important consequences. It led to an increasing shift of power back to the regions and to a rejection of transnational governance in inland navigation by the German government. On the other hand, mainly for economic reasons, Germany had a vested interest in a common agreement and was therefore dependent on the cooperation of the other governments – whether within the CCNR or not. The policy of appeasement in the mid-1930s led the French and Dutch governments to accept the German approach to the distribution of power in inland navigation. In the diplomatic note mentioned above, however, the German government stated, „that the traffic regulations agreed must not be modified unilaterally by one state, but only with the agreement of all others".[16] At the same time, economic actors such as private shipping companies and chambers of commerce intensified their transnational cooperation.

3. During the War: The "German" Rhine

With the German invasion of France, Belgium and the Netherlands in May 1940, the Rhine area became a battlefield. Important parts of the infrastructure were destroyed by both the German and Allied forces. In the Netherlands, 1.800 km (1.118 miles) of waterways became unusable, because damaged bridges and sunk vessels blocked the traffic.[17] After the surrender of the Dutch army on 15th May 1940, the reconstruction of transport infrastructures became paramount for the German army. The Wehrmacht needed a permanent and continual supply of coal and weapons from the Reich. In close cooperation with the Dutch waterways administration (Rijkswaterstaat), Germany embarked on a rapid reconstruction programme. Only a few days after the fighting had ended, the Rhine between the Ruhr area and the Netherlands was again fit for navigation. The whole waterways system in the Netherlands was re-established in only three months.

Along with this, the German occupiers reorganised the administration of inland waterways in the Netherlands. In May 1940, Nazi Germany ap-

---

16 Note verbal transmise par l'ambassade de l'Allemagne à Paris au Ministère des Affaires Etrangères de France, 3.8.1938, in: Commission Centrale pour la navigation du Rhin. 1938 Session extraordinaire, Protocole 2, Paris 24.8.1938, p. 9.

17 BA R5/10015, Organisationsfragen der niederländischen Binnenschifffahrt. (March 1943)

pointed Arthur Seyß-Inquart as „Reichskommissar" for the Occupied Netherlands and created a special department for inland navigation headed by a commissioner („Kommissar für See- und Binnenschiffahrt"). In the 1920s, Dutch inland navigation had been controlled by many different associations of ship owners competing on the transport market.[18] In May 1933, a new law created a „freight commission" tasked with distributing transport demand among the various companies. The transnational cooperation between the German and Dutch cartels intensified in 1937 due to the agreement mentioned above. Only a few days after the occupation of the Netherlands, the German administration gave the order to dissolve the existing cartels and establish a „Vereniging Centraal Bureau voor de Rijn- en Binnenvaart" as an umbrella organisation for all shipping companies and the „Particuliere", owner-operators of one single vessel. All ship owners and shipping companies were now obliged to join the „Centraal Bureau", which organised the transport on the Rhine. It was led by the Dutch Ministry of Waterways under German control. The Dutch Rhine navigation was therefore integrated into a pool, with membership compulsory for all ship owners and companies. While cartels of shipping companies and „Particuliere" existed in the Netherlands before 1940, membership had been voluntary. The reorganisation in 1940 integrated Dutch inland navigation into the German system. In the Reich, the cartel was organised on a national level by the „Reichsverkehrsgruppe Binnenschiffahrt" in a regional substructure for the Rhine, the „Transportzentrale Rheinschiffahrt" founded in January 1941 in Duisburg.[19] While its responsibilities were originally restricted to German territory, it immediately claimed authority over the entire transport system of the Rhine.[20] The Dutch shipping companies largely accepted German procedures, mainly for two reasons: ship owners still vividly remembered the severe crisis of the early 1930s and demanded stronger political and organisational support for inland navigation on the Rhine. Nazi Germany's occupation of the Netherlands generated a rising demand for transport due to the Wehrmacht's military supply

---

18 Ibid.

19 „Transportzentrale der Rheinschiffahrt. Zusammensetzung und Arbeitsweise", in: *Deutsche Verkehrs- Nachrichten*, 30.12.1940.

20 BA R5/684 Akten betr. die wirtschaftliche Lage der Rheinschiffahrt. Niederschrift über die Sitzung des Arbeitsausschusses der Transportzentrale der Rheinschiffahrt am 11.2.1941 in Duisburg.

needs and the increased transportation of food from the Netherlands to Germany.

In Belgium, the situation in inland navigation was similar. Most of the infrastructure had been destroyed in the spring of 1940. Re-establishing the system took about a year. The Albert Canal between Antwerp and Liège was reopened in January 1941 and the Canal de Louvain in October 1941. The most important challenge, however, was the lack of ships in Belgium. Many were destroyed during the fighting in May 1940. At the same time, many Belgian ship owners fled with their vessels from the German Wehrmacht into the South of France. After the occupation, the demand for ship transport boomed and could not be satisfied by the remaining Belgian transport capacity.[21] Similar to the Netherlands, the Belgian inland navigation system was now harnessed for German needs. It was now overseen by the German Ministry of Transport in close cooperation with the body responsible for German military transport in Belgium, the „Wehrmachtsverkehrsdirektion Brüssel". The powerful „Reichsverkehrsgruppe Binnenschiffahrt", the lobby organisation of German inland navigation in the Rhine region, also exerted considerable influence. As in the Netherlands and in Germany, Belgian shipping companies were now obliged to join a transport pool created in September 1940. The „Belgische Binnenvaart Centrale" had a similar role to the Dutch „Centraal Bureau". It was controlled by both the German military administration for Belgium and the „Reichsverkehrsgruppe Binnenschiffahrt" in Berlin. The Wehrmacht, the Ministry of Transport and the „Reichsverkehrsgruppe Binnenschiffahrt" quickly clashed over their responsibilities.[22]

German regional actors in the Rhineland immediately sought to integrate the Belgian transport system into the German network. After military action ended in the summer of 1940, it was again Karl Georg Schmidt, the mayor of Cologne, who took the initiative to connect the Belgian economy with the Rhineland.[23] He advocated the construction of a canal from Ant-

---

21 BA R5/10015, Belgien – Wieder leistungsfähige Binnenschiffahrt, 16.2.1942.

22 See for instance the report of the delegate of the Ministry of Transport who complained in Berlin about the dominant role of the Reichsverkehrsgruppe Binnenschiffahrt in Belgium. BA R5/71 Akten betr. die Organisation der Binnenschiffahrt in Belgien 1943 – 1944. Verkehrsdirektion Brüssel an Reichsverkehrsminister Berlin, 29.9.1943.

23 BA R5/291, Niederschrift. Besprechung über den Rhein-Maas-Schelde-Kanal im Reichsverkehrsministerium am 25. Oktober 1940.

werp to Cologne, a project that had been discussed previously, but never realised. In a meeting between the German Minister of Transport, Julius Dorpmüller, and representatives of the Rhine region in Berlin in October 1940, Schmidt argued for a rapid construction of the canal. Dorpmüller recognised that a closer connection of the Belgian territory to the Reich would require new transport infrastructures after the war. He therefore approved of the initiative in principle, although he was convinced that the canal could only be constructed after the war. A large majority of Belgian ship owners supported the German inland navigation initiatives. Like their Dutch counterparts, they greatly profited from the rising demand for transport after the crisis in the 1930s.

The situation on the Upper Rhine was different.[24] During the invasion in May 1940, several major bridges were destroyed and blocked the port of Strasbourg, which had been significantly enlarged by the French government after 1919. In the interwar period, the French had planned to develop Strasbourg into the most important port on the Upper Rhine to create an intermodal junction for inland navigation and rail transport. The war had interrupted the port's connection with the railway infrastructures in France and Germany. Germany took almost a year to rebuild the port of Strasbourg. In addition, the Upper Rhine was blocked by a series of pontoon bridges constructed by the Wehrmacht in the spring of 1940 to secure troop supply in France. The pontoons effectively also blockaded the ships docked in the port of Basel, which left them immobilised. From early 1941, however, the port of Strasbourg regained its position as the main junction for the transport of coal and other commodities to Switzerland and Italy.[25]

The inland navigation infrastructure of the Rhine was quickly integrated into the German system for two reasons: German policy on the Rhine was supported by the Dutch, Belgian and Swiss administrations. The „Centraal Bureau" and the „Binnenvaart Centrale" collaborated closely with the German authorities. While they were subjected to the control of the Wehrmacht and the German administration, they voluntarily accepted the German rule. Closely connected with this first point is that the influential

24 BA R5/684 Vol. 1, Der Oberpräsident der Rheinprovinz an den Reichsverkehrsminister, Bericht über die Reise an den Oberrhein, 6.8.1940.

25 Ministère des Affaires Etrangères, Archives Diplomatiques, Relations Commerciales Vichy, 17GMII/76.

shipping companies and their organisations supported the German dominance on the Rhine. Under wartime conditions, the navigation on the Rhine boomed and all the shipping companies were essential to meet the demand for transport services. For them, it was a stroke of luck as their sector had been in deep economic crisis in the 1920s and 1930s. Inland navigation had suffered from the competition of other modes of transport, namely road and rail. By contrast, since the outbreak of the war, transport capacities were badly needed and the shipping companies eagerly met the increasing German demand.

Under these circumstances, the CCNR became obsolete. Its archives and library had been transferred to Grenoble in November 1939 to protect them against possible war damage. In September 1940, the German Armistice Commission („Waffenstillstandskommission") in Wiesbaden asked the Vichy government to transfer the archives back to Strasbourg. The German authorities prohibited any further meetings of the CCNR, except one to decide its dissolution.[26] Its function was now assumed by the German authorities.

The system worked well until the autumn of 1944. When the allied troops reached the German border, they intensified their attacks on the country's infrastructure in order to prepare for the invasion. Once more, the Rhine became a combat zone. Allied planes attacked the ships on the river and German troops attempted to destroy the bridges to prevent the Americans and the British from crossing the river. In the autumn of 1944, Swiss shipping companies therefore tried to withdraw their vessels from the German Rhine to protect them from destruction. The German Secret Service („Sicherheitspolizei") considered this as a betrayal of Germany and responded by blocking Swiss ships on the German Rhine.[27] Nazi dominance over the river diminished and could only be maintained by military force.

26 Ministère des Affaires Etrangères, Archives Diplomatiques, Relations Commerciales Vichy, 17GMII/76. Note pour M. de Botsanger, 23.9.1943.

27 BA R5/303 Fol 1, Schnellbrief Auswärtiges Amt (Martius) to Reichssicherheitshauptamt, 30.8.1944.

4. *After the War*

After the German Wehrmacht's unconditional surrender in May 1945, the infrastructure of the Rhine region and the surrounding waterways lay again in ruins.[28] Considering the amount of damage, it is astonishing how quickly the river infrastructure was rebuilt. In the summer of 1945, the navigation between Rotterdam and Basel resumed despite obstacles including pontoon bridges in major cities and the wreckage of bridges and sunken ships in the water.

After resolving more practical issues such as clearing the obstacles and rebuilding the river infrastructure, the difficult decision on how to organise inland navigation after the period of Nazi hegemony on the Rhine had to be addressed. The CCNR had never been formally dissolved, but became inactive during the war. The first question was whether it should be restored. While the former member states quickly agreed to reinstate the CCNR, it was more difficult to decide what legal basis it should have. The Treaty of Versailles had profoundly changed its institutional structure, and the *modus vivendi* agreement of 1936 had introduced another reform. Finally, the Western Allies agreed a compromise. The Convention of Mannheim of 1868 was reinstated, with the exception that Switzerland and Belgium, which had not been members in the 19th century, were now included into the CCNR. France, the United Kingdom and the United States represented Germany, because their occupation zones bordered the Rhine. After the Federal Republic of Germany was founded in 1949, it was accepted as a member state and the United Kingdom and the United States left the commission. Compared with the political turmoil of the interwar period, the political cooperation between the riparian states of the Rhine now ran more smoothly.

After the surge in demand for transport facilities on the Rhine during the war, the market slumped after 1945. Shipping companies found themselves in a similar position to the 1920s and early 1930s. There was an oversupply of ships in the Rhine region, causing severe competition. In the 1930s, shipping companies had created pools in order to set standard prices for the transport of various commodities on a national level. During the war, these cartels had been reorganised under the leadership of the Ger-

---

28 Zentralkommission für die Rheinschifffahrt (ed.): *200 Jahre Geschichte*, Strasbourg 2015, p. 158.

man authorities with considerable influence from the lobby group. The idea of these cartels was revived in 1953, when the "Arbeitsgemeinschaft der Rheinschiffahrt" was founded in the Federal Republic of Germany.[29] As previously, the main task of this association was the distribution of transport commodities between the different shipping companies in order to avoid competition. The major difference was that the "Arbeitsgemeinschaft der Rheinschiffahrt" was a transnational organisation, while the cartels of the 1920s were organised only at the national level. The "Arbeitsgemeinschaft" was therefore to some extent a continuation of the cooperation between "Vereniging Centraal Bureau voor de Rijn- en Binnenvaart" and the "Reichsverkehrsgruppe Binnenschiffahrt" during the war and was strongly supported by national governments. While the Federal Ministry of Transport ("Bundesverkehrsministerium") was sceptical about the cooperation between German and Dutch shipping companies, the *Auswärtiges Amt* encouraged shipping companies to share capacities. The idea behind this decision was to avoid any conflict between German, Belgian and Dutch companies during the negotiations for a European Political Community and the European Defence Community. The close cooperation of shipping companies between the Netherlands and West Germany was now put under the auspices of European integration.

The end of the war therefore had an ambivalent impact on the infrastructure of inland navigation: on the one hand, the CCNR was restored and apart from minor changes resembled the form it had in the 19th century, while the changes imposed by the Treaty of Versailles and the *modus vivendi* were abandoned; on the other hand, the close relationship between national governments and lobby groups initiated in the interwar period and intensified during the war continued as before.

---

29 Tölle, Isabel: *Integration von Infrastrukturen in Europa im historischen Vergleich, Bd. 6: Binnenschifffahrt (Rheinschifffahrt)*, Baden-Baden 2016, p. 207 – 223; Thiemeyer, Guido: „Integration und Standardisierung in der internationalen Rheinschifffahrt nach 1945", in: Ambrosius, Gerold / Henrich-Franke, Christian / Neutsch, Cornelius / Thiemeyer, Guido (eds.): *Standardisierung und Integration europäischer Verkehrsinfrastruktur in historischer Perspektive*, Baden-Baden 2009, p. 137 – 153.

5. Conclusion

Without any doubt, the Second World War was a major hiatus for the history of the navigation on the Rhine. Political conflicts started in 1919 with the Treaty of Versailles and deteriorated in the early 1930s, when the CCNR failed to agree a new common convention for the Rhine. The *modus vivendi* agreement of 1936 was a Franco-German compromise that the Netherlands never accepted. The next decisive development occurred in November 1936 when Nazi Germany (and in its wake Italy) decided to leave the CCNR for political reasons. While the CCNR succeeded in drafting new traffic regulations and in resolving other technical issues in 1938, Germany now was the hegemon on the Rhine. The other riparian states accepted German dominance mainly for economic reasons. The Rhine was the backbone of Western European inland navigation and no government wanted to disrupt commercial interests because of political debates. The acceptance of German hegemony in the Rhine navigation also fitted comfortably into the general policy of appeasement. When German troops invaded Northern France, Belgium and the Netherlands in 1940, the entire navigable Rhine region (except for a small area in Basel) fell under direct German control. Although never dissolved, the CCNR became inactive and new standards were now set unilaterally by the German authorities. However, Germany left the traffic rules and other standards concerning the Rhine largely unchanged. Hence, there was a continuity in terms of technical, legal and administrative standards in the navigation on the Rhine, even though the institutional system changed completely.

In 1940, the CCNR only held two meetings in The Hague and Lausanne. By now, Nazi Germany had assumed complete control over the Rhine. Different institutions were involved in the administration of river traffic, in which the Wehrmacht assumed a major role. The German army needed a permanent supply line and dominated the transport on the river. Military needs were paramount during the entire war. Despite this, the Rhine system was formally under the supervision of the department of inland navigation in the Reich Ministry of Traffic in Berlin. In the Netherlands, the Wehrmacht closely collaborated with the German civil administration in The Hague. The Reichskommissar for the Occupied Netherlands Seyß-Inquart established a commissioner for waterways („Wasserstraßenbeauftragter") who, in turn, worked closely with the Dutch Ministry of Waterways. By contrast, the administration of the Belgian waterways was entrusted to the „Hauptverkehrsdirektion Brüssel", a subdepartment of the military administration in Belgium that was also responsible for Northern France.

It is interesting to see the pivotal role of cartels in inland navigation between 1936 and 1945. Shipping companies established these cartels in response to the severe economic crisis of inland navigation in the Rhine area. Their main objective was the distribution of transport orders among different companies to avoid cut-throat competition in inland navigation. The cartels were first created at the national level, but soon expanded across borders. In most cases, they were closely connected with the respective Ministries of Transport. During the Second World War, the German authorities supported the cartels, because they expected them to organise shipping transport more efficiently. In 1953, they were again supported by the Foreign Ministries of the Netherlands and Germany, because they were considered as vital to further the political integration of both countries into the European Coal and Steel Community. The organisation of transnational cartels is striking, because they are the most important factor of continuity in this whole period, formed to combat an economic crisis in the sector that emerged in the 1930s, continued during the war and reappeared in the early 1950s.

It is also important to point out that – in contrast to post and telecommunication – Germany had no plans to establish an international organisation for the navigation on the Rhine during the war. Since 1936, the Nazi government in Berlin circumvented the CCNR politically, although the German administration continued to cooperate with the other governments until 1940 via the „Strombauverwaltung Koblenz". After Germany's invasion of Western Europe, the Nazis considered the Rhine as a German river.

It is worth noting that most of the shipping companies supported the German hegemony in the navigation on the Rhine during the war. The main reason was that transport on the river increased significantly because of military needs. The transport boom greatly benefitted the shipping companies in the Rhine area that still remembered the deep crisis and the oversupply of transport capacities in the 1930s.

In contrast to the post and telecommunication sectors, there was little or no talk of „Europe" in inland navigation on the Rhine during the war. This is astonishing, because the notion of „Europe" was growing in the CCNR both in the interwar period and after 1945. Although the Reich had no „European policy" apart from German hegemony based on military power during the Second World War, many German officials attempted to promote a „New Europe" on different occasions – but this was never the case in the Rhine area.

6. References

Banken, Ralf / Wubs, Ben (eds.): *The Rhine. A Transnational Economic History*, Baden-Baden 2017.

Bloch, Charles: *Le IIIe Reich et le monde, nouvelle édition revue et augmentée d'une préface*, Paris 2015.

Boon, Marten / Klemann, Hein / Wubs, Ben (eds.): *Transnational Regions in Historical Perspective*, London/ New York 2020.

Conze, Vanessa: *Richard Coudenhove-Kalergi. Umstrittener Visionär Europas*, Gleichen/Zürich 2004.

Dumoulin, Michel (ed.): *Plans Des Temps De Guerre Pour L'Europe D'après-guerre*, Bruxelles 1995.

Fleury, Antoine (ed.): *Der Briand-Plan eines europäischen Bündnissystems. Nationale und transnationale Perspektiven, mit Dokumenten*, Bern 1998.

Freymond, Jean: *Le Troisième Reich et la réorganisation de l'Europe 1940 – 1942. Origines et projets*, Leiden 1974.

Kaiser, Wolfram / Schot, Johan: *Writing the Rules for Europe. Experts, Cartels, and International Organisations*, New York 2014.

Kießling, Friedrich: „Der Briand-Plan von 1929/30. Europa als Ordnungsvorstellung in den internationalen Beziehungen im 19. und frühen 20. Jahrhundert", in: *Themenportal Europäische Geschichte* (2008), www.europa.clio-online.de/essay/id-/fdae-1457.

Klemann, Hein / Wubs, Ben: „River Dependence. Creating a transnational Rhine Economy, 1850 – 2000", in: Hesse, Jan Otmar / Kleinschmidt, Christian / Reckendrees, Alfred / Stokes, Ray (eds.): *Perspectives on European Economic and Social History*, Baden-Baden 2014, p. 219 – 245.

Neulen, Werner: *Europa und das 3. Reich. Einigungsbestrebungen im deutschen Machtbereich 1939 – 1945*, Munich 1987.

Thiemeyer, Guido / Tölle, Isabel: „Supranationalität im 19. Jahrhundert? Die Beispiele der Zentralkommission für die Rheinschifffahrt und des Octroivertrages 1804 – 1832", in: *Journal of European Integration History* 17 (2011), p. 177 – 196.

Thiemeyer, Guido: „Die Zentralkommission für die Rheinschifffahrt und der Vertrag von Versailles", in: Schirmann, Sylvain / Libera, Martial (eds.): *La Commission centrale pour la navigation du Rhin. Histoire d'une organisation internationale*, Paris 2017, pp. 103 – 119.

Thiemeyer, Guido: „Integration und Standardisierung in der internationalen Rheinschifffahrt nach 1945", in: Ambrosius, Gerold / Henrich-Franke, Christian / Neutsch, Cornelius / Thiemeyer, Guido (eds.): *Standardisierung und Integration europäischer Verkehrsinfrastruktur in historischer Perspektive*, Baden-Baden 2009, p. 137 – 153.

Tölle, Isabel: *Europäische Integration der Rheinschifffahrt Mitte des 19. und Mitte des 20. Jahrhunderts im Vergleich*, Baden-Baden 2016.

Woehrling, Jean-Marie / Schirmann, Sylvain / Libera, Martial (eds.): *Central commission for the navigation of the Rhine 1815 – 2015, 200 years of history*, Strasbourg 2015.

Ziegerhofer-Prettenthaler, Anita: *Botschafter Europas. Richard Nikolaus Coudenhove-Kalergi und die Paneuropa-Bewegung in den zwanziger und dreißiger Jahren*, Vienna 2004.

Canalization of the Moselle River during the Second World War: Continuities or Departures between Nazi Policy and Long-Term River Improvement Plans?[1]

Martial Libera

Table of Content

River transport is a major economic consideration in Europe. The continent's development through industrial revolutions and subsequent interdependence between different markets in European countries enhanced the role of major river routes, especially for the transporting of heavy materials such as coal and coke, iron ore, sand, and steel. River transportation was a factor of production for these products, and often led to the definition of actual pricing policies. Such transport was also essential for developing the trade flows of producing companies. However, beyond its economic aspects, river transport contributed to the networking of territories, and therefore included "social, military, and most certainly political" facets as well.[2] Another distinctive feature of major river routes is that their improvement, which most often requires large-scale works and considerable financing, unfolds over the long-term, either because the works are completed in sections of waterways gradually rendered navigable, or be-

1 Translated from the French by Arby Gharibian.
2 Dumoulin, Michel: „Les transports: bastion des nationalismes", in: Dumoulin, Michel (ed.): *La Commission européenne 1958 – 1972. Histoire et mémoires d'une institution*, Luxembourg 2007, p. 457 – 469, here p. 457.

cause projects are planned, abandoned, and resumed on multiple occasions.

This was the case for the Moselle river, the main tributary of the Rhine, which it flows into at Koblenz. It also connects the major mining and steel producing areas of Western Europe, namely Lorraine in France, Luxembourg, as well as the Saar and the Ruhr, via the Rhine, in Germany.[3] The plan to canalize the Moselle, which was envisioned in the early nineteenth century in order to connect these industrial regions by a waterway, was completed only in 1964. The river's canalization owes much to the early efforts to construct the European Community. Improvement works were initiated to compensate Lorraine steelmakers—the De Wendels in particular—for their acceptance of the Schuman Plan.[4] In April 1952, Article 2 of the law authorizing the French president to ratify the European Coal and Steel Community (ECSC)[5] provided for the French government to initiate, "before the establishment of the Single Market [for coal and steel], negotiations with the respective governments for the rapid canalization of the Moselle between Thionville and Koblenz."[6] From that point forward, the matter was in the hands of the governments involved. The project was bogged down in various study commissions until 1955.[7] After the Saar referendum in October 1955,[8] Paris connected the future status of the Saar

3 The Moselle, whose source is in the Vosges Mountains, is 550 kms long. Berger, Françoise: „Les enjeux de la canalisation de la Moselle et de la Sarre jusqu'au Rhin pour les industriels sidérurgistes du bassin Lorraine-Sarre-Luxembourg (jusqu'aux années 1950)", in: Berger, Françoise / Rapoport, Michel / Tilly, Pierre / Touchelay, Béatrice (ed.): *Industries, territoires et cultures en Europe du Nord-Ouest XIXe-XXe siècles. Mélanges en l'honneur de Jean-François Eck,* Roubaix 2015, p. 137 – 145, here p. 138.

4 Libera, Martial: „La chambre de commerce et d'industrie de la Moselle face au plan Schuman", in: *Fare Cahier* 8 (2016), p. 35 – 48.

5 Spierenburg, Dirk / Poidevin, Raymond: *Histoire de la Haute Autorité de la Communauté européenne du charbon et de l'acier. Une expérience supranationale,* Bruxelles 1993, p. 43.

6 Chanrion, Fernand: *Une victoire européenne: la Moselle*, Paris 1964, p. 156.

7 Three commissions were created between 1952 and 1956: the Surleau commission (April 1952 – January 1953), the French-German-Luxembourger study commission (January 1952 – July 1953), and the French-German governmental commission (September1955 – February 1956).

8 Two thirds of its electors voted for the Saar's incorporation within the Federal Republic of Germany. See Poidevin, Raymond / Bariéty, Jacques: *Les relations franco-allemandes 1815 – 1975, seconde édition revue et augmentée*, Paris 1977, p. 334.

with acceptance of canalization of the Moselle in its negotiations with Bonn. After a year of bitter discussions, France, Luxembourg and the Federal Republic of Germany signed, in Luxembourg on October 27, 1956, the treaties and conventions on the Saar, the Canal d'Alsace, and canalization of the Moselle.[9] The improvement works were completed in 1964. The new navigable route was inaugurated on May 26 by Charlotte, Grand Duchess of Luxembourg, and Presidents Heinrich Lübke and Charles de Gaulle.[10] In order to allow 1,500 ton Rhine boats, with their draft of 2.5 meters, to navigate in all seasons, a channel was built along the bed of the Moselle river, reaching a width of 40 meters at its large bends. Seventeen dams equipped with locks were built between Metz and Koblenz to permanently maintain the three meters of water needed for navigation. Two years after its inauguration, annual traffic on the Moselle numbered 5 million tons.[11]

However, the history of the canalization of the Moselle stretches further back than postwar initiatives. Throughout the nineteenth century, and then again during the interwar period, various actors—the business community, chamber of commerce circles, town councilors, political and governmental staff in France, Luxembourg, and Germany—proposed a number of Moselle improvement projects, with the goal of making it navigable. At the beginning of the Second World War, these canalization projects were resumed by Nazi Germany. I will use a diachronic approach to focus on German wartime projects in order to explore the continuities of the Nazi project, or on the contrary to identify any departures from the projects that preceded and followed them. There were clearly elements of continuity over the *longue durée* with regard to the contents of preparatory work, feasibility studies, and the interest of such a waterway; the competition that canalization of the Moselle faced from the improvement of other waterways, as well as from other means of transportation, railways in particu-

9 *Convention du 27 octobre 1956 entre la République française, la République fédérale d'Allemagne et le Grand-Duché de Luxembourg au sujet de la canalisation de la Moselle*, p. 49, Archives départementales de la Moselle (hereafter ADM: Convention Between the French Republic, the Federal Republic of Germany, and the Grand Duchy of Luxembourg on the canalization of the Moselle), 1547 Wd 262.

10 Caffier, Michel: *La Moselle. Une rivière et ses hommes*, Nancy 1985. p. 125 – 127.

11 Ibid., p. 127.

lar; and remarkable long-term continuity, despite apparent differences, with respect to the political, economic, and even strategic considerations inherent to canalization of the Moselle.

1. Expert Assessments for the Moselle Improvement Project: Remarkable Long-Term Continuity

In 1939, just before the outbreak of the Second World War, Germany decided to reinitiate plans to improve the Moselle. The Reich Ministry of Transport tasked the Waterways and Navigation Board in Koblenz with developing a project to improve the navigability of the Moselle between Trier and Koblenz. After Germany's military victory and the armistice signed in June 1940, the project was even extended to the portion of the Moselle between Trier and Thionville on the French-German border,[12] which if it were carried out would make the waterway navigable until Metz, as the Moselle Iron Mines Canal running alongside the river between Metz and Thionville had been in service since 1932.[13]

The criteria identified in the Koblenz Memorandum, a preliminary study drafted by the Waterways and Navigation Board in Koblenz, explored the feasibility of the works, and provided projections for the flow of raw materials that could transit through the new waterway, and hence for its economic viability. The study clearly showed that the project was feasible. The improvement of the Moselle, which would regulate the river by widening the waterway and reducing its rapids, did not involve the large-scale works entailed by a genuine canalization. The construction of single locks, which are much less costly than double locks, would suffice for the planned improvements. The cost of the works would decrease as a result, as would their duration, estimated at 5 to 6 years, which is short for river improvements. Once navigable the Moselle would be a profitable transport corridor, firstly because boats would be loaded in both directions, with coal, coke, metal products and steel flowing toward Lorraine, and minette toward the Ruhr. The preliminary calculations for raw materi-

---

12 Vogel, Ludwin: *Deutschland, Frankreich und die Mosel. Europäische Integrationspolitik in den Montan-Regionen Ruhr, Lothringen, Luxemburg und der Saar*, Essen 2001, p. 68.

13 Berger: Les enjeux de la canalisation de la Moselle, p. 140 – 141.

als trade were particularly promising, and would make the Moselle, with nearly 7 millions tons of products transported annually, a leading transport corridor.[14]

The assessment of the Koblenz Memorandum was in keeping with the studies for canalization of the Moselle conducted during the nineteenth century. Under the German Empire, the steel producing interests of the Ruhr and Lorraine, which had advocated a canalization project for the Moselle and Saar rivers in the 1880s, came to the same conclusions. The cost of the works planned at the time, stretching nearly 300 km (240 km in Germany and 60 km in annexed Lorraine), would total 126,000 marks per kilometer, much less, for example than the 143,000 marks per kilometer needed to build the canal from Grondersingen to Sarreguemines. The duration of the works, which had already been estimated at 5 years, was considered an advantage. On an economic level, a navigable Moselle would considerably reinforce links and trade between the heavy industries of Lorraine, Luxembourg, and the Ruhr.

New projects were proposed after the Great War. Driven in 1919 by the French government, and then in 1926 by steelmakers from Luxembourg and the Trier Chamber of Commerce and Industry, these projects were also based on important technical and financial expertise. Their conclusions were positive.[15] For lack of agreement among the different parties involved, work ultimately began only on the French portion of the waterway. Construction of the canal between Metz and Thionville, which was launched in 1928 over a length of 30 km, was dug for a portion of its length in the bed of the Moselle, and ran laterally to the Moselle for most of its length. Its construction costs were given less consideration, for it was mostly financed by Germany as part of the reparations it owed France. Its cargo volume, under 1 million tons during its first three years of operation, was far below the projections made in 1927 by the Consortium for the Canalization of the Moselle, which had counted on an annual volume on the order of 7.5 million tons before the Great Depression.

After 1945, the project was quickly resumed and led by the Moselle, Saar, Trier, Koblenz, and Luxembourg Chambers of Commerce and Industry, which joined together to form the Communauté d'intérêts des chambres de commerce pour l'aménagement de la Moselle (Community

14 Vogel: Deutschland, Frankreich und die Mosel, p. 68 – 72.
15 Berger: Les enjeux de la canalisation de la Moselle, p. 140 – 141.

of Interests of the Chambers of Commerce for the Improvement of the Moselle).[16] The studies conducted by the chambers of commerce were very encouraging. On a technical level, the regularization of the Moselle did not present any obstacles. The digging of a channel—by reducing the river's current, flow, and slope—would establish the same depth everywhere, and would allow convoys to both be towed and pass one another. The construction of five dams and locks was also planned. The works proceeded in stages. Upon completion of the first stage, the Moselle would already be navigable for two-thirds of the year. In total, the regularization of the Moselle would be completed within eight years, a short time span for such projects.[17] The traffic seemed promising. The Moselle would connect "the steel and iron producing region of Lorraine, and the considerable industrial grouping of Nancy-Metz-Thionville, with the coalmining and industrial areas of the Ruhr, along with the major ports of the North Sea."[18] The rise and fall of overall traffic, consisting primarily of heavy goods and grains, would hover between 4 and 5 million tons per year, according to estimates that were voluntarily conservative in order to anticipate potential attacks. Given such cargo, the Moselle would be a highly profitable route, all the more so as the low cost of construction totaled, depending on estimates, between 8 and 12 billion francs in 1948, and would be paid by the Rhineland-Palatinate (nearly two-thirds), France (between a quarter and a third), and Luxembourg (approximately a tenth). The works would be carried out by an international corporation that would raise capital for that purpose. Financing would also be secured through tolls.[19] The feasibility studies conducted in 1952, when the project was taken over by the French government, were along the same lines.

In sum, the preliminary studies and work conducted for each of the projects came to the same conclusions as the assessments made by the Third

---

16 Libera: Diplomatie patronale, p. 151 – 174.

17 Deux notes relatives à l'aménagement de la Moselle, ministère de l'Economie nationale, Inspection générale, XIVe région économique (Nancy Metz), Fernand Chanrion (Two Notes Regarding the Improvement of the Moselle, Ministry of the Economy, General Inspectorate for Region 14, Nancy and Metz), 10.04.1948 and 30.07.1948, ADM 1547 Wd 245.

18 "Note relative à l'aménagement de la Moselle" (Note Regarding the Improvement of the Moselle), 30.07.1948; for details see the preceding footnote.

19 Libera, Martial: *Diplomatie patronale aux frontières. Les relations des chambres de commerce frontalières françaises avec leurs homologues allemandes (1945 – milieu des années 1980)*, Genève 2019, p. 168/69.

Reich during the Second World War. This continuity with regard to the essentially reassuring results of expert assessments for the project's viability proved that it was feasible and economically promising. This raises the question of why the canalization of the Moselle took so long to complete. The first reason, which also unfolded over the long-term, was that the canalization of the Moselle had to systematically compete with other river improvement projects, as well as with other types of transport.

2. *A Project Systematically and Continually Subject to Competition*

This was the case at the beginning of the Second World War. The Third Reich hesitated between two river improvement projects in its southwestern territory: the project involving the Moselle, and the construction of a canal from the Saar river to the Rhine river through the Palatinate, which would flow into the Rhine at Mannheim, and would eventually be extended to the west from Saarbrücken to Metz. This project, dating back to the interwar period and primarily supported by industrial actors in the Saar, presented a number of advantages. The primary one was that it would bring the Rhine within 133 km of Saarbrücken, or 161 km less than the route via the Saar and the Moselle. In addition, considering that the primary markets for the heavy industry of the Saar were, beginning in the interwar period, in Southern Germany, the distance would be reduced even further, by about 314 km, with Koblenz and Mannheim each being 153 km away via the Rhine route. The canal from the Saar river to the Rhine river would subsequently lead to major savings in terms of transport cost, thereby making the products of the Saar's heavy industry all the more competitive, especially compared to those from the Ruhr. However, the digging of a canal raised three problems. It would cost much more than the works planned along the Moselle, and the duration of these works was estimated by experts from the Waterways and Navigation Board in Koblenz to be 10 years, nearly double that planned for the improvements of the Moselle. Second, it would convey less cargo than the Moselle (5.22 million tons per year for the canal from the Saar to the Rhine, as opposed to 6.63 million tons per year for the Moselle). There was bitter competition between the two projects at the beginning of the war. Competing expert reports regarding the economic impact of the two waterways resulted in a confrontation between 1940 and 1942, between supporters for improving the Moselle and supporters for digging a canal from the Saar to the Rhine, with the latter believing that cargo projections for the Moselle, based on statistics from the 1930s, were outdated and overly optimistic.[20] However, the need to quickly increase the Third Reich's supplies in coal and minette from Lorraine ultimately led German authorities to favor improvement of the Moselle, and to postpone the digging of the canal from the Saar river to the Rhine river. In 1940, work began on the Moselle route by breaking the rapids and deepening the riverbed. Upstream in Triers and Koblenz, dams were built to provide electricity. Unfavorable military developments prompted Germany to stop the improvement works in 1944.[21]

The Third Reich's decision to initiate works on the Moselle was a major departure from earlier decisions. Previously, the projects competing with improvement of the Moselle had always won out, as was the case at the turn of the nineteenth century. The German Empire gave priority to constructing the canal from the Rhine river to the Weser river, with support from industrial actors in Northern Germany, rather than improving the Moselle, which was defended by the steelmakers of Lorraine and the Ruhr. At the time, improvement of the Moselle also faced dual opposition from the Alsace-Lorraine and German railways, with the latter planning the construction of a railway on the same route running alongside the river. In short, the project initiated in 1888 was dead and buried in 1912.[22]

During the interwar period, the Moselle improvement project was revived by various actors,[23] and once again subject to stiff competition. In Germany it was deemed to be of secondary interest, and hence was not given priority. The development of waterways was limited to three major canal projects at the time: the Rhine-Danube link, which advanced via a dual effort, one along the Main river until Würzburg (completed in 1940), the other along the Neckar river until Heilbronn (completed in 1935); and the central canal, operational in 1938, which set out from the Ems river and connected a series of cities in the country's center before reaching Magdeburg in 1938. The regulation of the Rhine river between Strasbourg and the Istein bar, which was completed in 1938, also took precedence over the Moselle, as did the construction of a canal running lateral to the Rhine from Kembs to Basel, which began service in 1932. In the late 1930s, the Moselle improvement project, which had the support of various

---

20 Vogel: Deutschland, Frankreich und die Mosel, p. 63 – 72.

21 Berger: Les enjeux de la canalisation de la Moselle, p. 141.

22 Ibid., p. 139.

23 See the first part of this article.

actors and had received conclusive expert assessments, was still considered secondary.[24]

This was also true after 1945, at least initially. Led locally in Moselle by the De Wendels, with backing from industry and officials in Metz, the river project was far from garnering unanimous support in France. With the support of their elected officials, the inland shippers and industrial actors of Strasbourg, who depended on trade along the Rhine river for their supplies and exports, represented a headwind for the Moselle improvement project, which would divert part of the Rhine traffic away from the port of Strasbourg. They countered by proposing a large canal that would closely connect the Rhine and Moselle departments to France, and Strasbourg to Metz and then Mézières. However, in the aftermath of the war, competition for canalization of the Moselle did not solely come from France. Within the Western European space, there were actors in inland shipping, represented in particular by the Rhine Union of Chambers of Commerce (RUCC), who pushed to complete the Rhine-Danube connection via the Main river, the Neckar river, and even through Switzerland and Austria via the Lake of Constance and the Inn river. While representatives from chambers of commerce bordering the Moselle river, or highly interested in its improvement—namely Moselle, Trier, Koblenz, and Luxembourg—made their voices heard, the priorities of the RUCC remained focused on trans-European links between the Rhine and Danube rivers, and then the Rhine and Rhône rivers. The Moselle project did not garner unanimous support in Germany either. The Saar business community hesitated to support it, for it was still counting on the construction of the canal from Saarbrücken to the Rhine river via the Palatinate.[25] Given these circumstances, the decision to proceed with canalization of the Moselle would require a miracle, but it actually occurred through a radical transformation of the geopolitical balance in the Rhine region between 1871 and 1945, one that was remarkably steady in terms of its essence.

---

24 Vogel: Deutschland, Frankreich und die Mosel, p. 59.

25 Libera: Diplomatie patronale, p. 151 – 175.

3. Similar Strategic Projects Over the Medium-Term

In French-German border regions, and hence along the course of the Moselle river, geopolitical patterns repeated from 1871, the date the German Empire was created, to the 1950s. Two overlapping factors were the cause: the growing interdependence between the steel producing areas of Lorraine, the Saar, and Luxembourg with those of the Ruhr, in addition to the alternating domination by France and Germany over the Rhine region. I will first examine interdependence within the Rhine steel industry. First, it was long-standing in nature—Lorraine traditionally depended on shipments of coke from the Ruhr and coal from the Saar to produce its steel—and increased during the 1880s, when the development of the Gilchrist-Thomas process made it possible to use minette from Lorraine, which was low in iron and remained untapped. From that point forward, the Ruhr, which did not produce enough iron ore for its steel production, and had to import it from Luxembourg, also bought minette from Lorraine. Power relations alternated cyclically throughout the period. Either Germany or France had domination over a region that included both the Upper Rhine (Alsace and Baden) and the left bank of the Rhine river (Moselle, the Saar, and what became after 1945 the Land of Rhineland-Palatinate). The stages are fairly familiar. In 1940, Nazi Germany proceeded with a de facto annexation of Alsace and Moselle. German hegemony followed the period from 1918 and 1935, when France—to which the Saar was economically connected—tried to make the Rhine region along the French-German border into a French space. The French policy was partly conducted in reaction to the German Empire's annexation of Alsace and Moselle following the Franco-Prussian War in 1870, one that was maintained over time, and came to an end only in 1918. The same pattern began after 1945 as France, which was one of the four powers occupying Germany, maintained an occupation zone in the country's southwest until 1949, and secured the economic and monetary attachment of the Saar until 1955. Each time the dominant power tried, with greater or lesser success, to impose its institutions on this space, and to create, with varying degrees, a unified political and economic region for which the Moselle naturally represented the shortest trade route between the interdependent industrial centers, as well as a powerful symbolic link.[26]

26 Poidevin / Bariéty: Les relations franco-allemandes, passim.

This was the case in 1940. The project, which began in the summer of 1939 exclusively on the German section of the Moselle, was extended to the French portion of the river after the Third Reich's de facto annexation of the Alsace and Moselle. Germany's political control over Alsace and part of Lorraine allowed it to initiate economic projects: the improvement of the Moselle sought to facilitate trade between the steel producing and coal mining Lorraine and the Ruhr as part of a relation of subordination, in which products from the Lorraine, minette in particular, would meet the Ruhr's supply needs and help grow the Third Reich's steel production.[27] The organization of the Rhine economic region under German domination was part of a much larger plan for a "new Europe." On the economic level, Nazi Europe planned to integrate the Rhine regions — Belgium, Luxembourg, and the Netherlands — as well as Denmark and Norway within a close union with Greater Germany.[28] In light of this vast plan, the reserves that Saar-based industrial actors in steel and coal had regarding the profitability of the Moselle route, however justified — as well as their alternative proposition for a canal from the Saar river to the Rhine river via the Palatinate — seemed very secondary, and were swept aside. Without the external constraint of the evolving military situation, the German project for the canalization of the Moselle would have proceeded.[29]

This was a genuine departure from the situation that prevailed before 1914. The German Empire nevertheless enjoyed considerable advantages: the left bank of the Rhine — Alsace and Moselle — was lastingly German, and the acceleration of the industrial revolution led to the development of trade and integration between the Empire's primary steel-producing areas, which prompted a rethinking of plans to improve the most direct waterway between the Ruhr, Luxembourg, the Saar, and Lorraine. The failure of the Moselle canalization project can be attributed to different actors: firstly to industrial actors in Northern Germany, who resisted the economic realignment of the German space around the Rhine, to the detriment of the traditional territories of Prussia[30]; secondly to the German administration, which hindered "the development of the Lorraine metalworking industry by preventing it from cheaply obtaining the coke it

---

27 Vogel: Deutschland, Frankreich und die Mosel, p. 68 – 72.

28 Bloch: Le IIIe Reich et le monde, passim, cited by Schirmann: Quel ordre européen, p. 263 – 265.

29 Vogel: Deutschland, Frankreich und die Mosel, p. 68 – 72.

30 Berger: Les enjeux de la canalisation de la Moselle, p. 138 – 139.

received from Westphalia"[31]; and finally German railways, which "transported minette to Westphalia at a very low price, but imposed very high rates for German coke headed for the Lorraine."[32]

After the First World War, it was now the turn for Paris to impose its views over the Rhine region. As a result of its military victory, France tried to inverse the power relations between the French and German economies, and to replace its rival as the leading steel-producing power of Europe.[33] The Treaty of Versailles made the Rhine into a French region, to the detriment of Germany: Alsace and Moselle were reintegrated, while the Saar was economically connected to France for fifteen years, and Luxembourg was no longer part of the Zollverein. Germany thus saw itself deprived of "80% of its resources in iron ore, over 40% of its cast-iron production capacity, and over 30% of its steel production capacity."[34] The treaty's economic clauses facilitated the development of the French steel industry, to which they lent considerably advantages. The industry also would enjoy, as part of war reparations, substantial shipments of German coal for many years. Canalization of the Moselle emerged as an option to facilitate transport from the Ruhr to Lorraine, and subsequently became a priority. This explains why after the war the Moselle canalization project received support from French interests, especially those from Moselle, as represented by the Moselle Chamber of Commerce. This time it was Germany's rapid disinterest in canalization of the Moselle that made the project falter. For obvious strategic reasons, Germany preferred improving exclusively German river regions rather than canalizing the Moselle, which would notably benefit France. In addition, the German steel industry, now deprived of minette from Lorraine and ore from Luxembourg, quickly pivoted to Sweden for its iron ore supplies,[35] which further reduced its interest in improving the Moselle. The failure could also be attributed to French policy. Concerned, with understandable political rea-

31 Levainville, Jacques: „La canalisation de la Moselle", in: *Annales de géographie* 206 (1928), p. 180 – 184, here p. 181.

32 Ebd.

33 Bariéty: Les relations franco-allemandes après la Première Guerre mondiale, passim.

34 Poidevin / Bariéty: Les relations franco-allemandes, p. 231.

35 Berger: Les enjeux de la canalisation de la Moselle, p. 140 – 141.

sons, about "orienting Lorraine toward France,"[36] at a time when it had been part of Germany for nearly half a century, the French government did not provide enough support for the Moselle improvement project, as the country's economic interest should have prompted it to do.[37] The only moment of the interwar period in which the project seemed likely to be completed was a brief political window that emerged in Western Europe after Locarno, when cooperation between Europeans seemed possible. The French, Germans, and Luxembourgers who helped create the International Steel Cartel in 1926 agreed to complete canalization of the Moselle.[38] The bright spell did not last, as the economic crash of 1929 and the rise to power of the Nazis brought an end to any joint project to improve the Moselle.

The postwar period proceeded along the same lines as the interwar period. France once again dreamed of replacing Germany as Europe's leading steel-producing power.[39] The conditions for the French dream to become a reality appeared to be in place this time: Germany was occupied by the Allies and disarmed, with its steel production severely limited, and its steel Konzerne broken up.[40] Also, as in the aftermath of the First World War, France obtained control over the Rhine region with the return of Alsace and Lorraine, the economic and monetary connection of the Saar, and Germany's granting of an occupation zone along the right bank of the Rhine, including the entire course of the Moselle. Similarly, the canalization of the Moselle responded to French economic needs and interests, which expected large shipments of German coal as part of war reparations. However, this time the project was directly led by inhabitants of Lorraine. In 1948, foundry owners pressured the French government—via the Moselle Chamber of Commerce and Industry, and with support from local political authorities—to quickly proceed with canalization of the Moselle. The government procrastinated. In Alsace, the business community concerned by activity along the Rhine was strongly opposed to improving the Moselle, which would considerably reduce traffic in the port of Strasbourg. To counter this project, Strasbourg town councilors and business

36 Chanrion: Les aspects internationaux de la canalisation, p. 158, cited by Berger: Les enjeux de la canalisation de la Moselle, p. 141.

37 Berger: Les enjeux de la canalisation de la Moselle, p. 141.

38 Ebd.

39 Libera: Un rêve de puissance, passim.

40 Bitsch: Un rêve français, p. 313 – 329.

leaders in Alsace proposed constructing a large Northeast Canal that would connect Strasbourg to Metz, and later to Charleville-Mézières. Paris refused to decide between the two competing projects and delayed for two years, between 1948 and 1951.[41]

The situation changed as a result of the Schuman Plan. Beyond the French government's decision to canalize the Moselle, which was first and foremost done as compensation to Lorraine steelmakers for their acceptance of the Schuman Plan,[42] the improvement project for the Moselle was made possible because, for the first time in nearly two hundred years, the Rhine economic region was not unified by a power using it as a base to dominate other countries along the river, but rather in the common interest of all interested parties. In this respect, the future implementation of the European Coal and Steel Community was a major departure in terms of objective. Some long-standing business leaders, such as Albert Houpert, the Secretary General of the Moselle Chamber of Commerce and Industry from 1919 to 1960, who had been following this issue since the interwar period, clearly perceived this historic change. They were all the more determined to see it through.[43]

4. *Conclusion*

The Nazi project for canalization of the Moselle was clearly in keeping with earlier initiatives to make the Rhine's primary tributary navigable. By facilitating trade between the Ruhr and Lorraine, canalization would enable the dominant power of the moment—in this case the Third Reich—to impose the economic unity of the Rhine region solely to its advantage, and to use the coal and steel-producing resources of neighboring countries as part of a "center-periphery" logic of domination. Other elements of continuity also emerged. As in the past, preparatory work and feasibility studies emphasized the interest of such a waterway. The project also had to compete with other river improvement projects as well as other means of transport, on both the national and international level. Finally, once again as in the past, the decisions were difficult to make. In the end, Nazi policy

41 Libera: Diplomatie patronale, p. 151 – 175.

42 See the introduction to this article.

43 Libera: Diplomatie patronale aux frontières, p. 413.

clearly took its place within the *longue durée* of the Moselle improvement project. Nevertheless, while the latter was undeniably European by virtue of its route and implications, it was not at all in terms of its spirit. It is because of this reversal of paradigm that the canalization project conducted by the Third Reich during the Second World War cannot be compared with the project completed in 1964, a little less than twenty years after the war. For the first time in over a century, the unification of the Rhine economic region was envisioned within a truly European framework.

5. References

Bariéty, Jacques: *Les relations franco-allemandes après la Première Guerre mondiale, 10 novembre 1918 – 10 janvier 1925. De l'exécution à la négociation*, Paris 1977.

Berger, Françoise: „Les enjeux de la canalisation de la Moselle et de la Sarre jusqu'au Rhin pour les industriels sidérurgistes du bassin Lorraine-Sarre-Luxembourg (jusqu'aux années 1950)", in: Berger, Françoise / Rapoport, Michel / Tilly, Pierre / Touchelay, Béatrice (ed.): *Industries, territoires et cultures en Europe du Nord-Ouest XIXe-XXe siècles. Mélanges en l'honneur de Jean-François Eck*, Roubaix 2015, p. 137 – 145.

Bitsch, Marie-Thérèse: „Un rêve français: le désarmement économique de l'Allemagne (1944-1947)", in: *Relations internationales* 51 (1987), p. 313 – 329.

Bloch, Charles: *Le IIIe Reich et le monde, nouvelle édition revue et augmentée d'une préface*, Paris 2015.

Bonnefont, Jean-Claude: „La réalisation d'un ancien projet: la canalisation de la Moselle", in: Châtelier, Louis (ed.): *La France de l'Est et l'Europe du Moyen Âge à nos jours*, Nancy 1995, p. 163 – 176.

Caffier, Michel: *La Moselle. Une rivière et ses hommes*, Nancy 1985.

Cahn, Jean-Paul: *Le second retour. Le rattachement de la Sarre à la France 1955 – 1957*, Berne / Francfort-sur-le-Main / New York 1985.

Chanrion, Fernand: „Les aspects internationaux de la canalisation de la Moselle", in: *Politique étrangère* 19 (1954), p. 157 – 168.

Chanrion, Fernand: *Une victoire européenne: la Moselle*, Paris 1964.

Dumoulin, Michel: „Les transports: bastion des nationalismes", in: Dumoulin, Michel (ed.): *La Commission européenne 1958 – 1972. Histoire et mémoires d'une institution,* Luxembourg 2007, p. 457 – 469.

Freymond, Jean: *Le Troisième Reich et la réorganisation de l'Europe 1940 – 1942. Origines et projets*, Leiden 1974.

Levainville, Jacques: „La canalisation de la Moselle", in: *Annales de géographie* 206 (1928), p. 180 – 184.

Libera, Martial: *Un rêve de puissance. La France et le contrôle de l'économie allemande (1942 – 1949)*, Bruxelles 2012.

Libera, Martial: „La chambre de commerce et d'industrie de la Moselle face au plan Schuman", in: *Fare Cahier* 8 (2016), p. 35 – 48.

Libera, Martial: *Diplomatie patronale aux frontières. Les relations des chambres de commerce frontalières françaises avec leurs homologues allemandes (1945 – milieu des années 1980)*, Genève 2019.

Meddahi, Bernard: *La Moselle et l'Allemagne 1945 – 1951, thèse de troisième cycle (dir. Raymond Poidevin)*, Université de Metz 1979.

Poidevin, Raymond / Bariéty, Jacques*: Les relations franco-allemandes 1815 – 1975, seconde édition revue et augmentée*, Paris 1977.

Schirmann, Sylvain: *Quel ordre européen? De Versailles à la chute du III*[e] *Reich*, Paris 2006.

Spierenburg, Dirk / Poidevin, Raymond: *Histoire de la Haute Autorité de la Communauté européenne du charbon et de l'acier. Une expérience supranationale*, Bruxelles 1993.

Vogel, Ludwin: *Deutschland, Frankreich und die Mosel. Europäische Integrationspolitik in den Montan-Regionen Ruhr, Lothringen, Luxemburg und der Saar*, Essen 2001.

Navigating the Middle: Integration of Inland Navigation in Central Europe and the Second World War[1]

Jiří Janáč

Table of Content

1. Introduction

The traditional narrative on the history of integration in Central Europe tends to focus on the successive periods of empire-building rather than the formation of transnational and international cooperation. It is often implicitly assumed that the rise of nineteenth-century imperialism followed by Nazi and Soviet empire building left only a brief window between the two world wars during which unrestricted cooperation among Central European nation states could develop before their entry in the EU in the twenty-first century.[2] But from the perspective of infrastructural integration, the situation seems rather more complex. Empire building efforts require efficient infrastructural networks and push for their extension even beyond

1 Acknowledgments: This work was supported by the European Regional Development Fund project "Creativity and Adaptability as Conditions of the Success of Europe in an Interrelated World" (reg. no. CZ.02.1.01/0.0/0.0/16_019/0000734).

2 See e.g. Loth, Wilfried / Pãun, Nicolae (eds.): *Disintegration and Integration in East-Central Europe: 1919 – Post-1989*, Baden-Baden 2014.

the imperial core. Furthermore, military economy associated with imperial wars provided an additional stimulus for a maximally efficient management of available capacities. Indeed, empire building clearly often leads to a facilitation of implementation of administrative rules that enable high-performing operational regimes of existing networks even on an international level.[3] When arguing along these lines, Schot and Schipper even suggest that a certain continuity in cross-border integration of transport, which was maintained during the Second World War and during the period of Nazi empire building efforts, provided the foundation for a relatively fast launch of Western and pan-European transport integration after 1945.[4] Similarly, scholars of the Soviet Bloc have recently shifted their focus from repression and conquest towards studying the role of socialist internationalism and integration, thus challenging the narrative of a centrally controlled empire and opening space for a debate about the role of experts and institutions.[5]

This contribution focuses directly on continuities and discontinuities in ideas, actors, and procedures of cross-border operation of inland waterways in Central Europe during the Second World War. This chapter follows generally the actor perspective of contemporary experts and focuses on issues related to cross-border operation of shipping vessels. First, it discusses operational harmonisation achieved via establishment of an international regulatory regime (production and content of rules for cross-border transport). The second subchapter deals with changes in actual use of cross-border waterways by shipping companies, and the final part of this contribution focuses on efforts aimed at material connectivity (the construction and maintenance of waterways). In terms of territories covered, the present analysis is restricted to the three central European rivers which the Versailles Treaty declared to be international, namely the Elbe, Oder and the Danube. In part, this delimitation draws also on visions ex-

3 Högselius, Peer / Kaijser, Arne / Vleuten, Erik van der: *Europe's Infrastructure Transition: Economy, War, Nature*, New York 2018.

4 Schipper, Frank / Schot, Johan: "Infrastructural Europeanism, or the project of building Europe on infrastructures: An introduction", in: *History and Technology* 27/3 (2011), p. 245 – 264.

5 Müller, Uwe: "Introduction: Failed and forgotten? New Perspectives on the history of the Council for Mutual Economic Assistance", in: *Comparativ: Zeitschrift für Globalgeschichte und vergleichende Gesellschaftsforschung* 5 – 6 (2017), p. 7 – 25.

pressed by contemporary actors. Since mid-nineteenth century, variously defined notions of Central Europe (*Mitteleuropa*) provided a conceptual framework for the process of cross-border integration within this region, which consists of roughly the abovementioned three river basins. Chronologically, the paper's aim is to trace the transition from the liberal interwar period, characterised by tensions between national state geopolitics and border building on one side and the development of international and transnational initiatives aiming at cooperation on the other, to the Nazi "empire-building", itself torn between search for a new cooperative international order on the continent and German domination, and finally on to the ensuing formation of the Soviet Bloc.[6]

The majority of the limited number of existing academic studies which discuss inland navigation in Central Europe from the perspective of integration were written by economic historians. They tend to understand Nazi military system-building efforts as a major rupture in the integration process, which is why scholars interested in waterway integration usually focus on the interwar/post-war period and approach the issue from the perspective of either national history[7] or geopolitics.[8] Somewhat in parallel, experts on internationalism and international organisations follow the history of major international organisations, which either disappeared at the beginning of the Second World War or were bypassed by other, more direct forms of negotiations.[9] Rather tellingly, one recently published account of history of the European Danube Commission discusses developments during the war hardly at all and the short chapter dealing with the twentieth century outlines the "institutional metamorphosis during the in-

---

6 Kirk, Tim: "Nazi plans for a new European order and European responses," in: Dafinger, Johannes / Pohl, Dieter (eds.): *A New Nationalist Europe Under Hitler: Concepts of Europe and Transnational Networks in the National Socialist Sphere of Influence, 1933 – 1945*, Abingdon 2019, p. 71 – 92.

7 Jakubec, Ivan: *Železnice a labská plavba ve střední Evropě 1918 – 1938: Dopravněpoli-tické vztahy Československa, Německa a Rakouska v meziválečném období*, Prague 1997.

8 Tulus, Arthur: "Geopolitics and Trade at the Danube Mouths during the Interwar Period: A Study Case on the German-British Rivalry", in: *Transylvanian Review* 22 (2013), p. 277 – 286; Teichova, Alice / Ratcliffe, Penelope: "British Interests in Danube Navigation after 1918", in: *Business History* 27/ 3 (1985), p. 283 – 300.

9 E.g. Jeřábek, Miroslav: *Za silnou střední Evropu: Středoevropské hnutí mezi Budapeští, Vídní a Brnem v letech 1925 – 1939*, Prague 2008.

terwar period and in post-war times".[10] Inversely, a large part of older literature on the Danube focuses almost exclusively on Cold War disputes.[11] Last but not least, there exists a vast body of historical accounts focusing on the technical development of inland navigation on individual rivers and/or histories (biographies) of major companies. These accounts are usually written by experts in the field rather than by trained historians. This literature, however, while marginalised in academic debates, at least implicitly points to continuities across the Second World War.[12]

At this point, it should be noted that this contribution is only a fraction of the originally planned full-length paper. Due to Covid pandemic-related difficulties, several archives (and especially sources related to Danube commissions) have not been fully consulted and explored. As a result, this paper offers only a brief outline of the situation based mainly on author's previous research in Archives of the Czechoslovak Ministry of Foreign Affairs, trade journals dealing with inland navigation in Central Europe, and secondary literature. To make up for this shortage of primary sources, I have decided to look in more detail on the Czechoslovak experts and engineers who were involved in efforts to make and keep Central Europe navigable. In the following, I also occasionally quote their opinions and describe their careers to illustrate the expert perspective.

Parts of the paper draw on my dissertation thesis, which attempted to analyse the long-term process of waterway integration in Europe through the lens of the Danube-Oder-Elbe canal, the never constructed but throughout the twentieth century negotiated connection between the Black, the North and the Baltic Sea.[13] The central argument of the thesis focused on the continuity of technocratic efforts across political shifts – such as the Second World War. But this paper significantly transcends the argumentation offered in the dissertation, especially on two levels. First, it corrects one of the major flaws in the original argumentation, namely the

10 Ardeleanu, Constantin: *The European Commission of the Danube, 1856 – 1948: An Experiment in International Administration*, Leiden 2020, p. 28.

11 Gorove, Stephen: *Law and Politics of the Danube: An Interdisciplinary Study*, The Hague 1964.

12 Švarc: Sedmdesát pět let Československé plavby; Hubert: Dějiny plavby v Čechách II; Völkl: Vom Biedermeier ins dritte Jahrtausend; Grössing / Binder / Fink / Sauer: Rot-Weiss-Rot auf blauen Wellen.

13 Janáč, Jiří: *European Coasts of Bohemia: Negotiating the Danube-Oder-Elbe Canal in a Troubled Twentieth Century*, Amsterdam 2012.

chosen chronology. The aim of the thesis was to show how technocratic ideas and projects survive and absorb political turbulences, how they deal with being reinterpreted by their carriers, that is, experts, again and again to fit ideological goals of changing political representations and ideologies. For that reason, I opted for a strictly political chronology. While that approach proved fruitful (plans indeed survived, albeit altered), I have realised that this framing had partly obscured the continuity of planning, of experts, ideas, institutions, and forms of cooperation.[14] Secondly, this paper refocuses the original storyline: this time, the emphasis is on challenging the centrality of the Second World War also by extending the notion of integration, looking beyond the actors involved directly in the negotiations of canal construction, and on the formation of a regulatory regime for inland navigation in the region.

2. *Towards Riparian Internationalism: Institutions and Nation States*

The exact date of outbreak of the Second World War on Central European waterways seems difficult to determine. Still, it seems that the critical turning point, a radical assault on the interwar international regime introduced after 1918, came with the infamous note of 14 November 1936, which announced a German decision to disregard the provisions of the Versailles Treaty concerning international regime on waterways on its territory. On the other hand, the situation deteriorated gradually ever since the Nazi rose to power. Already in 1934, German representatives led by Arthur Seeliger withdrew from participation in the League of Nations' Committee on Communications and Transit in a move that was a harbinger of the eventual demise of the ambitious program of internationalisation of all European navigable rivers and development of universal regulatory regime guaranteed by the League of Nations.[15] That step was then compounded by the note of 14 November 1936, in which Germany reject-

---

14 Discussed for the Czechoslovak case by recent social and economic history literature. See e.g. Rákosník / Spurný / Štaif: *Milníky moderních českých dějin: Krize konsenzu a legitimity v letech 1848 – 1989.*

15 Letter from Vojtěch Krbec to the Ministry of Foreign Affairs from 14 February 1934 (AMZV, II, 617).

ed the concept of Articles of the Treaty of Versailles related to internationalisation of rivers.[16]

The Treaty of Versailles and subsequent Barcelona Convention and Statute on the Regime of Navigable Waterways of International Concern, which were concluded under the auspices of the League of Nations in April 1921, anticipated the formation of international administration (a river commission) for selected "river systems" "of international concern". These river systems were those of Oder, which was formerly entirely German but now would serve also Czechoslovakia and potentially Poland by via its tributaries, the Elbe, which would serve Czechoslovakia and Germany, and the Danube, which used to flow through three empires but after 1918 flowed through seven countries: Germany, Austria, Czechoslovakia, Hungary, the Kingdom of the Serbs, Croats and Slovenes (S.H.S), Bulgaria, and Romania. This arrangement would cover the mainstream as well as some of the transboundary tributaries. Instead of traditional particularism characterised by domination of riparian countries and reciprocal arrangements, the new approach aspired at a formation of a universal "general regime" for future internationalisation of all (European) rivers.[17] This intention was clearly present in the repeatedly submitted (but failed) proposals for extension of the new regime to all navigable (i.e. not only transboundary) European rivers.[18]

All in all, the new regime introduced on the Elbe, Oder and Danube rested on two major premises: First of all, the laissez-faire articulation of the principle of freedom of navigation as a freedom of commerce ("communication and transit", including free trading between ports of each riparian country), which limited the sovereignty of riparian countries over their use of the rivers (restrictions on tolls and taxes, prohibition of preferential treatment of domestic shipping companies, etc.) and virtually eliminated differences between vessels operating under the flags of riparian and

16 *Documents on German Foreign Policy 1918 – 1945: Nov. 1936-Nov. 1937*, Washington 1983, p. 49.

17 Uprety, Kishor: *The Transit Regime for Landlocked States: International Law and Development Perspectives*, Washington, D.C. 2006, p. 40.

18 Report by Czech representative at the CCT Vojtech Krbec from 27 December 1933. Archives of the Czechoslovak Ministry of Foreign Affairs (AMZV), archival group II, box 617.

non-riparian countries.[19] Secondly, the introduction of a multilateral regulatory and administrative regime based on international river commissions formed on the basis of the principle of technocratic internationalism (in theory a depoliticised expert governance), which was designed to promote universalist principles and trade cooperation over national politics and protectionism.[20] The river commissions, consisting in theory of representatives of all countries (i.e. also non-riparian) interested in taking part in navigation on the river in question, were supposed to act as permanent and independent administrative bodies governing the use and development of navigation on a particular river and develop river-specific navigation acts that would reflect the specific situation within each river system.

Germany, as well as other riparian countries, had right from the start openly manifested their dissatisfaction with such envisioned "universal" international regime and successfully blocked its full implementation. As a consequence, the newly formed International Commission of the Danube (CID), which administered the upper, fluvial, part of the river, was not granted the same powers as the European Commission of the Danube (CED), an older body which had been governing the mouth (the maritime Danube) ever since 1856.[21] Similarly, the final articulation of the Elbe Acts ratified in 1922 fell short of the original visions when Germany successfully blocked the formation of a permanent secretariat of the Elbe Commission (International Elbe Commission, CIE), which consequently instead of administering the river functioned merely as a supervisory body.[22] On the Oder, German and Polish delegates in the International Commission of the River Oder (CIO) even managed to prevent the ratification of new acts of navigation altogether, referring to the fact that at the time, the entire navigable stretch of the river between Gliwice (Gleiwitz) and Szczecin (Stettin) was located in German territory (internationalisation operated with an envisioned extension of the navigable stretch up-

19 Vitányi: The Regime of Navigation on International Waterways. See also *Convention and Statute on the Regime of Navigable Waterways of International Concern*, League of Nations document C.479. M.327. 1921. VIII.

20 Lagendijk, Vincent / Schot, Johan: "Technocratic Internationalism in the Interwar Years: Building Europe on Motorways and Electricity Networks", in: *Journal of Modern European History* 6/2 (2008), p. 196 – 217.

21 Ardeleanu: The European Commission of the Danube, p. 313.

22 Jakubec: Železnice a labská plavba, p. 100.

stream to Czechoslovak borders; see Figure no.1).[23] Indeed, disputes between the riparian countries, who bickered about conceding parts of state sovereignty over rivers, and the non-riparian parties significantly hampered the development of the international regime. Otto Popper, a leading Czechoslovak expert and the first secretary of the International Commission of the Danube (CID), in retrospect noted that the result was a dissatisfactory compromise trapped in-between grand visions and the dull practice of power politics.[24]

German rejection of the international regime established at Versailles was not driven by a refusal to accept the principles of internationalisation and infrastructural integration as such. German critique focused on the fact that the regime was discriminatory, citing among other things especially disproportional representation in commissions and non-reciprocal character of the multilateral regime. In fact, though, the limited power of riparian states in international river commissions in Central Europe – especially when compared to the situation on the Rhine, which was mostly administered by the Central Commission for Navigation on the Rhine, the CCNR (by 1929, 70% of delegates) – contributed to a revival of initiatives aimed at a formation of Central European, as opposed to pan-European network. Riparian countries' participation in the two Danubian commissions was 25% (European Commission of the Danube, CED) and 73% (International Commission of the Danube, CID), while in the Elbe and Oder commissions, they controlled 60% and 45% of seats, respectively.[25] Especially German experts voiced concerns over Central Europe being exploited by Western powers. As Fritz Krieg put it already in 1929: "How long must the law of parity and equality of all subjects of international law be infringed? How much longer must *Mitteleuropa* alone keep its currents, the heart of its territories, open to foreign ships?"[26]

---

23 Jednání o německém přístupu k oderské plavební aktě v Drážďanech v únoru 1934. National Archives of the Czech Republic (NAČR), archival group Czechoslovak Office for Inland Navigation (ČPÚ), box.

24 Popper, Otto: "The International Regime of the Danube", in: *The Geographical Journal* 5 – 6/102 (1943), p. 240 – 253, here p. 244/45.

25 Krieg, Fritz: "Das Weltbinnenschiffahrtsrecht und die Ströme Mitteleuropas", in: Hantos, Elemer (ed.): *Mitteleuropäische Wasserstrassenpolitik: Referate und Beschlüsse der Mitteleuropäischen Wasserstrassenkonferenz, Budapest, 11.– 13. Mai 1929,* Vienna 1929, p. 81 – 101, here p. 89.

26 Ibid., p. 94.

German representatives argued that international administration should be limited to technical issues of hydraulic structures, customs, navigation police, and social security of the personnel.[27] Actually, a German proposal for a revision of navigation acts for Elbe and Oder, which was finalised before the Note of November 14 in autumn 1936 and later revoked, replaced virtually all competences of the Elbe Commission with bilateral treaties and the principle of reciprocity. At the same time, though, it respected the principles of the freedom of navigation and even confirmed the validity of the Czechoslovak lease of the port area in Hamburg enshrined in the Treaty of Versailles. Furthermore, the proposal was accompanied by a draft of a new German navigation act that would allow free shipping on all German waterways also for foreign vessels under same conditions on the basis of reciprocity.[28]

After the Anschluss of Austria and the Munich Agreement, Germany became the dominant power on the Danube, Elbe, and Oder, and took steps towards developing a new mechanism of governance that would respect the Nazi vision of international character of rivers. In 1938, German delegate at CED Georg Martius proposed a far-reaching transformation of the existing regime. It was driven by the two crucial objections against the existing one and suggested that riparian countries would take control over the river and the commission would be replaced by an ad hoc summoned technical council consisting of representatives of riparian states.[29] Despite the initially rather reluctant response, this proposal was soon transformed into less radical Sinaia Agreements, which transferred most competencies of the European Commission of the Danube (CED) to Romania in a solution that roughly corresponded to the situation on the Elbe after 1937 and downgraded the commission to a status of consultative body.[30]

Administration of the now "German" fluvial Danube changed accordingly and brought a complete resetting. At a conference on the Danube, which was held in Vienna in September 1940, representatives of the riparian countries and fascist Italy disbanded the International Danube Commission (CID) and replaced it with a newly established "council of fluvial

27 Jakubec: Železnice a labská plavba ve střední Evropě 1918 – 1938, p. 103.

28 Ibid., p. 100.

29 Kastory, Agnieszka: "Problem obecności Niemiec w Komisjach Dunajskich w okresie międzywojennym", in: *Studia z Dziejów Rosji i Europy Środkowo-Wschodniej* 42 (2007), p. 75 – 89, here p. 80 – 83.

30 Gorove: Law and Politics of the Danube, p. 32.

Danube". This council was supposed to administer the stretch of Danube between Bratislava and Braila as well as the mouth of the Danube (thus forming a single commission for the entire international Danube), which was international, but not the upper part of Danube from Bratislava, which was now German. A month later, the new body convened in Bucharest and discussed the formation of a new international regime along the lines of the previous German proposal – by then, the CED still formally existed.[31] After a dispute concerning the role of the USSR and persisting separation of administration of the maritime and fluvial Danube (since the European Danube Commission, the CED, still formally governed the mouth of the Danube), a new regime was drafted. It was based on a single commission for all of Danube and included the riparian states and Italy.[32] In 1941, the war broke out between Nazi Germany and the USSR and while it was still winning, Germany tried again to assume control of maritime Danube at another conference in November 1942. However, Romania, a Nazi ally, managed to prevent full implementation of the agreement by its more or less tacit obstruction.[33]

Soon after the turn of events on the war fronts in 1942, Gustav Königs, vice-secretary of state for inland navigation at the Reich Ministry of Transport, articulated a programme of post-war organisation of waterways in Europe, which reflected and summarised previous debates among German experts. He emphasised the crucial role of inland shipping in bringing about an economic integration of "Europe of nations states" under German leadership and repeatedly called for creation of a strictly international waterway system in Europe. Such system, described in opposition to interwar internationalism and river commissions, would grant freedom of shipping on national waterways to all nations "living in peace with Germany" and

31 Ghisa, Alexandru: "Romania and the first cracks in the implementation of the Hitler-Stalin pact of 1940: Germany's guarantees granted to Romania at the Vienna Award and the Danube issue", in: *Valahian Journal of Historical Studies* 16 (2011), p. 95 – 106.

32 Focas, Spiridon G.: *The Lower Danube River: In the Southeastern European Political and Economic Complex from Antiquity to the Conference of Belgrade of 1948, Boulder,* CO 1987.

33 Ardeleanu: The European Commission of the Danube, p. 318.

extend from the Atlantic to the Black and Caspian seas via newly built canals connecting the Rhine and Danube basins.[34]

Post-war geopolitical realities were not favourable to a return to any type of descendant of the liberal interwar international regime of administration of inland shipping in Europe that had been promoted by the Americans. In his speech at the Potsdam Conference, Truman even argued that "free and unrestricted navigation" on international (cross-border) rivers was an necessary prerequisite of peace and security on the continent.[35] Erection of the Iron Curtain, which stretched across the Danube and Elbe river basins and cut off the uppermost stretch of the Danube and the estuary of the Elbe from the rest of their systems, made such visions impracticable. Instead of the interwar universalist internationalism, the Soviet Union used its dominant position in the now solidified Socialist Bloc to enforce a return to riparian particularism.

Developments on the Danube offer an illustrative example. Not surprisingly, the USSR, a riparian country on the Danube since 1940, strongly opposed any reinstitution of the pre-war regime.[36] Moreover, Soviet policy since 1940 focused on the formation of a single commission that would govern the entire navigable stretch of the Danube and include only representatives of the riparian countries.[37] Under a motto "Danube for Danubians", delegates of socialist riparian countries at a re-constitutive meeting of the Danube Commission accepted the Soviet proposal to limit participation in the unified Danube Commission to riparian states (thus following in the footsteps of the Nazi authorities). Moreover, competencies of this commission were to be limited to such an extent that it in effect functioned as merely a coordinator, while all real power remained in the hands of the riparian states.[38] Kaser in his seminal analysis on the working of the COMECON and socialist integration repeatedly mentions the European

34 Königs, Gustav: "Die Wasserstrassen im Europa-Verkehr", in: *Süddeutsche Wasserstrassen* 1 – 2/19 (1943), p. 2 – 4.

35 Truman, Harry: "Radio Report to the American People on the Potsdam Conference", in: Woolley, John / Peters, Gerhard (eds.): *The American Presidency Project*, available at https://www.presidency.ucsb.edu/documents/radio-report-the-american-people-the-potsdam-conference.

36 Paterson, Thomas G.: "Eastern Europe and the Early Cold War: The Danube Controversy", in: *The Historian* 33/ 2 (1971), p. 237 – 247.

37 Ghisa: Romania and the first cracks in the implementation.

38 Kaser, Michael: *Comecon: Integration Problems of the Planned Economies*, London 1967, p. 95.

Danube Commission (1856–1918) as the closest analogy to the setup of the Cold War Danube Commission, which likewise consisted of national nominees.[39]

Contrary to the general consensus among scholars, this outcome was not the result of a purely Soviet dictate accepted, tacitly and sheepishly, by delegates from the satellite countries.[40] There were cautious voices of dissent. Czechoslovak experts, such as Ladislav Vavrouch, recognised the need for cooperation and insisted that some form of supranational administration covering the cost of maintenance of some stretches of the river is necessary.[41] Ultimately, though, the final agreement placed the responsibility for improvement of navigation in the Iron Gates and the Danube delta under bilateral administrations. Moreover, the agreement took place just a month after Cominform's resolution on the Communist Party of Yugoslavia, which heralded the Tito–Stalin split. Agreement to collaborate on waterway integration is thus a rather unique example of cooperation between Yugoslavia (former S.H.S. and a riparian country on the Danube) and the USSR at the time.[42]

On the Danube, Oder, and the Elbe, the principle of freedom of navigation remained in place but in a restricted form. Neither Czechoslovakia nor East Germany expressed interest in reviving the Elbe Commission and its navigation acts. Oder became due to the post-war westward shift of the Polish frontier a fully "socialist" river and again, neither of the people's republics showed interest in multilateral administration.[43] Navigation on the Elbe and Oder was regulated by bilateral agreements between riparian countries: Czechoslovakia and the GDR in 1954 concluded an agreement on mutual use of inland waterways, Czechoslovakia signed a transport treaty with Poland in 1947 and updated it in 1956, agreement between

---

39 Ibid., p. 41, 167.

40 See e.g. Ardeleanu: The European Commission of the Danube, p. 320.

41 Ladislav Vavrouch in his report on the first session of the new Danube Commission, AMZV, MO-OMO 55-65 O, b. 126.

42 Gulić, Milan: "Belgrade Danube Conference 1948", in: *Tokovi istorije* 1 (2013), p. 173 – 202.

43 Techman, Ryszard: "Czechosłowacka żegluga na Odrze w latach 1947 – 1957. Part I", in: *Przegląd Zachodniopomorski* 33/1 (2018), p. 145 – 167; Techman, Ryszard: "Czechosłowacka żegluga na Odrze w latach 1947 – 1957. Part II", in: *Przegląd Zachodniopomorski* 34/1 (2019), p. 5 – 27.

GDR and Poland 1952)[44] and other minor agreements on customs on transit traffic (GDR – CZE 1959).[45] Moreover, on the Elbe, Czechoslovakia and West Germany operated their shipping until 1988 without it being based on any bilateral agreement at all and despite this – and although tariff policies favoured the socialist and now Polish Szczecin – Hamburg remained a primary trading centre for Czechoslovakia.[46]

3. *Towards International Coordination of Shipping: Cartels and Regulations*

Nazi transport policies were initially based on an introduction of state control through "transport coordination" and suppression of intermodal competition on the national level, thus reflecting a common reaction to the Great Depression in the transport sector in Europe.[47] These policies, introduced in the first half of 1930s in the form of compulsory cartelisation and harmonisation of tariffs (fixed rates) within individual river systems, naturally affected the operation of international waterways.[48]

It should be noted, though, that ideas aiming at harmonisation and more efficient management of competing transport systems and tariffs in politically fragmented interwar Central Europe were not a Nazi invention. Already before the Great Depression, experts on transport economics such as Elemer Hantos were convinced that closer cooperation of shipping companies and unification of the so far mutually competitive tariffs (on various goods and distances) is a primary and necessary instrument of achiev-

---

44 Hoblík, Karel: "Mezinárodní vnitrozemní vodní cesty", in: Teklý, Vratislav (ed.): *Plavební příručka,* Prague 1962, p. 178 – 181.

45 Benda, Václav: "Výtah celních předpisů týkajících se mezinárodní lodní plavby", in: Teklý, Vratislav (ed.): *Plavební příručka*, Prague 1962, p. 181 – 183.

46 Jakubec, Ivan: *Československo-německé dopravněpolitické vztahy v období studené války se zvláštním zřetelem na železnici a labskou plavbu (1945/1949 – 1989),* Prague 2007.

47 Millward, Robert: *Private and public enterprise in Europe: energy, telecommunications and transport, 1830 – 1990,* Cambridge 2008.

48 US Office of Strategic Services, Research and Analysis Branch. Organization of European Waterways of international concern, R & A No. 2476, Washington: s.n., 1945.

ing a greater prosperity of Danube shipping and the region en large.[49] Faced with a complicated geopolitical situation and economic problems associated with competition from railways, major shipping companies operating on the river in the 1920s started to form cartels and pools. In fact, the situation of traffic on all three rivers, but especially the Danube[50] and the Elbe,[51] deteriorated after 1918 and lagged far behind the pre-war numbers. In 1926, cartels of shipping companies were established on both the Elbe and the Danube. On the Elbe, it was the new Elbe Shipping Association (*Elbe- Schiffahrts-Vereinigung*),[52] which guaranteed to each company a given share on a particular transport route, while on the Danube, the newly established Association of Danube Shipping Companies (*Betriebsgemeinschaft der Donauschiffahrten*) aimed at joint utilisation of vessels, docks etc.[53]

Initially, the introduction of new transport policies of the Third Reich played out differently on different international rivers. On the Elbe, the original cooperation of large shipping companies consisted in accepting orders only through the cartel association in return for guaranteed shares in river operations. By 1932, the national cartel association became mandatory for German carriers and the state introduced a system of fixed rates. This move was disputed at German courts as being incompatible with the Elbe Acts, but the court ruled that an association of national carriers does not amount to discrimination of foreign companies.[54] In February 1934, introduction of a corporative system of government in by now Nazi Germany led to incorporation of the association (*Vereinigung)* into the corpo-

49 Hantos, Elemér: "Einleitung: Mitteleuropäische Wasserstrassenpolitik", in: Hantos, Elemér (ed.): *Mitteleuropäische Wasserstrassenpolitik: Referate und Beschlüsse der Mitteleuropäischen Wasserstrassenkonferenz*, Budapest, 11. bis 13. Mai 1929, Vienna, Leipzig 1929.

50 LON/CRID/AdmL/342/133/153 (1-3) Report by Walker D. Hines, 1925.08.01.

51 Kopper, Christopher: "Germany's National Socialist Transport Policy and the Claim of Modernity: Reality or Fake?", in: *The Journal of Transport History* 34/2 (2013), p. 162 – 176.

52 Hinsch, Werner: "The River Elbe — International: A Historical Perspective", in: *Geo-Journal* 1/2 (1977), p. 45 – 48, here p. 47.

53 Švarc, Bohumil: "Vývoj podniku ČSPLO Děčín", in: Košťál, Miloslav (ed.): *Historie plavby a obchodu po Labi*, Prague 1971.

54 US Office of Strategic Services, Research and Analysis Branch. Organization of European Waterways of international concern, R & A No. 2476, Washington: s.n., 1945.

rative organisation of the transport sector. Already prior to this decision, Czechoslovak *Československá plavební akciová společnost Labská* (ČPSL), the only major non-German operator on the Elbe, withdrew from the association citing as its reason that the guaranteed share of 30% of traffic to Czechoslovakia (calculated based on data from 1929–1931) fell far below the real potential of the company.[55]

On the Oder, the Czechoslovak Oder Shipping Company (*Československá plavební akciová společnost oderská*, ČSPO), owned by the state and the mining industries of the Ostrava coalfield, was since its establishment in 1924 highly dependent on cooperation with German shipping companies co-owned by the same mining industries, the *Ostreederei GmbH*, and *Oppelner Verlade und Lagerhaus Oppeln*, and its transport capacities served mainly German customers. While it did not directly participate in the reorganisation of transport introduced on the German Oder after 1932, it profited from it through its close contacts with the German operators.[56]

Unlike Oder and Elbe, Danube traffic experienced hardly any direct effects in consequence of introduction of the new transport policies in the Third Reich until the Anschluss of Austria in 1938. The pool formed initially by Austrian (*Donaudampfschiffahrtsgesellschaft*, DDSG) and Hungarian (MFTR) companies was early on joined by their German (*Bayerischer Lloyd*) and Dutch competitors (COMOS), and by 1934 also by virtually all major (seminational) fleet operators on the river, that is, the Czechoslovak Danube Shipping Company (*Československá plavba dunajská*, ČSPD), S.H.S.'s JRP, Romanian N.F.R., and the Bulgarian DUNAV (which was itself owned by Austrian and Hungarian companies). Simultaneously, there formed three major associations for oil transport, cereals, and other goods, which operated under freight-allocation agreements.[57] Soon, however, a struggle for dominance within the organisation

55 Švarc, op.cit.

56 Jakubec, Ivan: "Odra jako 'československá' řeka", in: Jančík, Drahomír (ed.): *Pocta profesoru Zdeňku Jindrovi. K sedmdesátým narozeninám*, Prague 2003, p. 179 – 190, here p. 183 –185.

57 Hexner, Ervín: "Československé kartely – přednesl JUDr. Ervín Hexner ve schůzi společnosti pořádané dne 27. února 1933", Prague 1933, p. 28.

between the leading (largest) fleet operators hampered cooperation and with the Anschluss, this cartel ended altogether.[58]

In practice, the immediate impact on transport of the German withdrawal from international regime in 1936 was quite moderate. This was in part due to the fact that Germany continued to adhere to the principle of freedom of transit, which was now agreed upon on a bilateral rather than multilateral or international basis.[59] While Czechoslovak experts feared that dissolution of the international regime would have a negative impact on river transport, the situation of Czechoslovak shipping companies on the Oder, Elbe, and the Danube remained virtually unchanged, although at least in the case of Oder and the Elbe, the companies concerned clearly depended on close cooperation with the German fleet.[60]

After the Anschluss of Austria, the Munich Agreement, and Nazi occupation of Czechoslovakia, the situation had significantly changed. The ČPSL and ČSPO both came gradually more and more under control of German capital and became fully integrated in the transport sector of the Third Reich (as *Böhmisch-mährische Elbeschiffahrtsgesellschaft*). Czechoslovak Danube fleet passed to the Nazi puppet state of Slovakia.[61] On the Danube, all national shipping companies concerned – with the exception of the British Anglo-Danubian Lloyd and the French SFND, which, however, practically ceased operating on the Danube in 1939 – formed a compulsory *Betriebsgemeinschaft*. It was a cartel designed to make shipping on the Danube more efficient and centrally planned and controlled. It was headed by the DDSG, a formerly Austrian company, which was nationalised in 1938 now owned directly by the Third Reich as a part of the Hermann-Göring-Konzern. Under direct control of the Nazi Transport Ministry, the DDSG assigned all shipping companies their tasks and they had to

---

58 Enderle-Burcel, Gertrude: "Konkurrenz auf der Donau – Anfang und Ende der Betriebs-gemeinschaft der Ersten Donaudampfschifffahrtsgesellschaft mit der königlich ungarischen Fluß- und Seeschifffahrts A.G. in der Zwischenkriegszeit", in: Matis, Herbert / Resch, Andreas / Stiefel, Dieter (eds.): *Unternehmertum im Spannungsfeld von Politik und Gesellschaft. Unternehmerische Aktivitäten in historischer Perspektive*, Vienna 2010, p. 171 – 184.

59 Jakubec, Ivan: "Via Danubiana. Význam Dunaje pro Československo v letech 1918–1938", in: Šouša, Jiří / Jančík, Drahomír (ed.): Kolize, řevnivost a pragmatismus. Československo-rakouské hospodářské vztahy 1918 – 1938, Prague 1999, p. 219 – 246, here p. 226.

60 Jakubec: Odra jako 'československá' řeka, p. 186/187.

61 Hubert: Dějiny plavby v Čechách. Part II, p. 216.

make all their capacities available for the cartel.[62] The operation and use of virtually all transport capacities were coordinated: in addition to this cartel, a tanker pool and general cargo pool secured optimal utilisation of available vessels. In effect, they thus under different geopolitical circumstances maintained practices developed in the 1930s.[63] The fact that many shipping companies operating on the Danube reached record transport volumes in the early stage of the war, peaking in 1943, documents the relative success of such centralised organisation of trade on the river.[64] Similarly, transport statistics for the Elbe show a peak in 1941–1944 (for the period 1920–1960).[65] In practice, such arrangement served the needs of Nazi military efforts, which turned especially the Danube into a supply route for armies fighting on the Eastern Front.

After the war, Czechoslovak experts pleaded for a normalisation of transport relations and repeatedly argued for a broader cooperation in shipping, speaking especially against the dominant position of the USSR on the Danube, which was a direct outcome of the advance of Soviet troops.[66] Until 1954, the USSR had directly controlled the Romanian, Hungarian, and Austrian fleet and on top of that formed its own Danube shipping company, the DSGP. In 1950, Czechoslovakia initiated talks about a reinstitution of a consortium, *Betriebsgemeinschaft*, on the Danube. It emphasised the efficiency and profitability of such an arrangement in comparison with a "competition", thus giving the proposal a proper "socialist" ideological underpinning. While some form of a cartel has been in place since the First World War, it was never as complex as the arrangement introduced by the Nazi Germany in the early 1940s, when the *Deutsche Schiffahrtsgruppe* was de facto in full control. Czechoslovak experts argued that "while induced by political and war events, it is impossible to deny the practicality of such an arrangement".[67] It took another five years before the Bratislava Agreements, signed by state-controlled nation-

---

62 Sobol, Miroslav: "Hospodársky význam bratislavského prístavu do 1. pol. 20. storočia", in: *Verbum Historiae* 2 (2015), p. 28 – 64, here p. 40 – 43.

63 Gorove: *Law and Politics of the Danube*, p. 21

64 This was true for especially for the DDSG.

65 Švarc: Sedmdesát pět let Československé plavby.

66 Svatopluk Hlava in the debate on "normalisation" of transport relations, AMZV MO-45-55 T – boxes 2 and 8.

67 Spolupráce plavebních podniků SSSR a lidových demokracií na Dunaji, 1950. AMZV, MO-OMO 45-55, b. 2.

al shipping companies of the Danube basin, provided for fixed tariffs and allocation of transport volume between the participating states, thus following on the path which the *Deutsche Schiffahrtsgruppe* had opened.[68] The positive effect of the renewed arrangement became soon apparent: between 1955 and 1956, transport performance of the ČSPD grew by 66%.[69]

On the Elbe and Oder, the development followed a different path: it relied on strictly bilateral arrangements, where state-owned companies cooperated mainly on the basis of intergovernmental treaties or direct agreements between shipping operators. On the Oder, Československá plavba labsko-oderská (ČSPLO, a national shipping company established in 1952 by a merger of previous national operators on the Elbe and Oder) renewed its activities under the Czechoslovak–Polish Transport Treaty of 1947. Its operation, however, remained highly unprofitable, mostly because the navigable stretch of the river did not reach the Czechoslovak territory. After a direct agreement between the ČSPLO and the Polish carrier Żegluga na Odrze (ŻnO), concluded in 1956, failed to limit the losses, despite guaranteeing the ČSPLO a fixed share in domestic transport of Polish coal and prices not below those of the railways on the same route, the Czechoslovak company limited its activities to the connection from the Polish port of Szeczin to the Elbe (via canals).[70] On the Elbe, which unlike the Oder cut across the Iron Curtain, the cooperation was based on tacit acceptance of the principle of internationalisation between the BRD and the Socialist Bloc (especially Czechoslovakia). State-socialist shipping companies, such as the ČSPLO, were allowed to use the West German part of the Elbe, but only for transit to Hamburg, and could not enter other West German waterways. [71]

4. *Towards an Integrated Waterway System: Projects and Experts*

From the start, the expansionist policies of the Third Reich built upon the idea of a New Order for Europe and envisaged the continent in terms of *Grossraumwirtschaft*, that is, an integrated economy with Germany as its

68 Krajčovič (ed.): Bratislavské dohody.

69 Hubert: 75 let československé plavby na Dunaji. Part II, p. 8.

70 Techman: Czechosłowacka żegluga na Odrze w latach 1947 – 1957. Part II.

71 Jakubec: Československo-německé dopravněpolitické vztahy.

core.[72] Not to be dismissed as pure propaganda, the Nazi vision of a "New Order" for Europe built upon a long tradition of conservative right associated with the concept of *Mitteleuropa* (German-led Central Europe) and it had significantly influenced both political and economic decisions of the Nazi authorities throughout their existence. Starting from a traditional vision of a Central European framework, the territorial delimitation of *Grossraum* in the politics of the Third Reich gradually, in connection with the initial success on the war fronts, expanded so as to cover the entire continent.[73]

While historians identified various, often conflicting, strands in the Nazi discourse on Europe and international cooperation, ranging roughly from pure dominance to some sort of cooperative framework for selected nations,[74] the development of waterways (and transport infrastructure in general) occupied a central position in such visions.[75] Nazi *Grossraumpolitik* urged for a further development of technical standardisation of an envisioned transportation network that would facilitate *Grossraumwirtschaft* and focused on enlargement of transport capacities and construction of new canals interconnecting hitherto separate river basins with their diverse regulative regimes (especially Danube and Rhine) into a single system. The planners were well aware that their success depended largely on the quick development of the ties binding the territory.[76] The Danube has traditionally played a central role here as a gateway to the Balkans both as a resource of agricultural products and raw materials and a potential market for German industrial goods. [77]

---

72 Bauer, Raimund: "'Auch die neue europäische Wirtschaft muß organisch wachsen' Walther Funks Rede 'Die wirtschaftliche Neuordnung Europas' vom 25. Juli 1940 im Kontext zeitgenössischer Europavorstellungen", in: *Themenportal Europäische Geschichte* 2016, available at www.europa.clio-online.de/essay/id-/fdae-1669.

73 Janáč: European Coasts of Bohemia, p. 94.

74 Bauer, Raimund: *The Construction of a National Socialist Europe During the Second World War: How the New Order Took Shape*, London 2020.

75 Haushofer, Karl: "Grossdeutsche Wasserstrassen Geopolitik", in: *Zeitschrift für Binnenschiffahrt 1940*, p. 1.

76 Mierzejewski, Alfred C.: *The Most Valuable Asset of the Reich. Vol. 2: A History of the German National Railway, 1933 – 1945*, Chapel Hill, NC 2003.

77 See e.g. Hamlin, David: "Water and Empire – Germany, Bavaria and the Danube in World War I", in: *First World War Studies* 3/1 (2021), p. 65 – 85.

Such considerations underlay the Rhein–Main–Donau Gesetz of 16 May 1938, which one can view both as an expression of Nazi geopolitics and a revival of a traditional vision of navigation experts and economic circles in the region whose ai was to develop a standardised transnational waterway network in central Europe. Since late-nineteenth century, they continually discussed the technical and regulatory aspects of the future integrated network on various international – or rather transnational – fora, such as the *Deutsch – Österreichisch – Ungarischen Verband für Binnenschiffahrt* (est. 1896) or the *Mitteleuropäischer Binnenschiffahrtsverband* (est. 1930) with the aim to overcome political and geographical boundaries limiting the development and integration of waterways in Central Europe. The concept identified three bottlenecks, three missing links, in the envisioned Central European network: Danube – Rhine, Oder (Elbe) – Danube, and Danube – Dniester – Bug – Vistula.

German domination on the formerly international Danube, Oder, and Elbe after 1938 initially speeded up constructions aimed at an improvement of shipping capacities and development of an interconnected waterway system in Central Europe. This ambition was clearly manifested in a large-scale investment programs for rapid enlargement of transport capacities on the river, the so called *Donau-Neuprogramms* and *Donau-Sofortprogramms*, which were introduced in 1939.[78] Construction of hundreds of new vessels should secure the Third Reich a position of clear dominance on the Danube, while a transfer of ships from the Oder and Rhine underscored the importance of connection to the Balkans in Nazi plans.[79] Enlargement of the port of Bratislava, which was designed as a future hub at the intersection of the Danube and a canal connecting the Elbe with the Oder,[80] as well as construction of the initial stretches of the envisioned Danube – Oder connection in Vienna (Lobau) and Gliwicze (so-called Adolf-Hitler-Kanal) launched in 1939 represented clear and decisive steps towards the development of an integrated infrastructural network, basically modelled on proposals of older initiatives centred around

78 Binder, Johannes: "Aufstieg, Größe und Ende – Die Donau-Dampfschifffahrts Gesellschaft seit 1829: Ein Resümee des letzten Generaldirektors", in: *Völkl, Susanne (ed.): Vom Biedermeier ins dritte Jahrtausend – Versunken in der blauen Donau: 175 Jahre Erste Donau-Dampfschiffahrts-Gesellschaft 1829 – 2004*, Regensburg 2004, p. 25 – 70, here p. 29.

79 Grössing / Binder / Funk / Sauer: Rot-Weiss-Rot auf blauen Wellen, p. 139.

80 Sobol: Hospodársky význam.

the Rhine – Danube and Oder – Danube connections (see Figure 2). Julius Dorpmüller, the Reich Minister of Transport, in November 1939, in his celebratory speech at the opening of the Adolf-Hitler-Kanal (which was an upstream extension of the navigable Oder) painted a picture of a pan-European system stretching across the entire continent.[81] Centralisation of jurisdiction over water in the Reich territory under a newly established office of Inspector General for Water and Energy (*Generalinspektor für Wasser und Energie*) in 1941,[82] as well as the subsequent launch of the Reich waterway standardisation programme, clearly manifested the goal of establishing a broad and integrated system that would overcome the historically evolved differences in technical standards especially in the Rhine and Danube basins.

Organisation of the process largely followed in the footsteps of traditional internationalism, despite the fact that Nazi Germany either controlled or directly occupied formerly independent states in the region. Preparations for the construction of the Danube–Oder–Elbe Canal illustrate this rather well. In the mid-1930s, Germany reopened bilateral negotiations with Czechoslovak authorities on the construction of a link between the Oder and the Danube as a possible extension of the Danube waterway into German hinterland. It was part of a lavishly designed infrastructural development program. For most of the interwar period, the Czechoslovak authorities were rather reserved with respect to this project because it was perceived as benefitting the German rather than Czechoslovak interests. Nevertheless, Czechoslovak business circles and hydraulic experts along with their counterparts from Upper Silesia and Vienna, as well as "prophets" of integration of Central Europe, such as Hantos, continued to promote the plan. Following the Munich Agreement and occupation of Czechoslovakia a year later, the Czech authorities were forced to sign a protocol on inland navigation, which – alongside resignation from the Elbe and Oder commission – included the construction of the Danube–Oder canal and envisioned the creation of a joint expert commission for its construction and operation. While the commission and its agenda were dominated by Germany and its political goals, Czechoslovak experts co-

81 Anonymous: Otevření průplavu Adolfa Hitlera.

82 Stier, Bernhard: "Nationalsozialistische Sonderninstanzen in der Energiewirtschaft: Der Generalinspektor für Wasser und Energie 1941 – 1945", in: Hachtmann, Rüdiger / Süss, Winfried (eds.): *Hitlers Kommissare: Sondergewalten in der nationalsozialistischen Diktatur*, Göttingen 2006, p. 138 – 158.

operated and some even welcomed the ability of Nazi Germany to finally realise the project. In particular, they noted with satisfaction that "negotiations in [technical] subcommittees continue smoothly".[83]

The ambivalent nature of Nazi policies, which tended to oscillate between collaboration and extermination while, in the meantime, facing the contingencies of war, did not allow for actual implementation of the New Order.[84] On the other hand, it was this tension that eventually left a significant space to manoeuvre for experts who – as was the case of for instance most Czech hydraulic engineers and transport economists – embraced the idea of Nazi-led waterway integration and adjusted their particular technocratic visions of construction of a waterway network so as to be compatible with it.[85] Figures such as Kliment Velkoborský, Ladislav Vavrouch, Svatopluk Hlava, or Jan Smetana remained in high positions within the state administration before and after 1945. They kept promoting the idea of canal-building even in the new Cold War geopolitical context and represented Czechoslovakia at various platforms. On the other hand, individuals associated with the interwar internationalism lost their positions within the state administration of the Protectorate and never resurfaced in the future. This was the case of, for instance, Vojtěch Krbec, who even acted as head of the League of Nations transport commission, of Bohuslav Muller, originally a hydraulic engineer and later Czechoslovak representative in river commissions, or Otto Popper. This situation naturally hampered Czechoslovak participation in the post-war negotiations and undermined the position of liberally-minded experts within the Czechoslovak expert community.

A new chapter in the development of a material integration of waterways in Central Europe, delayed first by the war and then by the immediately post-war focus on reconstruction, had opened with the transition from a Soviet-led bilateralism towards a multilateral integration of the Soviet Bloc in the mid-1950s. This new approach was exemplified by creation of the COMECON (Council for Mutual Economic Assistance) whose explicit task was to overcome the economic nationalism of state social-

83 Zápis o poradě čs. plavebních expertů, konané dne 22/XI.38 v budově Čs. vyslanectví v Berlíně (Moravian Provincial Archive, (MZA), archival group Danube-Oder-Elbe Canal, b. 122, p. 5/6.

84 Klinkhammer, Lutz: "National Socialism and the Search for International Order: Comment", in: *Bulletin of the German Historical Institute* 50 (2012), p. 27 – 38.

85 Janáč: European Coasts of Bohemia, p. 91.

isms and develop a “socialist” integration. In mid-1950s, the COMECON adopted a programme aimed at a comprehensive utilisation of the Danube. The goal was to turn the river into an artery of development that would provide hydropower, transport, and water supply for the envisaged “socialist” industrialisation of Eastern Europe.[86] The programme also revived the idea of the trans-watershed canals that would extend the navigable Danube network to Poland and East Germany via connections between Danube, Oder, and the Elbe. Leading Czechoslovak hydraulic experts, such as Jan Smetana, who developed water management plan of the upper Elbe for the Nazi waterway integration project, even considered a Euro–Asian waterway connection that would link Siberian rivers through Volga, the Black Sea, and the Danube to the Rhine system. Eventually, though, the special COMECON Commission on the Danube, established rather tellingly as a subordinate body of the Standing Commission on Electric Power, fell victim to a collapse of the Soviet–Yugoslav relations.

The idea of a physical waterway integration was then taken up by the COMECON Standing Commission on Transport. Simultaneously, the Soviet Union simultaneously presented a broader plan of construction of a pan-continental waterway network to the Committee on Inland Navigation of the United Nations Economic Commission for Europe (UNECE) in 1957. Its aim was to relieve the overloaded railways in international transport within the Soviet Bloc.[87] While providing experts with a forum to discuss the technicalities of the proposed connections, these activities ultimately did not bear fruits. After lengthy debates, the COMECON dropped the waterway integration project in mid-1960s and focused instead on improving coordination of transport and other types of infrastructures.[88] Interestingly, the first and perhaps most visible result in the area of inland navigation was the intermodal tariff for rail–water transport on the Danube.[89]

86 Lagendijk: Divided Development.

87 Janáč: European Coasts of Bohemia, p. 167.

88 Flade, Falk: “The role of the CMEA in the construction of the transnational electricity grid Mir”, in: Jajeśniak-Quast, Dagmara / Müller, Uwe (eds.): *Comecon revisited. Integration in the Eastern Bloc and Entanglements with the Global Economy*. Comparativ 5 – 6 (2017), p. 48 – 64.

89 Agreement on International Direct Mixed Rail – Water Transport on the Danube, (MZhVS), 19 December 1961. Protocols of Comecon Standing Commission on

5. *Preliminary Conclusions*

While some authors situate the end of "internationalisation" of waterways in Central Europe to the 1936 and link it to the rise of Nazism (see e.g. Jakubec referring to the Note of 14 November),[90] others identify the arrival of the Iron Curtain as the decisive moment.[91] Some, like Kastory, combine the two, seeing the Sinaia Agreements of 1938 as a turning point leading to a "de-internationalisation", after which "the Danube became an internal river for countries of the Soviet Bloc".[92] From the perspective of history of infrastructural systems, it seems that the main discontinuity was not linked to the wartime regimes and organisations, but rather with implementation of the liberal international system during the interwar period. Before that time – and then again during and after the Second World War and at least until the 1960s – the development and management of infrastructures in the region was highly dependent on geopolitical aspirations of large empires, namely the Austro-Hungarian Empire, (Nazi) Germany, and the USSR. Development was characterised by dominance of the riparian states, focus on administration of particular river basins, bilateral negotiations and agreements, and preference for commercial utilisation of individual rivers by national authorities over the formation of a universal regulatory regime. In fact, international commissions on the Oder and Elbe were revived only after 1989 and this took place mostly in response to environmental concerns. On the Danube, despite limited success of COMECON joint transport policies which evolved since the 1970s, administration likewise remained largely dominated by bilateral negotiations among riparian countries until the collapse of Communism. This was the case despite the existence of the Danube Commission, which reflected criticism voiced by Germany during the interwar period and now, after the war, included only representatives of riparian countries and limited its activities to technicalities.

Transport no. 4 1960 (NAČR, archival group Ministry of Foreign Trade (MZO-FMZO), branch 20, box 5.

90 Jakubec: Železnice a labská plavba ve střední Evropě 1918 – 1938, p. 102

91 Binder: Aufstieg, Größe und Ende, p. 33.

92 Agnieszka / Zieliński, Bogdan: "The Diplomatic Dispute over the Rights of the European Commission of the Danube during the Interwar Period", in: *Politeja* 10/1 (2008), p. 165 – 174, here p. 174.

Let me now return to the issue of chronology, continuities, and discontinuities. Apparently, the gradual dissolution of the liberal international regime established by the Treaty of Versailles that was characterised mainly by multilateral administration of rivers through river commissions went hand in hand with a growing involvement of nation states in inland shipping. Mandatory cartels supervised by national authorities, first proposed by experts in the 1920s and gradually introduced by the Reich in international shipping in the region throughout the 1930s, clearly illustrate this shift. It did not amount to a rejection the principle of freedom of transit but it did severely limit its scope. This approach did not end with World War II: in fact, after the war it was again adopted by the state-socialist policies on the Danube and generally in the transport sector. Emphasis on efficiency and coordination required an elimination, or at least regulation, of market competition even on international level, which moreover in this case fully corresponded with the ideology of state socialism.

It would seem that the growing involvement of state authorities significantly restricted the room for experts, but many experts supported, rather than opposed, the transition to a more state-controlled regime of operation on cross-border rivers because that viewed it as the most efficient form of organisation. While existing scholarship on the subject often views the Second World War as the major interruption in the development of international cooperation within technocratic circles, an examination of careers of Czechoslovak experts involved in efforts to make Central Europe navigable calls such interpretation into doubt. In fact, careers of leading representatives of the official interwar Czechoslovak waterway policy who were active in institutions of the liberal internationalism of the League of Nations ended abruptly in 1938 and never recovered (Popper, Krbec, or Muller). On the other hand, experts who operated in less politically exposed positions during the interwar period and then during the Second World War actively participated in implementation of Nazi policies, survived and continued their careers, often promoting principles associated with dissolution of the liberal regime in the 1930s (Vavrouch, Smetana, Velkoborský).

In comparison to the Rhine, Central European waterways experienced a relatively slower and less intensive integration, although some features, especially cartelisation as a major agent of integration in the 1930s–1950s, were rather similar. It seems thus questionable whether one can attribute such difference in the quantity, rather than quality, to Cold War geopolitics, as some historians do. [93] While various initiatives aimed at closer cross-border cooperation (including the river commissions) indeed appeared swiftly after 1989, thus marking a rapid and clearly visible break with the state-socialist past, they were often driven my environmental concerns and roughly correspond to their counterparts on the Rhine. The intensity of transport on Central European rivers, and consequently also the need for more intense cross-border cooperation, has been more probably negatively affected by both the relatively less developed markets in the region (an argument mentioned in fact already by Hines and Popper during the interwar period) and by the fact that Central European rivers had not been developed to a level that would make it possible to consider them "natural" infrastructures in connection with which one could focus just on regulatory and control mechanisms, as it was the case in the Rhine basin especially after the Second World War.[94] Both the Elbe and Oder still constantly struggle with insufficient water levels in their navigable upstream stretches, i.e. in those parts that make them international, while shipping on the Danube remained split in three almost fully separate sections divided by the shallow stretch of Rajka – Gönyö and the Iron Gates well into the second half of the twentieth century.[95] Even today, the Danube Commission views deepening of the river as the best way of addressing the general dissatisfaction with a low (10%) usage of Danube's capacity for navigation.[96]

6. *References*

Anonyous: "Otevření průplavu Adolfa Hitlera a zahájení stavebních prací na Odersko-dunajském průplavu", in: *Zprávy veřejné služby technické* 21/ 2 (1939), p. 245 – 246.

---

93 Högselius / Kaijser / Vleuten: Europe's Infrastructure Transition, p. 306.

94 Henrich-Franke, Christian / Tölle, Isabel: "Competition for European competence: the Central Commission for Navigation on the Rhine and the European Economic Community in the 1960s", in: *History and Technology* 27/3 (2011), p. 331 – 352.

95 Chmelár, Vladimír: *Dunaj historický a dnešný,* Žilina 1993.

96 Louka, Elli: *Water Law and Policy: Governance Without Frontiers*, Oxford 2009, p. 104.

Ardeleanu, Constantin: *The European Commission of the Danube, 1856 – 1948: An Experiment in International Administration*, Leiden 2020.

Bauer, Raimund: "'Auch die neue europäische Wirtschaft muß organisch wachsen' Walther Funks Rede 'Die wirtschaftliche Neuordnung Europas' vom 25. Juli 1940 im Kontext zeitgenössischer Europavorstellungen", in: *Themenportal Europäische Geschichte* 2016, available at www.europa.clio-online.de/essay/id/fdae-1669.

Bauer, Raimund: *The Construction of a National Socialist Europe During the Second World War: How the New Order Took Shape*, London 2020.

Benda, Václav: "Výtah celních předpisů týkajících se mezinárodní lodní plavby", in: Teklý, Vratislav (ed.): *Plavební příručka,* Prague 1962, p. 181 – 183.

Binder, Johannes: "Aufstieg, Größe und Ende – Die Donau-Dampfschifffahrts Gesellschaft seit 1829: Ein Resümee des letzten Generaldirektors", in: Völkl, Susanne (ed.): *Vom Biedermeier ins dritte Jahrtausend – Versunken in der blauen Donau: 175 Jahre Erste Donau-Dampfschiffahrts-Gesellschaft 1829 – 2004*, Regensburg 2004, p. 25 – 70.

Chmelár, Vladimír: *Dunaj historický a dnešný*, Žilina 1993.

Enderle-Burcel, Gertrude: "Konkurrenz auf der Donau – Anfang und Ende der Betriebsgemeinschaft der Ersten Donaudampfschifffahrtsgesellschaft mit der königlich ungarischen Fluß- und Seeschifffahrts A.G. in der Zwischenkriegszeit", in: Matis, Herbert / Resch, Andreas / Stiefel, Dieter (eds.): *Unternehmertum im Spannungsfeld von Politik und Gesellschaft. Unternehmerische Aktivitäten in historischer Perspektive,* Vienna 2010, p. 171 – 184.

Flade, Falk: "The role of the CMEA in the construction of the transnational electricity grid Mir", in: Jajeśniak-Quast, Dagmara / Müller, Uwe (eds.): *Comecon revisited. Integration in the Eastern Bloc and Entanglements with the Global Economy. Comparativ* 5 – 6 (2017), p. 48 – 64.

Focas, Spiridon G.: *The Lower Danube River: In the Southeastern European Political and Economic Complex from Antiquity to the Conference of Belgrade of 1948*, Boulder, CO 1987.

Ghisa, Alexandru: "Romania and the first cracks in the implementation of the Hitler-Stalin pact of 1940: Germany's guarantees granted to Romania at the Vienna Award and the Danube issue", in: *Valahian Journal of Historical Studies* 16 (2011), p. 95 – 106.

Godard, Simon: "The Council for Mutual Economic Assistance and the Failed Coordination of Planning in the Socialist Bloc in the 1960s", in: Michel, Christian / Kott, Sandrine / Matejka, Ondrej (eds.): *Planning in Cold War Europe. Competition, Cooperation, Circulations (1950s – 1970s),* Berlin 2018, p. 187 – 210.

Godard, Simon: *Le Laboratoire De L'internationalisme: Le Caem Et La Construction Du Bloc Socialiste (1949 – 1991)*, Paris 2021.

Gorove, Stephen: *Law and Politics of the Danube: An Interdisciplinary Study*, The Hague 1964.

Grössing, Helmuth / Binder, Johannes / Funk, Ernst-Ulrich / Sauer, Manfred: *Rot-Weiss-Rot auf blauen Wellen: 150 Jahre DDGS*, Vienna 1979.

Gulić, Milan: "Belgrade Danube Conference 1948", in: *Tokovi istorije* 1 (2013), p. 173 – 202.

Hamlin, David: "Water and Empire – Germany, Bavaria and the Danube in World War I", in: *First World War Studies* 3/1 (2021), p. 65 – 85.

Hantos, Elemér: "Einleitung: Mitteleuropäische Wasserstrassenpolitik", in: Hantos, Elemér (ed.): *Mitteleuropäische Wasserstrassenpolitik: Referate und Beschlüsse der Mitteleuropäischen Wasserstrassenkonferenz*, Budapest, 11. bis 13. Mai 1929, Vienna – Leipzig 1929.

Haushofer, Karl: "Grossdeutsche Wasserstrassen Geopolitik", in: *Zeitschrift für Binnenschiffahrt* 1940, p. 1.

Henrich-Franke, Christian / Tölle, Isabel: "Competition for European competence: the Central Commission for Navigation on the Rhine and the European Economic Community in the 1960s", in: *History and Technology* 27/3 (2011), p. 331 – 352.

Hexner, Ervín: "*Československé kartely – přednesl JUDr. Ervín Hexner ve schůzi společnosti pořádané dne 27. února 1933*", Prague 1933.

Hinsch, Werner: "The River Elbe — International: A Historical Perspective", in: *GeoJournal* 1/2 (1977), p. 45 – 48.

Hoblík, Karel. "Mezinárodní vnitrozemní vodní cesty", in: Teklý, Vratislav (ed.): *Plavební příručka,* Prague 1962, p. 178 – 181.

Högselius, Peer / Kaijser, Arne / Vleuten, Erik van der: *Europe's Infrastructure Transition: Economy, War, Nature*, New York 2018.

Hubert, Miroslav: "75 let československé plavby na Dunaji. Part II", in: *Vodní cesty a plavba* 5/1 (1994), p. 5 – 11.

Hubert, Miroslav: *Dějiny plavby v Čechách II*, Děčín 1997.

Janáč, Jiří: *European Coasts of Bohemia: Negotiating the Danube-Oder-Elbe Canal in a Troubled Twentieth Century,* Amsterdam 2012.

Jakubec, Ivan: "Odra jako 'československá' řeka", in: Jančík, Drahomír (ed.): *Pocta profesoru Zdeňku Jindrovi. K sedmdesátým narozeninám,* Prague 2003, p. 179 – 190.

Jakubec, Ivan: "Via Danubiana. Význam Dunaje pro Československo v letech 1918–1938", in: Šouša, Jiří / Jančík, Drahomír (ed.): *Kolize, řevnivost a pragmatismus. Československo-rakouské hospodářské vztahy 1918 – 1938*, Prague 1999, p. 219 – 246.

Jakubec, Ivan: *Československo-německé dopravněpolitické vztahy v období studené války se zvláštním zřetelem na železnici a labskou plavbu (1945/1949 – 1989)*, Prague 2007.

Jakubec, Ivan: *Železnice a labská plavba ve střední Evropě 1918 – 1938: Dopravněpolitické vztahy Československa, Německa a Rakouska v meziválečném období*, Prague 1997.

Jeřábek, Miroslav: *Za silnou střední Evropu: Středoevropské hnutí mezi Budapeští, Vídní a Brnem v letech 1925-1939*, Prague 2008.

Kaser, Michael: *Comecon: Integration Problems of the Planned Economies,* London 1967.

Kastory, Agnieszka / Zieliński, Bogdan: "The Diplomatic Dispute over the Rights of the European Commission of the Danube during the Interwar Period", in: *Politeja* 10/1 (2008), p. 165 – 174.

Kastory, Agnieszka: "Problem obecności Niemiec w Komisjach Dunajskich w okresie międzywojennym", in: *Studia z Dziejów Rosji i Europy Środkowo-Wschodniej* 42 (2007), p. 75 – 89.

Kirk, Tim: "Nazi plans for a new European order and European responses," in: Dafinger, Johannes / Pohl, Dieter (eds.): *A New Nationalist Europe Under Hitler: Concepts of Europe and Transnational Networks in the National Socialist Sphere of Influence, 1933 – 1945*, Abingdon 2019, p. 71 – 92.

Klinkhammer, Lutz: "National Socialism and the Search for International Order: Comment", in: *Bulletin of the German Historical Institute* 50 (2012), p. 27 – 38.

Königs, Gustav, "Die Wasserstrassen im Europa-Verkehr", in: *Süddeutsche Wasserstrassen* 1–2/19 (1943), p. 2 – 4.

Kopper, Christopher: "Germany's National Socialist Transport Policy and the Claim of Modernity: Reality or Fake?", in: *The Journal of Transport History* 34/2 (2013), p. 162 – 176.

Krajčovič, Jozef (ed.): *Bratislavské dohody*, Bratislava 1988.

Krieg, Fritz: "Das Weltbinnenschiffahrtsrecht und die Ströme Mitteleuropas", in: Hantos, Elemer (ed.): *Mitteleuropäische Wasserstrassenpolitik: Referate und Beschlüsse der Mitteleuropäischen Wasserstrassenkonferenz, Budapest, 11.– 13. Mai 1929*, Vienna 1929, p. 81 – 101.

Lagendijk, Vincent / Schot, Johan: "Technocratic Internationalism in the Interwar Years: Building Europe on Motorways and Electricity Networks", in: *Journal of Modern European History* 6/2 (2008), p. 196 – 217.

Lagendijk, Vincent: "Divided Development: Post-War Ideas on River Utilisation and their Influence on the Development of the Danube", in: *The International History Review* 1/37 (2015), p. 80 – 98.

Loth, Wilfried / Păun, Nicolae (eds.): *Disintegration and Integration in East-Central Europe: 1919 – Post-1989*, Baden-Baden 2014.

Louka, Elli: *Water Law and Policy: Governance Without Frontiers*, Oxford 2009.

Mierzejewski, Alfred C.: *The Most Valuable Asset of the Reich. Vol. 2: A History of the German National Railway, 1933 – 1945*, Chapel Hill, NC 2003.

Millward, Robert: *Private and public enterprise in Europe: energy, telecommunications and transport, 1830 – 1990*, Cambridge 2008.

Müller, Uwe: "Introduction: Failed and forgotten? New Perspectives on the history of the Council for Mutual Economic Assistance", in: *Comparativ: Zeitschrift fur globalgeschichte und vergleichende Gesellschaftsforschung* 5 – 6 (2017), p. 7 – 25.

Paterson, Thomas G.: "Eastern Europe and the Early Cold War: The Danube Controversy", in: *The Historian* 33/ 2 (1971), p. 237 – 247.

Popper, Otto: "The International Regime of the Danube", in: *The Geographical Journal* 5 – 6/102 (1943), p. 240 – 253.

Rákosník, Jakub/ Spurný, Matěj / Štaif, Jiří. *Milníky moderních českých dějin: Krize konsenzu a legitimity v letech 1848 – 1989*, Praha 2018.

Schipper, Frank / Schot, Johan: "Infrastructural Europeanism, or the project of building Europe on infrastructures: An introduction", in: *History and Technology* 27/3 (2011), p. 245 – 264.

Sobol, Miroslav: "Hospodársky význam bratislavského prístavu do 1. pol. 20. storočia", in: *Verbum Historiae* 2 (2015), p. 28 – 64.

Stier, Bernhard: "Nationalsozialistische Sonderninstanzen in der Energiewirtschaft: Der Generalinspektor für Wasser und Energie 1941 – 1945", in: Hachtmann, Rüdiger / Süss, Winfried (eds.): *Hitlers Kommissare: Sondergewalten in der nationalsozialistischen* Diktatur, Göttingen 2006, p. 138 – 158.

Švarc, Bohumil: "Vývoj podniku ČSPLO Děčín", in: Košťál, Miloslav (ed.): *Historie plavby a obchodu po Labi*, Prague 1971.

Švarc, Bohumil: *Sedmdesát pět let Československé plavby*, Děčín 1997.

Techman, Ryszard: "Czechosłowacka żegluga na Odrze w latach 1947 – 1957. Part I", in: *Przegląd Zachodniopomorski* 33/1 (2018), p. 145 – 167.

Techman, Ryszard: "Czechosłowacka żegluga na Odrze w latach 1947 – 1957. Part II", in: *Przegląd Zachodniopomorski* 34/1 (2019), p. 5 – 27.

Teichova, Alice / Ratcliffe, Penelope: "British Interests in Danube Navigation after 1918", in: *Business History* 27/ 3 (1985), p. 283 – 300.

Truman, Harry: "Radio Report to the American People on the Potsdam Conference", in: Woolley, John / Peters, Gerhard (eds.): *The American Presidency Project*, available at https://www.presidency.ucsb.edu/documents/radio-report-the-american-people-the-potsdam-conference.

Tulus, Arthur: "Geopolitics and Trade at the Danube Mouths during the Interwar Period: A Study Case on the German-British Rivalry", in: *Transylvanian Review* 22 (2013), p. 277 – 286.

Uprety, Kishor: *The Transit Regime for Landlocked States: International Law and Development Perspectives*, Washington, D.C. 2006.

Vitányi, Béla K.J.: "The Regime of Navigation on International Waterways: Part III: Substantive Rights and Duties", in: *Netherlands Yearbook of International Law* 7 (1976), p. 3 – 90.

Völkl Susanne (ed.): *Vom Biedermeier ins dritte Jahrtausend – Versunken in der blauen Donau: 175 Jahre Erste Donau-Dampfschiffahrts-Gesellschaft 1829 – 2004*, Regensburg 2004.

7. *Appendix*

Figure no. 1:
Waterways between Oder and Vistula, League of Nations, 1930.

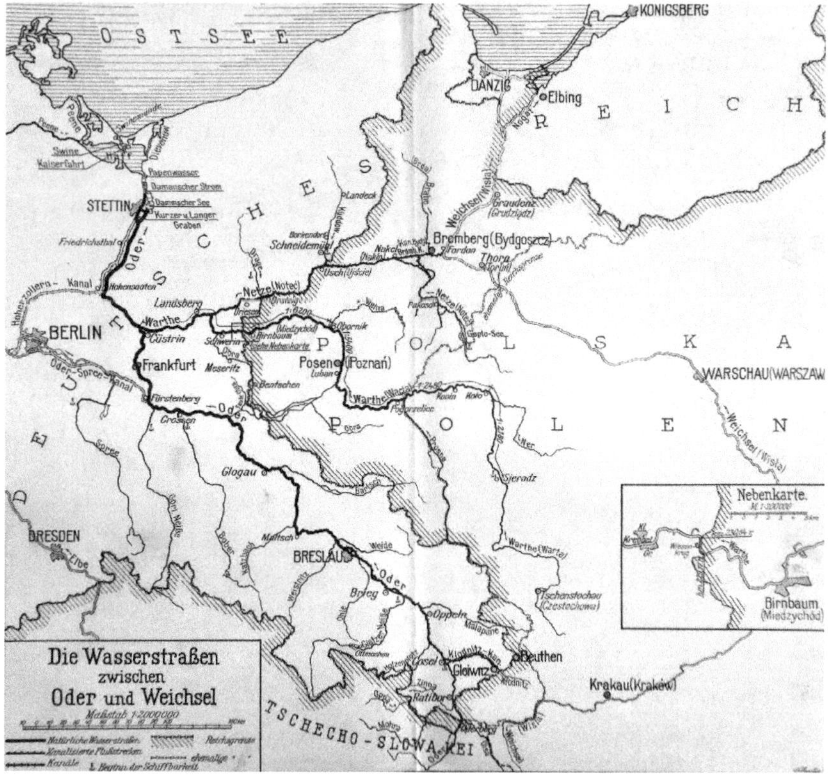

Figure no. 2:
Waterways in Central Europe, Czechoslovak Map from 1930s.

Railways: Halted Multilateral Cooperation, Valid Multilateral Agreements

Léonard Laborie

Table of Content

1. Introduction

Since Raul Hilberg's work in the 1960s, railways have been identified as a crucial cog in the wheel of the Final Solution[1]. This chapter will not focus on that particular aspect of Second World War railway history, which "remains distorted and hugely sensitive"[2], but on the framework of international agreements that made cross-border railway traffic of all kinds possible during the period. This includes deportee trains, which represent-

---

1 See Hilberg, Raul / Pehle, Walter H. / Schlott, René: "The indispensability of the railroads", in: *The Anatomy of the Holocaust: Selected Works from a Life of Scholarship*, New York 2020, pp. 53 – 55. I rely here on the historiographical synthesis of Broch, Ludivine: "Professionalism in the Final Solution: French Railway Workers and the Jewish Deportations", in: *Contemporary European History* 23 (2014), pp. 359 – 380. See also: Hildebrand, Klaus: "Die Deutsche Reichsbahn in der nationalsozialistischen Diktatur, 1933 – 1945", in: Gall, Lothar / Pohl, Manfred (eds.): *Die Eisenbahn in Deutschland*, Munich 1999, pp. 165 – 244.

2 Broch: Professionalism, p. 364.

ed a tragic and tiny fraction of it; in Hilberg's words, freight cars were loaded with Jews and then "sealed, dispatched, emptied, and cleaned, to be filled with new, perhaps altogether different cargoes, in the circulatory flow"[3].

On the eve of the war, international rail exchanges were governed by numerous conventions and international organisations established during their first century of existence. How did this framework evolve and function during the war? Were other mechanisms planned or implemented to complement or replace it in Europe, possibly bridging post-war developments in this field?

2. *Fragmented international governance*

A variety of conventions governed international rail exchanges. In fact, in the mid-twentieth century, a single key (the so-called Bern key) that could open all wagons and carriages across Europe had already existed for several decades, avoiding convoys changes at border crossings, and sparing agents from having to carry an inconvenient key ring. Although they overlapped to a large extent, these conventions and the organizations responsible for governing them differed in terms of purpose, stakeholders, and geography. Two generations of arrangements were intertwined: the first dated back to the 1870s and 1880s, and gave a pre-eminent role to small neutral states; the second dated back to the aftermath of the First World War, and were implemented at the instigation of the Allies[4].

While companies had been coordinating their freight train timetables since the early 1860s, the Bern Key was developed in 1886 at the Second International Conference of the Technical Unity of Railways, held in the Swiss capital[5]. At the same time, the Swiss Federal Council, together with all those who "use, benefit from and live off the railways"[6], also pushed

---

3 Hilberg: The Anatomy, p. 55.

4 Dienel, Hans-Liudger: "Die Eisenbahnen und der europäische Möglichkeitsraum 1870-1914", in: Roth, Ralf / Schlögel, Karl (eds.): *Neue Wege in ein neues Europa. Geschichte und Verkehr im 20. Jahrhundert*, Frankfurt 2009, pp. 105 – 123.

5 Ribeill, Georges: "Aux origines de l'utopie du réseau ferroviaire européen intégré", in: *Histoire & Sociétés* 21 (2007), pp. 44 – 59, here pp. 50 – 52.

6 Tissot, Laurent: "Les modèles ferroviaires nationaux et la création d'un système international de transports européens, 1870 – 1914. Coordination, intégration ou

for the development of international law to replace the domestic law of the various parties involved, in order to settle disputes between companies, and between companies and their customers. The aim was to make shippers and carriers more secure by facilitating direct shipments with no transhipment, and by establishing clear and common liability rules, regardless of origin and destination. The International Convention for the Carriage of Goods by Rail was adopted in 1890[7]. Celebrated at the time as "one of the most important and happy events of the century"[8], it was overseen by a Central Office for International Carriage by Rail. It was largely inspired by the provisions adopted by the member companies of the Verein Deutscher Eisenbahnverwaltungen (Association of German Railways Companies), which had enabled the development of cross-border traffic in a highly fragmented area, doing so first in Prussia beginning in 1846, and subsequently throughout the German states[9]. The last cornerstone of this complex edifice was the International Railway Congress Association, founded after a first congress held in Brussels in 1885 for the purpose of offering the public a continuity of service "as if there were a single network"[10]. Initially ignored by German companies, who saw it as a French platform aiming to counterbalance the influence of the Verein, it became the international forum for public and private operators to discuss all technical aspects relating to the construction and operation of railways[11].

---

unification?", in: *Relations internationales* 95 (1998), pp. 313 – 327, here pp. 324 – 325.

7 Tissot, Laurent: "Naissance d'une Europe ferroviaire: la convention internationale de Berne (1890)", in: Merger, Michèle / Barjot, Dominique (eds.): *Les entreprises et leurs réseaux: hommes, capitaux, techniques et pouvoirs, XIXe – XXe siècles,* Paris 1998, pp. 283 – 295.

8 Lyon-Caen, Charles: "La convention du 14 octobre 1890 sur le transport international des marchandises par chemins de fer", in: *Journal du droit international privé et de jurisprudence comparée* 20 (1893), p. 465.

9 Kaiser, Wolfram / Schot, Johan: *Writing the Rules for Europe. Experts, Cartels and International Organizations*, London 2014, pp. 121 – 128. Kaessbohrer, Adolf: "Der Verein Mitteleuropäischer Eisenbahnverwaltungen", in: *Archiv für Eisenbahnwesen* 56 (1933), pp. 12 – 380.

10 In the words of the Belgian Fassiaux, quoted by Williot, Jean-Pierre: "Aux sources d'une Europe partagée: la médiation ferroviaire au XIXe siècle", in: Démier, Francis / Musiani, Elena (eds.): *L'Europe: une autre nation?* Bologna 2020, pp. 47 – 62, here p. 55.

11 Ribeill: Aux origines, p. 50.

Following the defeat and disintegration of the central empires, thousands of kilometres of new borders challenged the pre-war circulation of goods and people. To face the challenge and, at the same time, shift the European rail network's centre of gravity from the German Verein to the West and the victorious Allies, France and Italy initiated an international re-organisation after the Armistice, which was incidentally signed in a sleeping-car belonging to the Compagnie internationale des wagons-lits. New acronyms were created: RIC for Regolamento Internazionale delle Carrozze, and RIV for Regolamento Internazionale dei Veicoli, which in 1921 and 1922 respectively gave rise to what was sometimes called the International Union of Wagons and the International Union for International Direct Car Services; UIC for the International Union of Railways, founded in 1922 in Paris[12]. Seeing the latter simply as the result of a French desire to dominate the new railway order obscures the fact that German companies also supported the operation, and considered it preferable to the creation of a body attached to the League of Nations, which was deemed overly political. The UIC would be independent of the League of Nations. All in all, the UIC ultimately had a weak grip on the supervision of international trade, which remained essentially determined by pre-war conventions and organisations. Only the conference of the Technical Unit went closer to the UIC, which was clearly not the driver of the international regulatory convoy[13].

This complex, fragmented, and to some extent competitive landscape, gave experts great influence in international rail governance, insofar as they circulated most of the time from one arena to another, and were the only ones capable of holding the various regulations together[14]. Kaiser and Schot conclude that "The war then provided a new opportunity to rethink the position of the various organisations"[15]. While I agree, I would suggest focusing less on reflections in London, and more on what was actually happening in continental Europe.

12 On this second phase see Anastasiadou, Irene: *Constructing Iron Europe: Transnationalism and Railways in the Interbellum*, Amsterdam 2012.

13 Kaiser / Schot: Writing, pp. 144 – 145.

14 Idem, p. 173.

15 Idem, p. 147.

3. *The International Railway Union During the War: An Organisation Overseen by the SNCF, Itself Involved in Economic Collaboration with the Reichsbahn*

The UIC operated normally in the first few months after the declaration of war, from September 1939 to the invasion of Belgium in May 1940[16]. Its Central Clearing Office, based in Brussels, carried out clearing transactions between members.

The General Secretariat of the UIC then went into dormancy. Its *Bulletin* was no longer published, nor were its statistics. Staff numbers and expenses were reduced to a minimum, although the UIC formally continued to exist in order to "prepare for the resumption of activities", as it was said after the war[17]. Designated as administration president of the management committee in 1938 for a period of three years, the young SNCF—a semi public company resulting from the merger and partial nationalisation of French private companies—fulfilled this role throughout the period. In the absence of contributions from members, the company advanced the funds on its own. Its director, Robert Le Besnerais, presided over the UIC, and was assisted by another Frenchman, the organisation's secretary general since its foundation, Gaston Leverve. Together they ensured "the execution of a reduced service during a difficult period"[18], "keeping in touch with the Central Clearing Office, either by correspondence, or by visits of the Director of the Central Clearing Office to the headquarters of our Union in Paris"[19]. As for the Verein, it remained active and even expanded geographically. Its statutes had allowed for the participation of associate members outside German speaking countries since 1929[20]. While Danish, Swedish and Norwegian railways had joined the organization before the war, Central European railways had not, in spite of the explicit invitation extended by its renaming as Verein Mitteleuropäischer Eisenbahnen in

---

16 See *Bulletin de l'Union international des Chemins de fer* (April – May 1946).

17 "Rapport complémentaire du secrétaire général au comité de gérance de l'UIC", in: *Bulletin de l'Union internationale des Chemins de fer* (April – May 1946), p. 26.

18 *Bulletin de l'Union internationale des Chemins de fer* (April – May 1946), p. 20.

19 "Rapport complémentaire", p. 27.

20 Alfred Mierzejewski does not touch on the Verein in his book: *The Most Valuable Asset of the Reich: A History of the German National Railway*, vol. 2: 1933-45, Chapel Hill 2000. On what follows, see *Zeitschrift des Vereins Mitteleuropäischer Eisenbahnverwaltungen* (1939 – 1944).

1932 (Association of Central European Railway Administrations)[21]. Slovakia became a member during the war in 1942, followed by Romania in 1943. Both directly implemented the Verein's regulations. Since 1940, the Verein had postponed all meetings until the restoration of peace. In the meantime, coordination was carried out by mail under the Reichsbahn's leadership. Interestingly enough, there was no acrimonious rhetoric against the International Railway Union in the Verein's journal, quite the contrary. In 1941 the Verein for instance adjusted its freight calculations to adhere to UIC regulations, while many other issues were reported as being carried out in accordance with UIC regulations.

All in all, it is clear that the SCNF played a watchdog role within a sleeping UIC, while the Deutsche Reichsbahn exercised de facto supervision over the Verein. The relation between the two companies was thus formative during this period. In his synthesis on the history of French railways, François Caron focuses on three aspects of this relation[22]. The first is one of domination. The German occupation authorities supervised the SNCF. In stations and offices, there was one German agent (what their French counterparts called "*bahnofs*") for every 64 French agents at the end of 1942. Second, this relation became part of a wider French-German system of negotiation and collaboration between Vichy and the occupier. SCNF assets were key to both. They were run by the Vichy Ministry of Communications, itself bound to respect the terms set by the armistice commission. For the occupiers, the SNCF was key to their policy of wealth extraction, repression, and persecution. Finally, Caron stressed the development of an experiment in technical cooperation between the SNCF and the Reichsbahn, on the use of single-phase 50 Hz industrial current for electric traction. French engineers were authorised to follow experiments in the Höllental valley [23].

As Alfred Mierzejewski has pointed out: "The SNCF was brought into the continental railway system that the DRB had established"[24]. This idea generally mirrors what the historian Charlotte Pouly has called the "theory

---

21 Kaiser / Schot: Writing, p. 147. Mierzejewski, Alfred: *The Most Valuable Asset.*

22 In the last volume, published posthumously: Caron, François: *Histoire des chemins de fer en France, 1937 – 1997,* Paris 2017, pp. 72 – 109.

23 Idem, p. 93, and Armand, Louis: *Propos ferroviaires,* Paris 1970, p. 254. The 50 Hz single-phase solution for electric traction proved crucial in the French network after the war.

24 Mierzejewski: The Most Valuable Asset, p. 136.

of the double constraint (German and Vichy Diktat)"[25] with respect to the SNCF during the Second World War: German Diktat in connection with the Armistice and the occupation; Vichy Diktat in the form of tighter control over the economy and state-to-state collaboration. However, Pouly argues for a different perspective. The companies' archives reveal that they had preserved agency, and even secured greater leeway. As a result, they cannot be presented as the simple technical instrument of an overarching policy. The military diktat of 1940 laid down in the armistice commission was quickly overtaken and circumvented by a return to normal trade relations. After a brief phase of looting, during which French wagons were used as spoils of war and then requisitioned, SNCF equipment was rented rather than requisitioned (over the period, on average, a quarter of the SNCF's remaining wagon fleet was rented in Germany, while 14% of the fleet used by the company came the other way round from the Reichsbahn). The company was paid for the services rendered to the German military and civil authorities, whether for traffic within the country or in the form of transit (from or to Italy and Spain in particular). The SNCF "will carry out all transport for German interests in France (90% of traffic on average) in a contractual form in return for payment"[26]. This economic collaboration sacrificed the service due to the French public, but generated revenues, thereby avoiding budget deficits, a real spectre at the head of the SNCF; it reciprocally offered the Reichsbahn cheap service, thanks to an advantageous exchange rate and occupancy fees. On a more political level, it was also a means for the managers of these two companies to maintain a relative autonomy, preserving them from direct intrusion on the part of their respective guardianships. Proceeding as it had before -in a time of material shortage, occupation and a "controlled market economy"[27]- is what finally made "the SCNF (…) a secondary belt, a voluntary partner (*Freiwillige*) for the circulation in a vast *Kontinental-Europaïsche Zusammenarbeit* whose engine is the Reichsbahn"[28]. Ludivine Broch has

---

25 Pouly, Charlotte: "'Räder müssen rollen für den Sieg!' Regard franco-allemand sur la SNCF et la *Reichsbahn* (1940-1945)", in: *Revue de l'IFHA* 6 (2014). URL: http://journals.openedition.org/ifha/8070; DOI :https://doi.org/10.4000/ifha.8070

26 Ibid.

27 Ibid.

28 Pouly, Charlotte: "Penser les circulations économiques à travers la SNCF pendant l'Occupation: 'Circulez y a rien à voir' ?", in: *Hypothèses* 18 (2015), pp. 149 – 164, p. 164. DOI: 10.3917/hyp.141.0149.

emphasized the ambiguity of the situation, as well as the lack of a clear demarcation between good and evil for contemporaries:

> The occupation was a double-edged sword for the *cheminots*: by keeping the trains running, they fed both the French nation and the German military apparatus; they bridged two zones and ripped communities apart; they brought POWs home and deported children. In general, there was no obvious side on which to stand[29].

In any case, what is important from our perspective is that all of this happened in accordance with international law as established before the war. According to Pouly, bilateral relations reframed by the wartime context developed "in the continuity of the international peacetime agreements (RIM [sic] and RIV of 1935, among others)"[30]. The rules were seemingly neither suspended nor transformed, but carefully applied, at least in the French-German case. This fits with the idea that both companies managed to carve out their own sphere of autonomous regulation.

4. *Technical integration, from the war to the post-war period*

It is within this framework that further technical cooperation, joint work on operational standardization (e.g. registration and securing of international traffic), and projects such as the "European wagon community" developed[31]. The latter touched on the thorny problem covered by RIC and RIV regulations, namely that of the movement of rolling stock across borders. In order to reduce the cost of international transport, it is obviously preferable not to unload a convoy at the border before re-shiping it to another one: the convoy must be allowed to continue to its destination. Once there, should the wagons be sent back as soon as possible, even if they have to travel empty, in order to quickly return them to their original network and protect them from possible damage? Would it not be more economical to use them at their point of arrival, even if it means paying a rental fee and drawing up a balance sheet at the end of the year? Better still, could part of the fleet be pooled for international transport? This is the last option that the European wagon community project was pursuing, along with the idea of extensive standardisation of equipment. And it is on this project—less grandiose than Hitler's plan for a new super-broad

29 Broch: Professionalism in the Final Solution, p. 380.
30 Pouly: 'Räder müssen rollen für den Sieg!'
31 Ibid.

gauge network—that the Reichsbahn focused its attention. While the Reichsbahn opposed the Breitspurbahn, which it saw (like Transport Minister Albert Speer)[32] as pointless, the idea of a wagon pool was supported by the head of the Main Car Office in the Reichsbahn Central Office Berlin, Johannes Schultz, who had to allocate freight cars throughout Germany. This was even more the case given that the idea was discussed by the Verein's technical committee in June 1939, before the war broke out. Further discussions of the matter were postponed in 1940, in order to hold them in conjunction with the UIC's revision of the RIV, and then actively resumed once again[33]. The course of the war stopped both projects. "History does not say whether [Schultz] was led to participate in the elaboration of the 'EUROP pool' some ten years later"[34].

The UIC resumed its activities as soon as the war was over, amid the turmoil of returning prisoners and deportees, and the beginning of reconstruction. The idea of a wagon pool gradually resurfaced. A first general assembly was held in Paris in February 1946 (44 delegates representing 16 countries), and a double conference was held in Montreux (on timetables and direct services) in October. Some of them were meeting after years of interruption, while others had disappeared, such as the historic Secretary General, Gaston Leverve, who passed away in 1945. President Robert Le Besnerais remained. Members of the management committee warmly thanked him[35], even though he had resigned from his functions as director of the SNCF in autumn 1944, worried about the legal repercussions from the organisation's persecution of communist railway workers at the begin-

---

32 Högselius, Per / Kaijser, Arne / Vleuten van der, Erik: *Europe's Infrastructure Transition. Economy, War, Nature,* London 2016, p. 46.

33 *Zeitung des Vereins Miteleuropäischer Eisenbahnverwaltungen* (1941).

34 "L'histoire ne dit pas si l'intéressé fut amené à participer à l'élaboration du 'pool EUROP' une dizaine d'années plus tard". Picard, Jean-François: "Des réquisitions de la Wehrmacht à la création du 'Pool EUROP', une histoire de wagons de marchandises (1940-1950)", in: *Correspondances* 14 (2004). Online: http://archivchemindefer.free.fr/wagons/poolEurop.html.

35 "Malgré les lourdes tâches que lui imposait la période de guerre, M. Le Besnerais a suivi avec une particulière vigilance la vie ralentie de l'UIC, assumant la responsabilité que n'était plus à même de prendre le Comité de Gérance lui-même, avec le souci constant de permettre à notre organisation de reprendre sa vie normale dès que la victoire des Alliés le permettrait". "Rapport du comité de gérance à l'assemblée générale", in: *Bulletin de l'Union internationale des Chemins de fer* (April – May 1946), pp. 48 – 49.

ning of the war and during the Occupation[36]. As persona non grata at the SNCF, Le Besnerais remained at the head of the Union until his death in 1948. He helped strengthen this institution in the European railway landscape in the aftermath of the war, having himself pointed out that a grouping of the various international organisations around the UIC would be advisable[37]. New players on the techno-political scene, such as the European Central Inland Transport Organisation (ECITO) and its successor, the United Nations Economic Commission for Europe's Inland Transport Committee, supported this trend[38]. Set up by the Allies before the war was over, ECITO brought together the transport experts who had to manage the return of wagons and locomotives scattered across Europe[39]. While the UIC woke up, pre-war international peace agreements were paradoxically suspended. As railway companies argued for the ownership and redistribution of rolling stock, several conventions regulating its circulation across borders simply did not apply. Hence the need for a Wagon Exchange Commission, based in Paris from late 1945 to the spring of 1948, and the idea of a temporary pooling and compensation system. It is in this context that discussions between the SNCF and the West German Deutsche Bahn resumed in the late 1940s[40]. They led in 1951 to the establishment of a bilateral pool of freight wagons for cross-border traffic called EUROP, with the blessing of the High Commission for Occupied Germany[41]. The success of the operation, which quickly led to a significant reduction in operating costs through a drop in empty returns, attracted the interest of West-

---

36 Pouly, Charlotte: "Les agents et dirigeants de la SNCF, épurés sous Vichy, épurés après Vichy. Regard croisé autour de la reintégration", in: *Histoire & Mesure* XXIX-2 (2014), pp. 135 – 154, here p. 148. https://doi.org/10.4000/histoiremesure.5115.

37 Le Besnerais, Robert: "Les grands organismes ferroviaires internationaux", in: *Bulletin de l'UIC* (January – February 1947), pp. 24 – 28, here p. 28.

38 Kaiser / Schot: Writing, pp. 159 – 161.

39 Ibid., pp. 149 – 158.

40 Kopper, Christopher: "Die internationale Zusammenarbeit der Deutschen Bundesbahn (1949-1992)", in: Ambrosius, Gerold / Henrich-Franke, Christian / Neutsch, Cornelius (eds.): *Internationale Politik und Integration europäischer Infratruktur in Geschichte und Gegenwart*, Baden-Baden 2010, pp. 213 – 232.

41 Henrich-Franke, Christian: "Europäische Verkehrsintegration im 19. und 20. Jahrhundert", in: Neutsch, Cornelius / Thiemeyer, Guido (eds.): *Internationalismus und Europäische Integration im Vergleich. Fallstudien zu Währungen, Landwirtschaft, Verkehrs- und Nachrichtenwesen*, Baden-Baden 2007, pp. 133 – 176.

ern European companies. They joined the pool, within the framework of a reinforced UIC[42].

The new director general (1949-1955) of the SNCF and president of the UIC, Louis Armand, was the driving force behind this dynamic. Although he himself had directly been involved in the resistance against the occupying forces, Armand readily extolled the cordial and professional relations between French and German railway workers, even during the war[43]. Numerous testimonies collected in France[44] confirm a kind of transnational professional camaraderie in the field which, combined with the application of international regulations in force and the absence of generalised breaks in the quarries, marked out a path of railway continuity from the pre-war to the post-war period. However, not all cooperation was successful. If the idea of the pool was successful, technical cooperation on electric traction—which continued in the French zone of occupation in Germany, under the leadership of Armand who had pushed for it on the French side during the war—came up against "technological chauvinism"[45]. German industry abandoned the path of industrial direct current, and despite Louis Armand's insistence, its standardisation within the European Coal and Steel Community failed[46]. After leaving the SNCF and the UIC, from which he had launched a number of other institutional and commercial initiatives allowing railways to compete with other modes of transport through European cooperation, he chaired the European Atomic Energy Community (Euratom) for a year, and then became Secretary General of the International Union of Railways from 1961 to 1971. His extraordinary career embodies "the typical (and ultimately mythical) image of the apolit-

---

42 Kaiser / Schot: Writing, pp. 169 – 173. Armand: Propos, pp. 284 – 286. See also Henrich-Franke, Christian: "Louis Armand – Between United Atoms and Common Railways", in: Badenoch, Alexander / Fickers, Andreas (eds.): *Materializing Europe. Transnational Infrastructures and the Project of Europe*, London 2010, pp. 144 – 147.

43 Kaiser / Schot: Writing, pp. 166 – 167.

44 Cited in Broch: Professionalism, p. 368.

45 Armand: Propos, p. 210. On electrification of the railways in Western Germany, see Hascher, Michael: "Die Stromsystemfrage bei der Elektrifizierung der Eisenbahnen in Europa 1950 – 1955. Das Beispiel der Entscheidung in der Bundesrepublik Deutschland", in: Burri, Monika, / Elsasser, Kilian / Gugerli, David (eds.): *Die Internationalität der Eisenbahnen*, Zürich 2003, pp. 177 – 194.

46 Chevandier, Christian / Ribeill, Georges: "Louis Armand", in: Jean-Claude Daumas (ed.): *Dictionnaire historique des patrons français,* Paris 2010, pp. 29 – 31.

ical technical expert"[47], for whom the war paradoxically strengthened the feeling of belonging to a transnational technical community, and faith in its ability to build a peaceful Europe.

5. *Conclusion*

How can we characterize wartime cooperation in the railway sector? On the key issue of the transnational circulation of rolling stock, it was formally based on pre-war agreements, such as the RIC and RIV conventions — at least seen from France — or through the Verein regulations. The International Railway Union, a contested institution before the war, did not disappear; it went into dormancy under the French railways, but was not replaced by a new organization. Reading the Verein's *Zeitung*, the Union remained an important point of reference for members of the Verein during the war. This stood in sharp contrast to what happened in the postal and telecommunication sector, where a new organization replaced and complemented pre-war ones. In contrast, during the post-war period the Allies agreed to revive and strengthen the International Railway Union, while in the context of massive damage and the unanswered question of German reparations, they had to temporarily suspend the pre-war agreements regulating the transnational circulation of rolling stock. The Verein also came to an end, and with it the dual institutional setting of transnational railway governance in Europe. The project of a European wagon pool advanced across this divide, taking shape in the Western European sphere.

6. *References*

Anastasiadou, Irene: *Constructing Iron Europe: Transnationalism and Railways in the Interbellum*, Amsterdam 2012.

Broch, Ludivine: "Professionalism in the Final Solution: French Railway Workers and the Jewish Deportations, 1942-4", in: *Contemporary European History* 23 (2014), p. 359 – 380.

Caron, François: *Histoire des chemins de fer en France, 1937 – 1997,* Paris 2017.

47 Henrich-Franke: Louis Armand, p. 147.

Chevandier, Christian / Ribeill, Georges: "Louis Armand", in: Daumas, Jean-Claude (ed.): *Dictionnaire historique des patrons français,* Paris 2010, pp. 29 – 31.

Dienel, Hans-Liudger: "Die Eisenbahnen und der europäische Möglichkeitsraum 1870-1914", in Roth, Ralf / Schlögel, Karl (eds.): *Neue Wege in ein neues Europa. Geschichte und Verkehr im 20. Jahrhundert*, Frankfurt 2009, pp. 105 – 123.

Hascher, Michael: "Die Stromsystemfrage bei der Elektrifizierung der Eisenbahnen in Europa 1950 – 1955. Das Beispiel der Entscheidung in der Bundesrepublik Deutschland", in Burri, Monika / Elsasser, Kilian / Gugerli, David (eds.): *Die Internationalität der Eisenbahnen*, Zürich 2003, pp. 177 – 194.

Henrich-Franke, Christian: "Europäische Verkehrsintegration im 19. und 20. Jahrhundert", in: Neutsch, Cornelius / Thiemeyer, Guido (eds.): *Internationalismus und Europäische Integration im Vergleich. Fallstudien zu Währungen, Landwirtschaft, Verkehrs- und Nachrichtenwesen*, Baden-Baden 2007, pp. 133 – 176.

Henrich-Franke, Christian: "Louis Armand – Between United Atoms and Common Railways", in: Badenoch, Alexander / Fickers, Andreas (eds.): *Materializing Europe. Transnational Infrastructures and the Project of Europe*, London 2010, pp. 144 – 147.

Hilberg, Raul / Pehle, Walter H. / Schlott, René: "The indispensability of the railroads", in: *The Anatomy of the Holocaust: Selected Works from a Life of Scholarship*, New York 2020, pp. 53 – 55.

Hildebrand, Klaus: "Die Deutsche Reichsbahn in der nationalsozialistischen Diktatur, 1933 – 1945", in: Gall, Lothar / Pohl, Manfred (eds.): *Die Eisenbahn in Deutschland*, Munich 1999, pp. 165 – 244.

Högselius, Per / Kaijser, Arne / Vleuten van der, Erik: *Europe's Infrastructure Transition. Economy, War, Nature,* London 2016.

Kaiser, Wolfram / Schot, Johan: *Writing the Rules for Europe. Experts, Cartels and International Organizations*, London 2014.

Kopper, Christopher: "Die internationale Zusammenarbeit der Deutschen Bundesbahn (1949-1992)", in: Ambrosius, Gerold / Henrich-Franke, Christian / Neutsch, Cornelius (eds.): *Internationale Politik und Integration europäischer Infratruktur in Geschichte und Gegenwart*, Baden-Baden 2010, pp. 213 – 232.

Mierzejewski, Alfred: *The Most Valuable Asset of the Reich. A History of the German National Railway* 2 (1933 – 45), Chapel Hill 2000.

Pouly, Charlotte: "Les agents et dirigeants de la SNCF, épurés sous Vichy, épurés après Vichy. Regard croisé autour de la reintégration", in: *Histoire & Mesure*, XXIX-2 (2014), pp. 135 – 154 https://doi.org/10.4000/histoiremesure.5115.

Pouly, Charlotte: "Penser les circulations économiques à travers la SNCF pendant l'Occupation: 'Circulez y a rien à voir'?", in: *Hypotheses,* 18 (2015), pp. 149 – 164. DOI: 10.3917/hyp.141.0149.

Pouly, Charlotte: "'Räder müssen rollen für den Sieg!' Regard franco-allemand sur la SNCF et la *Reichsbahn* (1940 – 1945)", in: *Revue de l'IFHA* [Online] 6 (2014). URL: http://journals.openedition.org/ifha/8070; DOI: https://doi.org/10.4000/-ifha.8070.

Ribeill, Georges: "Aux origines de l'utopie du réseau ferroviaire européen intégré", in: *Histoire & Sociétés* 21 (2007), pp. 44 – 59.

Tissot, Laurent: "Les modèles ferroviaires nationaux et la création d'un système international de transports européens, 1870 – 1914. Coordination, intégration ou unification ?", in: *Relations internationales*, 95 (1998), pp. 313 – 327.

Tissot, Laurent: "Naissance d'une Europe ferroviaire: la convention internationale de Berne (1890)", in: Merger, Michèle / Barjot, Dominique (ed.): *Les entreprises et leurs réseaux: hommes, capitaux, techniques et pouvoirs, XIXe-XXe siècles,* Paris 1998, pp. 283 – 295.

Shaping Motorway Europe: Between War and Peace

Mathieu Flonneau

Table of content

1. *Introduction*

> The European card was the card to play—as M. Lucien Lainé remarked—to win the game. In this case more than any other, it was important not to neglect the mystical side of things, the psychological factor of this human endeavor.[1]

As indicated by the epigraph, which uses a diaphanous teleology of sorts, a motorway is much more than a motorway! "Some have sought to attribute a civilizing importance to the construction of motorways," noted Philippe Reine in his seminal work from 1944,[2] and it is true that the construction of Europe endowed them with this quality. Their highly political world was defined and codified as a coherent ecosystem for mobility by the World Road Association in 1957.

However, the foregone conclusion underscored by the green signage with which motorways were presented as links between territories and European countries should be put into perspective with their national origins, which became nationalist during World War Two and were accompanied by

1 First International Road Congress, Geneva 1931, cited by Sancery, Marcelle: *L'autoroute, voie de la prospérité et de l'unité européenne*, Clermont-Ferrand 1962, p. 75.

2 Reine, Philippe: *Trafic automobile et réseau routier. Les autoroutes en Allemagne, en Italie et en France*, Paris 1944, cited by Sancery: L'autoroute, p. 189.

supranational designs of domination. This period coincided with their intellectual construction, in other words their definition on paper before the start of their actual material construction.

2. The Roads toward Motorway Dependency

The intentionality and awareness of the motorway process was consequently in full effect, as the two decades between 1935 and 1955 saw the emergence and diffusion of institutional and technocratic measures for importing and adapting—albeit with some syncretism—foreign and especially European models, in this case Italian and German ones.[3] This phase of the history of motorway networks was indeed marked by an intense circulation of models for road traffic and techniques,[4] in addition to the national considerations that were often entangled with them.[5] A new general framework was built, from the founding of the Permanent International Association of Road Congresses (PIARC, which became the World Road Association in 1995) in 1909 after the Paris Congress of 1908, to the Milan Congress in 1926, which truly defined the motorway, in addition to the revelatory invention of l'Union Routière de France (French Road Union) in 1935, whose motto from the very outset — "*Route fréquentée crée prospérité*" (busy roads create prosperity) — did not emphasize the necessity of motorways.[6] The landscape was radically changed by the rapid acculturation of

3 On the contemporary American model see Seely, Bruce E.: *Building the American Highway System: Engineers as Policy Makers*, Philadelphia 1987; Ibid: "'Push' and 'Pull' Factors in Technology Transfer: Moving American-Style Highway Engineering to Europe 1945 – 1965," in: *Comparative Technology Transfer and Society*, 2/3 (2004), p. 229 – 246.

4 See Gardon, Sébastien: "Pour une histoire des circulations sur la circulation", in: *Métropoles* 6 (2009); Passalacqua, Arnaud / Schipper, Frank: https://metropoles.revues.org/4053; Schipper, Frank: *Driving Europe, Building Europe on Roads in the Twentieth Century*, Amsterdam 2008; Badennoch, Alexander / Fickers, Andreas (eds.): *Materializing Europe: Transnational Infrastructures and the Project of Europe*, 2010.

5 The example of Czechoslovakia bears mentioning in this dual national and international sense.

6 Which is to say the year after the Munich Road Congress and the enactment of the French coordination law; Ďurčo, Michal: "The shift in Slovakian road planning from Austria-Hungary to Czechoslovakia", in: *Encyclopédie d'histoire numérique de l'Europe* [online], published on 26/06/20. Permalink: https://ehne.fr/en/node/21300.

automobile technology coupled with the standardization of ecosystems (i.e., its political and geopolitical impact), as well as the enacting and learning of driving rules, as demonstrated by Codes de la route (Motorway Codes) in France in 1921.

At the same time, the universal presence of roads raised questions for nations everywhere with regard to the form they would take. In France, this was to an extent "interfered with" by the debate surrounding the coordination of transportation, which was rekindled by the issue of motorways.[7] The motorway option, which was sketched out in the early 1920s and for a time was seen as a pacifier of international relations — especially as part of the Geneva Spirit movement — returned in a different key, one that was connected to foreign experiences.[8] The First International Road Congress was held in Geneva in 1931, with Albert Thomas, the director of the International Labour Office, speaking in person.

3. *The Tumultuous and Opportunistic Motorway Transition*

As is often the case in history, periods of crisis—and even more so of war—can untangle complex questions that the status quo of times of peace cannot elucidate.

In 1944, the jurist and senior civil servant Philippe Reine wrote the following regarding such roads, which remained unknown in France at the time:[9] "The situation a few years ago was not as evident, which is why one

7 Neiertz, Nicolas: *La coordination des transports en France de 1918 à nos jours*, Paris 1999, p. 740. See our review in: *Annales. Histoire. Sciences Sociales* 6 (2001), pp. 1394 – 1396.

8 Marcelle Sancery's book (*L'autoroute, voie de la prospérité et de l'unité européenne*) includes information regarding this crucial congress. Also see Schipper: Driving Europe.

9 The uncertainty of the vocabulary is one constant of the road debate. See Desportes, Marc: *Paysages en mouvement*, Gallimard 2005; Desportes, Marc / Picon, Antoine: *De l'espace au territoire. L'aménagement en France XVIe – XXe siècles*, Paris 1997. On the genealogy of associated road forms, see Desportes, Marc: "The History of Highway Nodes," in: *History and Technology* 8 (1992), pp. 247 – 261; Lemone, Bertrand / Mesqui, Jean: „Un musée retrouvé, le musée des travaux publics 1939 – 1955", in: *Ministère de l'Equipement, du Logement, des transports et de la Mer* (ed.), 1991, p. 157. In 1955 the building was alotted to the Conseil

can speak, without arriving at a clear conclusion, of an opportunity for building motorways." His pioneering study sought to provide information about a subject that remained, in his own words, "widely unknown," one that was driven by "voices crying in the desert"[10] that had previously been on the margins of public policies. One had to wait for the state's resolute engagement on the topic with the essential law of 1955—and especially on programs that relied massively on private financing, with the creation of semi-public concessionary companies during the 1960s—for motorway civilization to truly be born in France.[11] This chronology of events suggests that if there was a French manner of converting motorways, it did not emerge for another fifteen years after World War Two.

At this stage, the genealogy of motorways calls for being broadened geographically, as well as for being resituated within socio-technical legacies and roads toward dependency. Despite early and occasional attempts in the United States or Germany, it truly emerged as an innovative road network in Italy in the early 1920s. The word used in French—at times hesitant in matters of terminology—was incidentally the translation of the Italian term (*autostrada*) used for the new continuous circulation road between Milan and the Great Lakes region, which was conceived by the engineer Piero Puricelli and inaugurated by King Victor Emmanuel III on September 21, 1924. Reserved exclusively for automobiles for reasons of safety, these parallel one-way restricted-access roadways saw their technical characteristics formalized during the Fifth Road Congress held in Milan in 1926.[12]

One of the reasons given in France for rejecting the motorway and maintaining and developing the former system was related to the history the

---

économique et social (Economic and Social Council). The work by Geneviève Zembri-Mari also bears mentioning: *Maillage autoroutier et territoire. Permanences et mutations du modèle français de développement autoroutier*, ENPC doctoral thesis 1999.

10 Sancery: L'autoroute, p. 12.

11 See Abraham, Claude: *Les autoroutes concédées en France. 1955 – 2010*, Paris 2011, p. 183.

12 On Italy see Moraglio, Massimo: *Driving Modernity: Technology, Experts, Politics, and Fascist Motorways, 1922 – 1943*, New York 2017; Ibid.: "Highway Network in Italy and Germany Between the Wars: A Preliminary comparative Study", in: Mom, Gijs / Tissot, Laurent (eds.): *Road history: Planning, Building and Use*, Neuchatel 2007; the following articles also deserve consideration: Ibid: "A Rough Modernisation: Landscapes and Highways in Italy in the 1900s," in: *Athens OH* 16 (2008), p. 108 – 124; Ibid: "Real ambition or just coincidence? The Italian fascist motorway projects in interwar Europe", in: *The Journal of Transport History* 19 (2009); Ibid: "Transferring Technology, Shaping Society. Traffic Engineering in PIARC Agenda, in the early 1930s," in: *Technikgeschichte* 19 (2013).

country set out upon in the initial phases of its demonstration. Its conclusions nevertheless came up against an apparently timeless legend, namely the pre-existence in France of the "the world's finest network."[13]

For that matter, amid the uncertainty of the technical vocabulary, the "best French roads" were referred to as *auto-routes* (motorways).[14] As roads designed for high speeds, motorways had not yet been truly defined, except by the textile entrepreneur Lucien Lainé assisted by Pigelet, the head engineer from the Ponts-et-Chausées, both of whom were behind projects in Northern France:

> The motorway is a road exclusively reserved for motor vehicles that does not pass through inhabited centers, crossing below or above ordinary roads, and accessible from these roads in specific areas, formed by straight lines connected by curves with large radiuses, in which all provisions have been made for perfect visibility, optimal stability, and ordered circulation.[15]

Later on in January 1943, the "motorway dispute" opposing "*philo-autoroutiers*" (motorway lovers) and their "enemies" in the automobile press—and at *La vie automobile* in particular—sketched out an alternative: "The rehabilitation of our road network. The case against golden roads." An illustrated brochure, apparently authored by Georges Gallienne,[16] was published at the time: "French motorways, a future problem." Charles Faroux, a talented journalist and eminent figure in the automobile world, vigorously opposed this assumption:

> The push in favor of 'Golden roads,' to use Georges Duhamel's colorful expression, is exerted solely through a few financial groups who could do no better than choose as spokesperson a man who wanted to regain his...virginity by working for these Transports Routiers, for whom he was once their worst enemy.

Reine then cited other arguments prevailing at the time:

> The defenders of motorways are none other than shady wheeler-dealers with a single ambition, eager above all to secure the privilege of building the new roads, as well as the power to collect the corresponding revenue.

---

13 This same argument also appears in Antonini, Jules: *Le Rail, la Route et l'Eau*, Paris 1937.

14 Yves Le Trocquer, the former minister of Travaux publics (Public Works) and a senator from the Côtes-du-Nord, still spelled it with a hyphen in his book: *La route et sa technique*, chapter "Les questions du temps présent," Félix Alcan, 1931.

15 Definition used by Reine in the *Bulletin quotidien d'études et d'informations économiques, 4 August 1942*. The role and innovative initiatives of Lucien Lainé, a textile industrialist from Beauvais who was not an engineer, deserve close study.

16 He would serve as the future president of l'Union Routière de France and was also the mayor of Chambourcy.

It should be noted that in his book, motorways are discussed only in part 3, entitled "Building The First Motorways of Europe: Italy," and in part 4, "Building a Comprehensive Motorway Program: *Autostrada* in Germany." French motorways first appear only on page 287 in part 5, which is entitled "The Building of a Partial Motorway Program: The Motorways of France." Toward the end of the book, in chapter 2 of part 5, after a lengthy reflection he directly raised the question: *Should motorways be constructed in France?* The question is explored prudently and with no clear-cut answer given the absence of what some — preoccupied with scientifically proving the necessity of motorways — subsequently called the "motorway coefficient."[17]

The German model served as the standard, with the Autobahn being a constant reference. Chancellor Hitler kicked off his policy on September 23, 1933 in Niederrad on the Frankfurt-Mannheim-Heidelberg section,[18] but the inspiration for the great Germanic network HAFRABA[19] stretched further back, with Reine tracing them in his general conclusion back to the very sources of German economic dynamism: „Inexpensive, rapid, and safe transport of people and merchandise is one of the most important levers of national well-being and civilization in all of its forms," wrote Frédérich List a century ago with the recent arrival of railroads in mind. The same sentence could quite rightly be applied today to motorways.

To conclude, it should be noted that these war years made a decisive contribution to the development of the technical object that is the "motorway," whose national, social, political, and geopolitical impact should under no circumstances be obscured.

---

17 Reine based his book on data such as network density (France 115 km of roads per 100 km², 52 in the United States, 39 in Germany, 57 in Italy, 90 in Great Britain, 73 in Holland, and 18 in Spain) and the number of cars per kilometer of road (3.5 in France, 6.4 in the United States, 9 in Germany, 57 in Italy, 9 in Great Britain, 6 in Holland, and 1.4 in Spain).

18 On the German model see Ziegler, Volker: „Les Autoroutes du IIIe Reich et leurs origines", in: Cohen, Jean Louis (ed.): *Les années 30. L'architecture et les arts de l'espace entre industrie et nostalgie*, Paris 1997. Zeller, Thomas: *Driving Germany: The Lansdcape of the German Autobahn. 1930 – 1970*, Berghahn 2010; Richard Vahrenkamp: *The German Autobahn. 1920 – 1945: Hafraba Vision and Mega Projects*, Lohmar 2010.

19 The origins of HaFraBa, which was was founded in 1928, go back to 1926: *Verein zur Vorbereitung der Autostraße Hansestädte – Frankfurt – Basel.*

4. Chronology

- *1924, first motorway built in Italy.*
- *1926, PIARC Congress and "motorway charter."*
- *1931, First International Road Congress in Geneva.*
- *1933, Hitler inaugurates the Frankfurt-Mannheim-Heidelberg section.*
- *1935, public utility declaration for the Western Paris motorway.*
- *1955, French law on the status of motorways.*
- *1957, the World Road Association provides an international definition for motorways.*
- *1970, inauguration of the Lille-Marseilles motorway*
- *1975, European agreement on major international traffic routes.*

5. References

Flonneau, Mathieu: "'Routes en or' et 'automobile pour tous'. Adosser l'archéologie des autoroutes françaises à l'horizon européen," in: Bouvier, Yves / Laborie, Léonard (eds.): *L'Europe en transitions. Energie, mobilité, communication XVIIIe – XXIe siècles*, Nouveau Monde 2016, p. 191 – 226.

Moraglio, Massimo: *Driving Modernity: Technology, Experts, Politics, and Fascist Motorways, 1922 – 1943*, Berghahn Books 2017.

Schipper, Frank: *Driving Europe, Building Europe on Roads in the Twentieth Century*, Amsterdam 2008.

Vahrenkamp, Richard: *The German Autobahn 1920 – 1945. Hafraba Visions and Mega Projects*, Lohmar 2010.

Karel Paul van der Mandele (1880 – 1975)

Martial Libera

During the postwar period, Karel Paul van der Mandele played an important role in river improvements for the Rhine and its tributaries through the Rhine Union of Chambers of Commerce, a the transnational interest group he headed from its creation in 1949 until 1965. The experience of the war and the German occupation prompted this banker to promote postwar European construction through strengthened economic cooperation between Western Europeans, which he believed would occur via the creation of a genuine network of rivers serving as the backbone for the Rhine corridor, and driving Western European trade.

Mandele was born in Delft on November 1, 1880, into a family of financiers. His father Willem Karel Samuel van der Mandele was a cashier and securities broker in this city, where his liberal-minded family was well-respected. Karel Paul van der Mandele earned his secondary school diploma from Delft high school, and then began studies in economics at the University of Lausanne with Vilfredo Pareto, which he quickly interrupted to study law at Leiden University, where he established a lasting friendship with his professor of international law, Cornelis van Vollenhoven. The difficulties that the family business experienced in 1901, and his father's subsequent disrepute, were a painful experience for the young Mandele. He devoted himself to paying back his family's creditors in full.

After completing his studies in 1902, Mandele first worked as a lawyer in a law office in the Hague. In 1906 he married Hermine Sophie Marie van Bosse. The couple had four children (three daughters and a son). Mandele settled in Rotterdam in the same year, and was hired as the secretary for the board of directors of Rotterdamsche Bank Vereeniging (Robaver), one of the most powerful investment banks in Rotterdam. Four years later he became its director, and held this position until 1940. Beginning in 1932, Mandele also became a member of the Rotterdam Chamber of Commerce and Industry, and was easily elected to be its president in 1938 thanks to his commitment to transforming the city, serving in this capacity until 1960. During the interwar period he invested in embellishing the city, conserving nature in the province, and developing the sciences in Rotterdam. He did so by helping secure financing for a number of striking monuments, including the Boijmans Museum, a stadium, the stock exchange, and the port hospital, which were completed in the 1930s.

During the Second World War, Mandele was in a complicated position, as it was difficult to represent the interests of Rotterdam and its population, and simultaneously satisfy those of its occupiers. Mandele was nevertheless able to conserve the duties of the chamber of commerce. Thanks to the chamber's many branches in the province, he was even able to assist the general population and companies, and especially to preserve the chamber as a site for the Dutch to meet and exchange, at a time when the collaboration of town councilors with the occupier was on the rise. In 1943 Mandele joined a resistance group—the Patriotic Committee—created upon the request of the British government, and in this context helped finance the railway strike of 1944-1945. During the occupation, he began to think about the postwar period and the plans needed for the recovery. He believed in a world founded on new values. He benefited from the analyses of his compatriot Lilli Hedwig van der Schalk-Schuster, who was close to German business circles hostile to the war, and informed him of their international plans for the postwar period, as well as the secret contacts they had abroad.

Mandele was at the height of his career during the postwar period. In Rotterdam he served as president of the chamber of commerce, working with the city's administration to rebuild the city as a hub for global maritime traffic, thereby consecrating the principle of joint action by government services and private initiatives. The monthly meetings between city administrators and representatives from the business class also led to the organization, every five years, of festivities to publicize the city, such as Rotterdam Ahoy in 1950, E55 in 1955, and the Floriade in 1960. In order to complete these projects, Mandele helped create a number of foundations tasked with fundraising.

He was also active on the international scene. In Western Europe, Mandele was hostile to the construction of a political order. He believed more in functional reforms, and called for uniting European economic interests within international corporations, in which Dutch companies could play a leading role. He rubbed shoulders with the directors of Unilever, including Paul Rijkens and David Mitrany, who served as the company's international affairs officer, and was more known for his academic duties and as a theorist of international functionalism. They were both interested in Mandele's ideas, and encouraged him. Mandele implemented his projects by creating and promoting the Rhine Union of Chambers of Commerce (RUCC) in 1949, which in its beginnings included approximately forty chambers of commerce from the seven Rhine countries: Austria (connected to the Rhine basin by the Inn River and Lake Constance), Belgium (connected to the Rhine by the Meuse River), France, Luxembourg, the Netherlands, Switzerland, and the Federal Republic of Germany. By creating this union that he presided over until 1965, Mandele achieved another of his objectives, namely reintegrating Western Germany within the European scene by granting its representatives the same rights as those from other countries. With the RUCC, he unsuccessfully sought to create a "greater Europe" that would move beyond the borders of the Cold War through navigable links between the Rhine and Danube rivers. Mandele also failed in his attempt to create an international corporation uniting the economic interests of the Rhine. His vision of instituting the Rhine Development Corporation within the RUCC remained in the planning stages due to a lack of support from many chambers of commerce. Mandele nevertheless remained attached to the functionalist method, which explains his reluctance toward the first European initiatives, the Organisation for European Economic Co-operation (OEEC), the Council of Europe, and even the European Coal and Steel Community. He did not think it was possible to build Europe from the top-down, or to create an institutional Europe whose initiative came primarily from the states; this would entail new forms of state intervention, international in this instance, that the experience of the preceding quarter century would definitely disqualify. For Mandele, Europe had to build itself from the bottom-up, a Europe of active forces driven by functional, flexible, and responsive economic actors that could quickly produce results. In 1957, he once again opposed the creation of the European Economic Community, which he doubted would be favorable to Dutch interests. However, Mandele was able to strengthen the role of river transport in Western Europe. The RUCC took an active part in works to make numerous Rhine tributaries navigable, including the Main river, the Meuse river, the Moselle river (canalized in 1964), and Neckar river.

During the 1950s and 1960s, Mandele promoted the international development of the port of Rotterdam. He helped create a number of specialized institutes to analyze international developments in relation to commercial activity. Under the auspices of the Overseas Institute, he pushed for institutes for Africa, Canada, the USSR, Scandinavia, Australia, and Latin America. He also laid the foundation for the future expansion of the Netherlandsche Economic High School (NEH), one of the schools that subsequently led to the creation of Erasmus University Rotterdam.

His late career was marked by honors. In 1955 he received the Silver Carnation, awarded each year to individuals who contributed to Dutch culture. He was also made a chamberlain in the special service of Queen Juliana, and in 1958 a doctor *honoris causa* of the Dutch School of Economics (today Erasmus University Rotterdam). While Mandele stopped serving as president of the Rotterdam Chamber of Commerce and Industry in 1960, he continued to be active on numerous boards of directors during the 1960s. He died on January 23, 1975 in Rotterdam.

References

Fockema, Andrea: "Mandele, Karel Paul van der (1880-1975)," in *Biografisch Woordenboek van Nederland,* The Hague 1985, online version, last modified on 11/12/2013 URL:http://resources.huygens.knaw.nl/bwn1880-2000/lemmata/bwn2/mandele

Devin, Guillaume: "Que reste-t-il du fonctionnalisme international," in: *Critique internationale* 38 (2008), p. 137 – 152.

Libera, Martial: *Diplomatie patronale aux frontières. Les relations des chambres de commerce frontalières françaises avec leurs homologues allemandes (1945 – milieu des années 1980)*, Geneva 2019.

Libera, Martial: "L'Union des chambres de commerce rhénanes et l'organisation du marché européen (1949 – 1975): entre Europe du libre-échange et Europe organisée," in: Boyer, Jean-Daniel / Carrez, Maurice (eds.): *Marchés, réseaux commerciaux et construction de l'Europe*, Paris 2016, p. 109 – 123.

Mitrany, David: *A Working Peace System: An Argument for the Functional Development of International Organization*, London 1944.

Prosperity and Identity: European Networks in *Signal* Magazine. An Argument used to promote the Nazi Project for the Continent's Unification

Claire Aslangul-Rallo

Table of Content

1. Introduction

Soon after the outbreak of the Second World War, German authorities mobilized unprecedented means for foreign influence, especially through the diffusion of newspapers and magazines throughout Europe and beyond. It was in this context that the bi-monthly magazine *Signal* was launched in April 1940, which drew inspiration from the attractive format of the recently created magazines *Life* (1936) and *Match* (1938), and used the extensive means at its disposal to promote a positive image of Germany through "soft" propaganda.[1] Between 1940 and 1945, its circulation rose to 2.5 million in 25 languages in neutral, occupied, and friendly countries (but not in Germany, even though the "matrix" translated into other languages was drafted in Berlin), with France being a leading country. The magazine addressed a wide audience and generally devoted approximately half of its contributions to reporting on the war and politics, supplemented by social and cultural topics with more or less neutral ideological content.

These subjects were often broached from a European perspective likely to attract the reader, especially in France, which offered particularly fertile ground for this approach: "The European ideal is deeply rooted in France. […] This ideology plays in our favor," Abetz noted in 1941.[2] The French-language version was even more "European" than the German original, as between late 1942 and the end of the magazine's diffusion in France in the summer of 1944, it offered specially conceived articles for the French public, with reflections on subjects with a French-German or European dimension in lieu of the more German-centric articles of the "matrix."[3] Europe's presence in *Signal* evolved over time, and it was only in the spring of 1941 that the topic started gaining quantitative importance (in texts, images, and advertisements).[4] After the start of the war against the USSR, articles on culture and "the reorganization of the European eco-

1 See Aslangul, Claire: "*Signal* et la France: 'vendre' par l'image le rapprochement franco-allemand sous l'Occupation," in: Aslangul-Rallo, Claire / Krapoth, Stéphanie (eds.): *Les relations franco-allemandes en perspective: sources, méthodes et temporalités pour une approche des représentations depuis 1870*, Besançon 2016, p. 259 – 318.

2 In a June 1941 report to Ribbentrop, cited by Bruneteau, Bernard: "*L'Europe nouvelle" de Hitler. Une illusion des intellectuels de la France de Vichy*, Monaco 2003, p. 17.

3 Especially a dozen articles on the LVF (Legion of French Volunteers Against Bolshevism), and a long article by René Vallet, "L'idée européenne chez les hommes d'État et les penseurs français" (The Idea of Europe Among French Statesmen and Thinkers), in: *Signal* 22 (1943). See Aslangul, Claire: "Le magazine *Signal* (1940 – 1945). Propagande 'universelle' ou adaptation à des publics hétérogènes? L'exemple de la version francophone", in: *Matériaux pour l'histoire de notre temps* 1 (2020), p. 56 – 67.

4 See Aslangul, Claire: "Les publicités dans le magazine Signal (1940 – 1945) entre promotion commerciale et propagande politique: apports d'une analyse quantitative", in: Aslangul, Claire / Zunino, Bérénice (eds.): *Die Presse und ihre Bilder / La presse et ses images*, Berlin/Bern 2021.

nomic area"[5] were supplemented by contributions on Europe as a community of values, culture, and race. The topic of a "crusade against Bolshevism," conducted under the aegis of Germany by "volunteers" from all countries, experienced a resurgence after the defeat of Stalingrad in February 1943. *Signal* engaged in outrageous dramatization, claiming that the conflict's outcome could determine whether Europe thrived or became permanently annihilated.

These articles with a European dimension contrasted the projects of the "former world", such as Paneurope and the "corpse" of the LN, with the future vision of a peaceful and prosperous "new community of nations,"[6] one that reserved a special role for transportation, energy, and communication networks. The latter enabled the exchange and free movement of goods,[7] persons, and ideas, and were presented as drivers of the continent's beneficial unification. These articles effectively contributed to a propagandist strategy seeking to falsify the reality of the national socialist project, with which they were nevertheless directly associated, namely the maximal exploitation of the continent's resources for the benefit of the German Reich.[8]

---

5 The title of Walther Funk's famous speech on July 25, 1940 (*Die wirtschaftliche Neuordnung Europas*, *Rede vor Vertretern der deutschen und ausländischen Presse)*, cited in the February 1941 article by Diether Heumann, "L'or est mort. Pourquoi l'or a-t-il passé de vie à trépas !" (Gold Is Dead: Why Gold Went From Life to Death!), in: *Signal* 4 (1941) (February): 8. Signal appeared bi-monthly beginning in April 1940, with sequential numbering per year, from 1 to 17 in 1940, and then 1 to 24 in 1941, 1942, and 1943; it appeared less regularly in 1944, with only 19 issues being published that year; in 1945 there were five issues for the German edition, and only four for the French edition (from January to March).

6 Von Oertzen, F.W.: "Société des Nations? Communauté des Nations. Ce qui est impossible aujourd'hui sera possible à l'avenir" (League of Nations? Community of Nations: What is Impossible Today Will Be Possible in the Future), in: *Signal* 13 (1941) (July): 8 – 11. See also Clauss, Max: "Le mauvais chemin de la Paneurope" (The Wrong Road of Paneurope), in: *Signal* 17 (1940), p. 4 – 5.

7 An eloquent article shows, through the use of an anecdote, how much customs duties increased the cost of an unremarkable product such as a watch, and concluded: "Unified Europe freed of these customs borders will become a single market, offering tremendous possibilities to sell its products," in: *Signal* 15 (1943) (August): 23: Anonymous "(Le nouvel aspect du monde: l'avenir de l'Europe) Soederstroem achète une montre" (The New Aspect of the World: Europe's Future — Soederstroem Buys a Watch).

8 See for example "Sitzung im Reichswirtschaftsministerium: Neuaufbau der europäischen Wirtschaft," July 22, 1940 (*Quellen zur Neuordnung Europas 1,*

While the topic of networks was present throughout the magazine's publication, it became the focus of a series of dedicated articles between the fall of 1941 and the summer of 1942. In May 1941, an article by Lehnau announced "the publication of a new series in which certain issues of interest to all of Europe will be discussed", based on concrete examples of real productions — not "utopias but actual facts."[9] Between September 1941 and July 1942, ten articles in this vein appeared at infrequent intervals, on average one article every two issues. They all evoked the topic of networks in more or less detailed fashion. Study of this corpus reveals the dual interest of networks for Nazi propagandists. First, this topic of apolitical belonging offered readers a positive and concrete vision, with the evocation of tangible results, coupled with prospects for economic prosperity and the construction of a lasting understanding between peoples. Second, the presentation of past and present German realizations in matters of infrastructure, as well as descriptions of its opponent's failures and shortcomings in the matter, were used to legitimize the Third Reich taking over "leadership of Europe."[10]

2. *An Ideal Subject for "Positive Propaganda"*

2.1 The Propagandistic Usefulness of Networks in the Context of "the European Continent's Unification" in 1941-1942

The publication of a series of articles on networks was in keeping with the pro-European editorial line defined in January 1941 by editor-in-chief Medefind, who emphasized subjects "of interest to a wide readership", "a

---

source 14, S. 7 – 11 available on the portal "Online Academy - the authentic records of the Nuremberg War Crimes Tribunal" <http://www.profit-over-life.org/books/books.php?book=37>), in addition to the different projects presented in Neulen, Hans Werner: *Europa und das Dritte Reich. Einigungsbestrebungen im deutschen Machtbereich 1939 – 1945*, München 1987.

9 Lehnau (pen name for Walther Kiaulehn): „L'Europe sera un jardin luxuriant" (Europe Will Be A Lush Garden), *Signal* 10 (1941) (May), p. 20 – 22 and p. 27, here 20.

10 Fischer, Rudolf: „Qui peut diriger l'Europe?" (Who Can Lead Europe?), in: *Signal* 11 (1941) (Juni), p. 22 – 27.

foreign audience in particular."[11] This option was reinforced in April 1941 by the Minister of Propaganda Joseph Goebbels's desire to underscore "the most attractive sides of human life" in propaganda publications.[12] Publication as a series was not implemented until September, with the decisive impetus for doing so seemingly coming from the initiation of Operation Barbarossa in the summer of 1941: plans to create an actual self-sufficient European economic area began to take shape after military successes in the West,[13] and the French defeat in particular[14]; beginning in June 1941, the East's raw materials, agricultural reserves, and industrial prospects, already presented as "immeasurable"[15] during the German-Soviet pact, seemed within reach. The start of the offensive against the USSR was, for that matter, perceived and presented in *Signal* as the moment when the endeavor to unify the European continent began.[16]

Propagandists now insisted on completing ideological and political mo bilization (the "crusade against Bolshevism") by using a more attractive component for the foreign audience. According to the recommendations of Karl Megerle,[17] the journalist and propaganda specialist for Joachim von

---

11 Rutz, Rainer: "*Signal." Eine deutsche Auslandsillustrierte als Propagandainstrument im Zweiten Weltkrieg,* Essen 2007, p. 253, 279, citing Medefind's notes, 28.1.1941, AA PA Presseabt. Lfd. Nr. 55 II.

12 Goebbels's diary, entry for April 30, 1941, cited in Rutz, "Signal", p. 279.

13 An article from June 1940 shows the beginning of the economic area's realization: "the Balkans [...] represent an economic whole, leaning most naturally toward Greater Germany," with "new interdependence" and an "economic symbiosis" of sorts: Anonymous: „L'Allemagne et les Balkans" (Germany and the Balkans), in: in: *Signal* 5 (1940) (Juni), p. 34 – 35.

14 The article Anonymous: „Hier – aujourd'hui – demain. Trois chapitres d'économie européenne" (Yesterday—Today—Tomorrow: Three Chapters from the European Economy), in: *Signal* 23/24 (1942) (December), p. 50 – 65 retrospectively looks back at this turning point, and points out that: "It was after the collapse of France that the broad outlines of the great European area emerged" (63).

15 Anonymous: „La porte s'ouvre sur l'Est" (The Door Opens onto the East), in: *Signal* 7 (1940) (Juli), p. 42 – 43.

16 See Wirsing, Giselher: „La naissance du soldat européen" (The Birth of the European Soldier), in: *Signal* 12 (1943), p. 8, 11, 13: "Something has existed since June 22, 1941 that had disappeared for centuries: the European soldier. [...] [The] appearance of the European soldier coincides with Europe's birth. [...] A shared destiny is the guarantor of the future happiness and abundance in which all peoples will participate as part of a unified continent."

17 Megerle, Karl: „Positive Presse- und Propagandathemen", September 27, 1941, in: *Quellen zur Neuordnung Europas 1,* source 14, p. 40 – 43. Megerle was also

Ribbentrop's Ministry of Foreign Affairs, a "positive propaganda [...] chiefly concerned with Europe's future" was essential; this would involve "building enduring peace and recognizing a shared destiny" with Germany playing the role of "protector" for European peoples destined for "collaboration," in addition to the "conservation and regeneration of Western culture" and "the creation of a great European economic area with an organic division of labor based on technical planning and the most modern transportation," thereby leading to a "Europe of prosperity." In the words of Bruneteau, who aptly describes the European idea's ability to "enchant" influential members of the French intelligentsia of all stripes[18] — its economic component in particular — it was the time of the "hymn to the 'great space.'"[19]

It was precisely from this program — editorial in nature for *Signal*, and corresponding to the general direction of policy—from which the articles appearing between the fall of 1941 and the summer of 1942 seemingly stemmed, evoking trans-European networks including railway infrastructure,[20] roads,[21] air traffic,[22] inland navigation,[23] wireless communica-

---

an active contributor to the magazine *Berlin-Rom-Tokio*, another important German press organ abroad; see Longerich, Peter: *Propagandisten im Krieg. Die Presseabteilung des Auswärtigen Amtes unter Ribbentrop*, München 1987, S. 79.

18 Bruneteau: L'Europe nouvelle, p. 70.

19 Ebd., p. 10.

20 Kapeller, Ludwig: „Le trafic international dans l'Europe sans frontières. (La solution future: voyages d'agrément et trains de luxe à la portée des travailleurs)" (International Traffic in Borderless Europe: The Future Solution — Affordable Leisure Travel and Luxury Trains for Workers), drawings by R. Hainisch, in: *Signal* 20 (1941) (October) , p. 41 – 45.

21 Anonymous: „Plus de routes droites ! Une nouvelle situation sociale pour l'Européen: conservateur des sites" (No More Straight Roads! A New Social Situation for the European: The Preserver of Sites), in: *Signal* 20 (1941) (October), p. 24/25, drawings by Manfred Schmidt.

22 Kapeller, Ludwig: „ ‚Le 'train aérien', express de l'avenir. L'Europe, centre du trafic aérien mondial (Le développement de l'aviation civile allemande depuis ses débuts jusqu'à l'époque actuelle)" (The "Air Train," The Express of the Future: Europe, The Center of Global Air Traffic—The Development of German Civil Aviation from its Beginnings to the Present), drawings by R. Hainisch, in: *Signal* 23 – 24 (1941) (Dezember), p. 53 – 55 and 58; and Kapeller, Ludwig: „L'Europe, centre de la circulation aérienne mondiale. Un voyage par avion dans l'Europe de demain" (Europe, The Center of Global Air Traffic: A Journey by Airplane in the Europe of Tomorrow), drawings by R. Hainisch, in: *Signal* 1 (1942) (Januar), p. 41 – 45.

tions,[24] and meteorological stations on the European continent,[25] along with methods for the allocation[26] and control[27] of energy. Eight of them were signed by Ludwig Kapeller (who was probably the author of the ninth one as well), the popular journalist and long-time contributor to the general interest magazines of the publisher Ullstein (which had been Aryanized in the meantime), as well as the author of novels of detective fiction and a specialist on radio, whose impact he theorized in influential publications.[28] With the exception of one article vilifying utopian enemy projects such as "heating Siberia" by "domesticating the Gulf Stream,"[29] his contributions conveyed an optimistic vision evoking concrete, practical, and technical economic aspects that perform the "invaluable function of depoliticizing the European 'question.'"[30] Like the exhibition "La France européenne" (European France, opened on June 1, 1941 at the Grand Palais), which sought to present the subject "in the most captivating

---

23 Ka. (Kapeller, Ludwig): „En bateau à travers l'Europe. A propos de canaux et de projets" (By Boat Through Europe: Regarding Canals and Projects), in: *Signal* 13 (1942) (July), p. 35 – 36.

24 Kapeller, Ludwig: „L'Europe vous parle! Le passé de la T.S.F. et son développement à venir" (This is Europe Talking! The Past and Future Development of Wireless Telegraphy), drawings by Rodolphe, in: *Signal* 6 (1942) (March), p. 42 – 45.

25 Kapeller, Ludwig: „Le temps qu'il fait en Europe" (The Weather in Europe), drawings by Manfred Schmidt, in: *Signal* 3 (1942) (Februar), p. 40 – 43; and Ludwig, Kapeller, Ludwig: „Le temps sur le continent" (The Weather on the Continent), drawings by Hainisch, *Signal* 4 (1942) (Februar), p. 41 – 43.

26 Anonymous: „Nouvelles énergies pour l'Europe. Un problème d'aujourd'hui et de demain" (New Energies for Europe: A Problem for Today and Tomorrow), drawings by R. Hainisch, in: *Signal* 18 (1941) (September), p. 40 – 45, Kapeller is probably the author.

27 Kapeller, Ludwig: „On voudrait domestiquer le Gulf-Stream!" (They Want to Tame the Gulf Stream!), sketch by Hans Liska, in: *Signal* 7 (1942) (April), p. 23 – 27.

28 See Bendig, Volker: *Die populärwissenschaftliche Zeitschrift Koralle im Ullstein und Deutschen Verlag 1925 – 1944,* Ph.D. diss., Ludwig-Maximilians-Universität, München 2014, S. 194. It should be noted that *Signal* presented itself as the "illustrated supplement" for the highly popular *Berliner Illustrierte Zeitung (BIZ)*, and was published by *Deutscher Verlag,* which was created by the Aryanization of the publisher Ullstein.

29 Kapeller: On voudrait domestiquer le Gulf-Stream!

30 Bruneteau: L'Europe nouvelle, p. 66 ff.

manner possible,"[31] Kapeller's articles complemented the many others that were highly political in nature.

This attempt to remain close to the reader, which pushed the ideological dimension of the Nazi European project to the background, used an attractive layout and always placed the articles in the second half of the volume dedicated primarily to "apolitical" subjects (Ill. 1). The popularization of technical subjects was first rate, with incredibly thorough maps and explanatory diagrams breaking up the text of these long and meticulous articles (up to 4.25 pages, or 1/10th of the publication's overall volume). They featured lively descriptions, with little caricatures or amusing drawings in color or in red, black, and white; charming anecdotes and details describe, for instance, the modernity and "full comfort" of mass air travel ("two millions travelers today with Lufthansa alone"), with "an ashtray and reading lamp on tray tables," as well as and a "comely 'stewardess'" who will bring you a glass of beer or a typewriter — "our radiotelegraph operator is at your disposal should you want to transmit a telegram."[32]

L'Europe, centre de la circulation aérienne mondiale

Ill. 1: "L'Europe, centre de la circulation aérienne mondiale" (Europe, The Center of Global Air Traffic), in: *Signal* 1 (1942) (January): p. 41– 45, here p. 40 – 41.

31 Notat, Léo: „L'exposition de la France européenne", in: *La Gerbe* 29 (1941), cited in Bruneteau: L'Europe nouvelle, p. 85.

32 Kapeller: L'Europe. Centre de la circulation aérienne, p. 41 – 42.

2.2 Networks as Drivers of Resource Exchange in the Service of Future Prosperity

Lehnau's article had already announced in May 1941 that transportation infrastructure was essential to "transform[ing] the heart of the continent into a vast flourishing garden," and emphasized the great wealth of "products that our tables could enjoy if Europe intensified its exchange of ideas and products." He already saw

> on the horizon, above the battlefields, the emerging vision of a future Europe transformed into a great garden, which through its talent for organization, love of nature, and strength of thought could and should become a paradise at the center of the world.[33]

This "vision" took very concrete manner in Kapeller's articles. Networks emerged as an essential way of compensating—to the benefit of all—for the productive shortfalls of certain European states,[34] on a continent marked by "airtight partitions [that] isolate the countries of a fragmented Europe."[35] In the field of energy for instance, one could "generously compensate for deficits by way of exchange, and distribute surplus energy according to needs. The high frequency cable […] has quickly and without traffic created a state of equilibrium in Europe"; a "European electrical network" should therefore be created, and the "collection points of various countries linked"[36] in order to do so (Ill. 2). What was true for energy also applied to goods: thanks to rail transport, "the European of the future would be neither mediocre nor starving," for there would be a "distribution of these resources" and of the "work enabling their exploitation."[37]

33 Lehnau: L'Europe sera un jardin luxuriant, p. 20.
34 Kapeller: En bateau à travers l'Europe, p. 35 – 36.
35 Anonymous: Nouvelles énergies pour l'Europe, p. 40.
36 Ibid., p. 43f.
37 Kapeller: Le trafic international, p. 44.

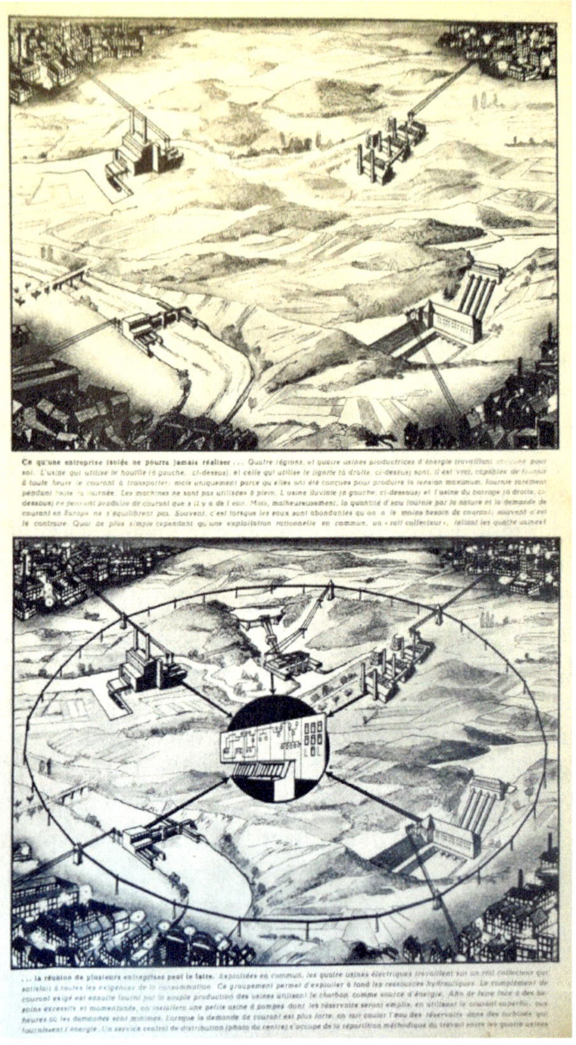

Ce qu'une entreprise isolée ne pourra jamais réaliser ... Quatre régions, et quatre usines productrices d'énergie travaillant [illegible] pour soi. L'usine qui utilise la houille (à gauche, ci-dessus) et celle qui utilise le lignite (à droite, ci-dessus) sont, il est vrai, capables de fournir à toute heure le courant à transporter; mais uniquement parce qu'elles ont été conçues pour produire la tension maximum, fournie seulement pendant toute la journée. Les machines ne sont pas utilisées à plein. L'usine fluviale (à gauche, ci-dessous) et l'usine du barrage (à droite, ci-dessous) ne peuvent produire de courant que s'il y a de l'eau. Mais, malheureusement, la quantité d'eau fournie par la nature et la demande de courant en Europe ne s'équilibrent pas. Souvent, c'est lorsque les eaux sont abondantes qu'on a le moins besoin de courant; souvent c'est le contraire. Quoi de plus simple cependant qu'une exploitation rationnelle en commun, un « rail collecteur », reliant les quatre usines!

... la réunion de plusieurs entreprises peut le faire. Exploitées en commun, les quatre usines électriques travaillent sur un rail collecteur qui satisfait à toutes les exigences de la consommation. Ce groupement permet d'exploiter à fond les ressources hydrauliques. Le complément de courant exigé est ensuite fourni par la souple production des usines utilisant le charbon comme source d'énergie. Afin de faire face à des besoins excessifs et momentanés, on installera une petite usine à pompes dont les réservoirs seront emplis, en utilisant le courant superflu, aux heures où les demandes sont minimes. Lorsque la demande de courant est plus forte, on fait couler l'eau des réservoirs dans des turbines qui fournissent l'énergie. Un service central de distribution (photo du centre) s'occupe de la répartition méthodique du [illegible] entre les quatre usines.

Ill. 2: "What one company alone could never produce... the confluence of multiple companies can", Anonymous: "Nouvelles énergies," in: *Signal* 18 (1941) (September): p. 40 – 45, here p. 43.

The prosperity presented in Kapeller's articles—generating exchange and thereby economic well-being, with a concern for just distribution—was based on the idea of a "shared rational exploitation" of complementarity as part of a "reasonable program based on the continent's general interest."[38] However, the rhetoric of the articles on networks also played greatly on the power of dreams; the persuasive nature of these articles was based on their capacity to project the reader beyond the painful present toward a future full of promises,[39] and it is not surprising that most of the articles were at least partly written in the future tense. Here is a representative but by no means isolated example:

> Yesterday, dream; tomorrow, no doubt, reality: the channeling of the Upper Rhine into the heart of the Alps. [...] These projects [for canals] have long been under study, and the new Europe will carry them out, for today it is convinced of one thing: it is fighting for both its security and well-being for centuries to come, and that everything it endeavors today can only be of benefit to future generations.[40]

By expanding this European project to include a global dimension,[41] Kapeller also indicated that for future generations,

> our globe will become too small [...] just as Europe no longer can satisfy the ambitious creative energy of our aviation pioneers, those who create and plan global air traffic, with Europe at the center. And we Europeans will all be proud one day that we dared to 'start' toward a new Europe.[42]

2.3 Networks, Drivers of "European Identity" through the Movement of Persons and Ideas

As we saw in last final quotation, the seeds of the European continent's unification also gave rise to the figure of "the European," the member of a

38 Anonymous: Nouvelles énergies, p. 40/43.

39 Here we see the appearance of a Nazi sociotechnical imaginary for Europe. On the notion of "sociotechnical imaginaries," see Jasanoff, Sheila / Kim, Sang Hyun (ed.): *Dreamscapes of Modernity: Sociotechnical Imaginaries and the Fabrication of Power*, Chicago 2015. I would like to thank Léonard Laborie for this bibliographical reference.

40 Kapeller: En bateau à travers l'Europe, p. 35f.

41 The global project was that of a "new global economy of large complementary spaces," as presented, for example, in the article by Prof. Dr. Hunke: "Le monde demande des produits et non des devises" (The World Wants Products Not Currency), in: *Signal* 4 (1940) (Juni), p. 35.

42 Kapeller: L'Europe centre de la circulation aérienne, p. 44/45.

community of belonging built on collaboration and exchange. This topic appeared frequently in Kapeller's articles, which emphasized the movement of goods as well as persons, which is to say relations between humans, for one day:

> Romanian barges from the Danube will move alongside those from the Spree, boatmen from the Rhine will visit their colleagues on the barges of the Dnieper, those from the Rhône will give accordion concerts on the barges of the Elbe. It will be in these internal ports that the continent's peoples will get to know one another, and the traffic of merchandise will be accompanied by the exchange of thought, goods, and cultures.[43]

The struggle against the shared Bolshevik enemy surely contributed — "blood spilled together unites" — to the nascent sense of shared destiny and a "European consciousness."[44] However, it was especially the growing movement of persons — soldiers and workers — during the war that would drive an "emerging personal knowledge" that could serve as the foundation for "future harmony."[45] Thanks to the "mixing of millions of people," each one can "have an idea of is happening with their neighbor in Europe."[46] Migrations would also bring about a beneficial acculturation, especially with respect to integrating populations from the East destined to rejoin Europe[47]; given that "the immense spaces of the East [...] expect the plane to bring about their spiritual and economic attachment to Europe,"[48] the key issue was to turn the "fertile lands that military operations have captured in the continent's East, Ukraine in particular," into "the breadbasket for all of Europe."[49]

---

43 Kapeller: En bateau à travers l'Europe, p. 36.

44 Wirsing: La naissance du soldat européen.

45 Seiler, Anton: „La Relève débourre les crânes" (La Relève Has Opened Minds) [La Relève was a system in which French workers were exchanged for French POWs], in: *Signal* 22 (1943) (November), p. 38. On this subject see especially the special issue of *Comparativ. Zeitschrift für Globalgeschichte und vergleichende Gesellschaftsforschung 28 1 (2018), hrsg. v. Barbara Lambauer and Christian Wenkel, on the topic "Entstehung und Entwicklung transnationaler Kommunikationsräume in Europa zu Kriegszeiten, 1914 – 1945."*

46 Wirsing, Giselher: „L'Europe sera-t-elle pauvre ?", in: *Signal* 15 (1943) (August), p. 8/11.

47 See Anonymous: „Nazalija. Fille de l'Ukraine", in: *Signal* 24 (1943) (Dezember), p. 42/43.

48 Kapeller: L'Europe centre de la circulation aérienne, p. 44/45.

49 Anonymous: Hier – aujourd'hui – demain, p. 60 – 65.

In addition to the exchange of goods and movement of persons, the immaterial exchanges made possible by telecommunication networks were presented as drivers for the sense of interdependence among European countries, which need one another to, among other things, make effective use of meteorological data.[50] Wireless telegraphy networks would create a vast space for cultural and "spiritual" sharing: the continent's radio network, an "instrument of harmony among peoples", had already transformed Europe into "a large audience hall where one could hear those great Europeans who had left their mark on human culture,"[51] with music playing a leading role among the productions that constitute a "European cultural community."[52] The tone becomes messianic toward the end of the article, and announces the projection of a self-aware "Europe" toward the exterior:

> A day will come when [...] Europe will become self-aware and will create its "great European broadcasting station," which will be a radiophonic representative before the court of the whole world; a day will come when the call to the whole world will ring out through the microphone: "This is Europe talking." Then the world will understand that Europe has been and is the cradle of human culture, and wants to remain so.

If networks enabled both material and immaterial contact — thereby creating a "vital European community space"[53] that is the bearer of an identity — they were presented as the initial result of a natural need to come together. Here we see the continent-wide application of a model inspired by Friedrich List,[54] one that was certainly relevant in the construction of the German nation-state: the need for exchange prompted the construction of (railway) networks, which in turn helped move beyond particularism and

50 Kapeller: Le temps qu'il fait en Europe.

51 Kapeller: L'Europe vous parle, p. 45.

52 See Burrin, Philippe: *La France à l'heure allemande: 1940 – 1944*, Paris 1995, p. 302.

53 To echo the expression used on a number of occasions, for instance in the article Anonymous: „Ni Roosevelt, ni Staline. L'Europe reste maîtresse de sa destinée" (Neither Roosevelt Nor Stalin: Europe Remains the Master of Her Destiny), in: *Signal* 7 (1943) (April 1943, French edition only), p. 25.

54 The subject, for that matter, of a long portrait that subsequently appeared in *Signal*: Anonymous: „Ses projets se réalisent aujourd'hui. Un européen voici cent ans: Friedrich List. Friedrich List à l'écran dans 'la route infinie'" (His Projects are Being Realized Today: A European 100 Years Ago: Friedrich List: Friedrich List on the Screen in "The Infinite Road"), in: *Signal* 5 (1943) (März 1943), p. 30/31.

toward political unification (Kapeller formulated it by describing "the importance of a network methodically built to produce the union of Germany").[55]

This dialectic allowed Kapeller to ultimately present nascent European unification as the result of a process initiated "from below" (and not by a dominant Germany), and as a response to the various needs of the protagonists (and not as the maximal exploitation of the continent's resources for the benefit of the Third Reich):

> while the egotism of capitalist powers and the short-term ideas of small states [...] tore at the framework uniting European nations, exchanges between people and the circulation of trains between all countries repaired this tissue, reconnecting the thread [....] well before statesmen ever imagined what Europe could become.[56]

Networks were thus central to a subtle argument that masked Germany's real objectives, and presented it not as a tyrant, but as a benevolent body for coordinating "natural" interests, a humble coordinator of a "large network of solidary interests, in the image of fruitful cooperation."[57]

3. *Networks and the Legitimization of Germany's "Leadership of Europe"*

3.1 A Proven Organizing Power

The recurring argument that these articles on networks used to explain why Germany could and must assume the natural leadership of European unification[58] was the emphasis placed on its organizational talents, which had proved worthy in the past and allowed it not only to develop its internal networks, but to also make European nations cooperate among themselves. Kapeller also offered a reminder of everything Germany had accomplished for "the development of civil aviation [...] from its beginnings to the present," notably with "Central Europe's first regular air connection between Vienna and Kiev" in 1918. He stressed that "from the beginning, Germany has endeavored to instill collaboration among European nations

55 Kapeller: Le trafic international, p. 42.

56 Ibid., p. 41.

57 Lorch, Wilhlem: „Huit extraits de presse et ce qu'ils cachent" (Eight Press Excerpts and What They Hide), in: *Signal* 16 (1943) (August), p. 36/37.

58 See the article cited in note 10.

in developing air travel," with "a service [...] combining within a single group German, Danish, and Dutch companies" in 1919. Mention was also made of the spirit of innovation, whose "daring conceptions embraced the entire continent, and whose ultimate goal was to make Europe the center for global air traffic."[59]

Germany's pioneering role in organizing railroad networks across the entire continent should spark the "admiration" of "today's European," for it was beginning in the nineteenth century that the "Union of German Railway Administration [...] established the methods for a traffic that benefits Europe":

> At the beginning of the World War, this Union included 90 companies, and its network extended across 11,300 kilometers, including 19 railways in Austria-Hungary, 5 in Holland and Luxembourg, 2 in Belgium, one in Russia, and the railroads of the Romanian state. The railroads of Denmark, Sweden, Norway, and Switzerland joined in 1929, and in 1932 the Union could proudly call itself the "Union of Central European Railway Administration." It was this organization that planned traffic in Europe and laid the groundwork for the international conventions [...] that became applicable across the entire European continent.[60]

The coordination of European actors was not the only condition for the emergence of continent-wide networks, for according to Kapeller, Germany had also thought out the connections between transport networks thanks to the effectiveness of its

> administration [which] was […] the first in Europe to arrange for its postal mailings to travel be airmail; it even went so far as instituting a home pick-up and drop-off service performed by employees on motorcycles.[61]

In pursuing these efforts, Hitler's Germany had allowed,

> through [its] wise and prudent administration, for the equitable division of merchandise transportation by road and rail in recent years," and with respect to "competition on river pathways," "the Reich once again paved the way, combining under one hand the administrations for both railways and water transport.[62]

The technical superiority visible in the realization of networks was another argument used to legitimize political and economic domination. In the intercontinental connections developed during the interwar period, and men-

59 Kapeller: Le 'train aérien, p. 58 und 55.

60 Kapeller: Le trafic international, p. 42/43.

61 Kapeller: Le 'train aérien, p. 55. The same argument is made in Kapeller, L'Europe, centre de la circulation aérienne, p. 42.

62 Kapeller: Le trafic international, p. 44.

tioned in the article “le train aérien” (The Aerial Train), Kapeller asserted that “German technical skill once again triumphed” with the production of “an airfield in the middle of the Atlantic.” The description made liberal use of superlatives:

> the transoceanic line of 13,500 kilometers [...,] the world’s longest. The planes serving it flew an average of 153 kilometers per hour, another record within a record. [...] It is therefore justified to say that the entrepreneurial spirit and inventive genius of German aviation pioneers had ultimately resolved the problems of transatlantic connections.[63]

With regard to wireless telegraphy, Kapeller observed that “Europe’s first [radio] concert” in 1920 was the work of a certain Schwarzkopf at the “central broadcasting station of the Reich’s postal service,” and that “soon Europe would grow accustomed, each Sunday, to the concerts of the Königswusterhausen.”[64]

The articles often stressed the formidable success of the past, proof of the country’s skill, which was also present in the field of road construction:

> when it comes to creating a new Europe, the experienced acquired by the defenders of German sites will be highly appreciated, experience that is essential in the struggle against Europe’s transformation into a sterile steppe.[65]

The present — that of an economic power and powerful political organization — also provided Germany with the means to achieve its ambitions. Emphasis was placed on the construction of networks, which include “installation costs [...] [that were] exceedingly high,” and call for “exceptional measures. They leave no place for the petty interests of particular individuals. The general interest is crucially important”; it is therefore imperative to leave behind the bygone conceptions “of the narrow-minded, those who support the fragmentation of Europe into little states.”[66] Dr. Todt was presented as an example of those who promoted and carried out this transition: “the creator of the *autostrades* [highways] and of the ‘Siegfried line’ [...] a far-sighted and energetic administrator,” he “shows all of Eu-

63 Kapeller: Le ‘train aérien, p. 58.

64 Kapeller: L’Europe vous parle, p. 42.

65 Anonymous: Plus de routes droites, p. 25. This specter of *Versteppung* (“steppification”) is related to the period’s imaginary that described the landscapes of the East as “models” of desolation; see for instance Kapeller’s use of it in his article, “Le ‘train aérien,’” cited above.

66 Anonymous: Nouvelles énergies, p. 42.

rope the path to follow."[67] Germany was also presented as showing the way for navigable routes: while waiting for the war's end

> to carry out Europe's centuries-old dream, a Suez canal of sorts for the continent, a river route that would connect the Atlantic to the Black Sea, Adolf Hitler announced the project, in a law dated May 11, 1938, for the rapid creation of this connection by channeling the Danube past Vienna and up to the Reich's border.[68]

The representations that *Signal* wanted to diffuse to its readership were best reflected in the metaphor of the orchestra conductor,[69] whose "understanding and authoritarian" presence was needed to "direct the voices and bring them into harmony." This metaphor appeared in Kapeller's article on wireless telegraphy.[70] The International Broadcasting Union created by broadcasting companies proved unable to tame the "confusion of the waves": "most European radio stations seek to lie and excite people. Instead of serving as a link, [...] radio [in the 1930s] only served to create new gulfs between peoples" until the Nazis took charge with the "shortwave receiver in 1933, diffusing German news in foreign languages" in order to "address listeners abroad in their own language." This image of the benevolent coordinator/reconciler/harmonizer implicitly pervaded the other articles on Europe, which strove to show that "the peoples of Europe are genuinely expecting the victor to totally reorganize the general conditions of existence and their projects."[71]

67 Ibid., p. 43.
68 Kapeller: En bateau à travers l'Europe, p. 36.
69 An archetypal figure that appeared regularly in *Signal.*
70 Kapeller: L'Europe vous parle, p. 42.
71 Clauss, Max: „1940. Décision européenne. L'Allemagne a débarrassé le continent de la guerre" (1940. European Decision. Germany Rid the Continent of War), in: *Signal* 15 (1940) (November), p. 4/5, 37.

Ill. 3: "L'Europe vous parle" (This is Europe Talking), in: *Signal* 6 (1942) (March): p. 42 – 45, here p. 44.

Being behind "most of the technical progress [...] and improvements in the administrative field,"[72] with a leader and political system able to make quick decisions and coordinate effectively — as well as the financial and technical means needed to create costly networks — Germany naturally must assume the leadership of Europe. This pro-German propaganda, which used a "virtue device," was coupled with a propaganda effort denigrating the enemy, which tried to act as a "poison device,"[73] and was meant to ultimately garner support for the Reich's ideas.

72 Kapeller: Le trafic international, p. 44.

73 "Virtue device" (promoting a person, idea, or party by associating it with "good" words and symbols) and "poison device" (the opposite, associating it with symbols of evil or detested values) is the terminology used by Clyde Miller, who was among the group of American scientists revolving around the Institute for Propaganda Analysis (1937 – 1942). See Bernard Huygue, François: *Maîtres du faire croire. De la propagande à l'influence*, Paris 2008, p. 60.

3.2 Contrasting Enemy Networks

In conformity with *Signal*'s Manichean strategy, the legitimization of German hegemony was also based on discrediting the enemy, with the issue of networks offering numerous arguments in this respect. The systematic denigration of adversaries was aimed at the Soviet enemy in particular.[74] Reports on the USSR presented the state of "Soviet roads" (Ill. 4) and compared them with the exemplary constructions of Hitler's Germany,[75] thereby giving the editors very concrete elements to justify the civilizing mission directed toward the peoples of the East (knowing that the "new and self-aware Europe will absorb [...] the great spaces of the East, which will have to be initiated in European culture and civilization").[76] Kapeller's articles forcefully developed arguments found elsewhere in *Signal*, which pointed out that the "means of transportation are not even at the level of those found in Europe 50 years ago."[77] Kapeller the observer, who contributed to the "Central Europe's first airmail line" in 1918, scornfully related how while flying over Russia he saw "the famous Vienna-Kiev, which when everything went well, took forty hours to make its journey," "crawl[ing] miserably through the forest" and "mournful steppes."[78]

---

74 On the USSR's image in *Signal*, see Saur, Sébastien: *"Signal" et l'Union soviétique 1940 – 1944*, Parçay-sur-Vienne 2004.

75 These were abundantly present right from the launch of *Signal*, for instance in June 1940 when "the Inca road" — made possible through "mandatory labor service and constant cooperation of all efforts" — was described as a "precursor of the Reich's highways." See Uberlohde-Doesing, Heinrich: „La 8e merveille du monde. Les routes interminables des Incas" (The Eighth Wonder of the World: The Neverending Roads of the Incas), in: *Signal* 4 (1940) (Juni), p. 23 – 25, 34.

76 Kapeller: Le trafic international, p. 44.

77 Graf, Engelbert: „Des espaces sans fin. La configuration géographique de l'Europe orientale" (Endless Spaces: The Geographical Configuration of Eastern Europe), in : *Signal* 1 (1942) (Januar), p. 8.

78 Kapeller: Le 'train aérien, p. 54.

Ill. 4: "Comment nous avons pris d'assaut Kichinev" (How We Took Kichinev by Storm), in: *Signal* 17 (1941) (September): p. 12 – 17, here p. 16/17.

England was primarily attacked on another front, being designated as a selfish, petty, and cowardly power jealous of German success, and completely anti-European in its approach to networks. For instance, in his remarks on the development of air networks, Kapeller described, for the period succeeding the Treaty of Versailles (especially targeting England), how enemies restricted "the German spirit of initiative,"[79] and how at the same time the English "allowed Lufthansa and Air France to assume the risks of flights over the Atlantic."[80] With respect to railways, England "could have joined the European network, but scornfully [...] conserved its attitude of splendid isolation," and "sabotaged" various European projects.[81] For air networks, "collaboration has been established between various companies," whereas "Imperial Airways remains in its ivory tower."[82] While the "organization [of the] meteorological service is a European undertaking."

79 Ibid., p. 55.
80 Kapeller: L'Europe, centre de la circulation aérienne, p. 41/42.
81 Kapeller: Le trafic international, p. 43.
82 Kapeller: L'Europe, centre de la circulation aérienne, p. 41/42.

> at a meteorological congress in Friedrichshafen, the English delegate declared with a haughty smile that his compatriots preferred not to participate in the meteorological service of Europe [rather] than renounce their habit of measuring temperature in degrees Fahrenheit... [...] England also persisted in its 'splendid isolation' [in English] in the field of meteorology, as it did in the European conventions for railways and aviation.[83]

Another kind of rhetoric was used for the American enemy, which was simultaneously discredited and presented as a danger for Europe. In an article from its series on Europe and large-scale network and infrastructure projects, Kapeller exposed the ineptitude of American projects to tame the Gulf Stream, which reflect the "bluff of American science" seeking to deprive Europe of "the central heating carried by the distant conduits of the Gulf-Stream." "The American E. F. Gagott declared that 'The Gulf Stream belongs to us!' and with a straight face asserted that it is possible, for the benefit of America, to capture this current vital for life in Europe just as it exits the Gulf of Mexico."[84] In an article from the same period, but not signed by Kapeller, ridicule was heaped on the American project to connect the "USA" and the "UdSSR" [sic] using the ice road through Alaska,"[85] in an effort to supply their "Bolshevik friends" with "war materiel" to the detriment of Europe caught between the two powers.

83 Kapeller: Le temps qu'il fait en Europe, p. 42/43.

84 Kapeller: On voudrait domestiquer le Gulf-Stream, p. 26.

85 Anonymous: „Le grand plan de Roosevelt: la route de glace par l'Alaska" (Roosevelt's Great Plan: The Ice Road Via Alaska), in: *Signal* 11 (1942) (Juni), p. 4/5.

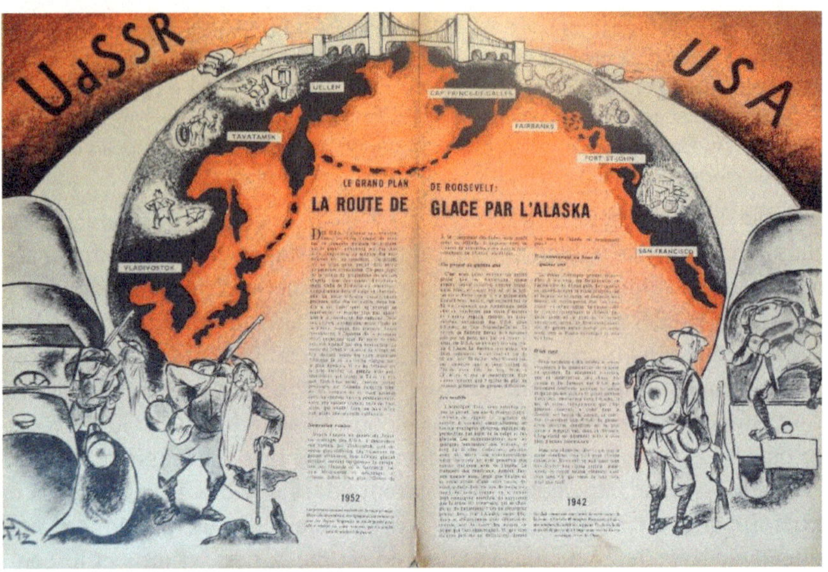

Ill. 5: "Le grand plan de Roosevelt: la route de glace par l'Alaska" (Roosevelt's Great Plan: The Ice Road Via Alaska), in: *Signal* 11 (1942) (June): p. 4/5.

American networks in particular were represented by highly specific metaphors, first with evocations of "the dollar's imperialism extend[ing] across the globe, like the tentacles of a giant octopus,"[86] and then by representing "the air network encircling the globe"[87] like a spider web (Ill. 6). Repeating codes used in anti-Semitic productions,[88] these images proposed an implicit parallel between supposed Jewish domination and "the United States coldly building its power,"[89] striving to obtain "a monopoly

86 Johann, A. E.: „Roosevelt, empereur du monde ?" (Roosevelt, Emperor of the World?), in: *Signal* 18 (1941) (September), p. 4/5, 33/34.

87 Anonymous: „Bases aériennes et suprématie mondiale" (Airbases and Global Supremacy), drawings by R. Hainisch, in: *Signal* 9 (1943) (Mai), p. 4 – 6.

88 See Aslangul, Claire: „Faire peur, faire 'vrai': *Der ewige Jude.* Objectifs, procédés et paradoxes d'un 'documentaire' antisémite," in: *ILCEA. Revue de l'Institut des langues et cultures d'Europe, Amérique, Afrique, Asie et Australie* 23 (2015). URL: https://ilcea.revues.org/3402. Also see the examples proposed by Joël Kotek, "Qu'est-ce qu'une caricature antisémite? Essai d'explication historique et politique," available at: https://isgap.org/flashpoint/quest-ce-quune-caricature-antisemite-essai-dexplication-historique-et-politique/ (accessed on August 4, 2020).

89 Anonymous: Bases aériennes et suprématie mondiale.

over global communication lines," and especially "to achieve global supremacy in navigation" and aviation.[90]

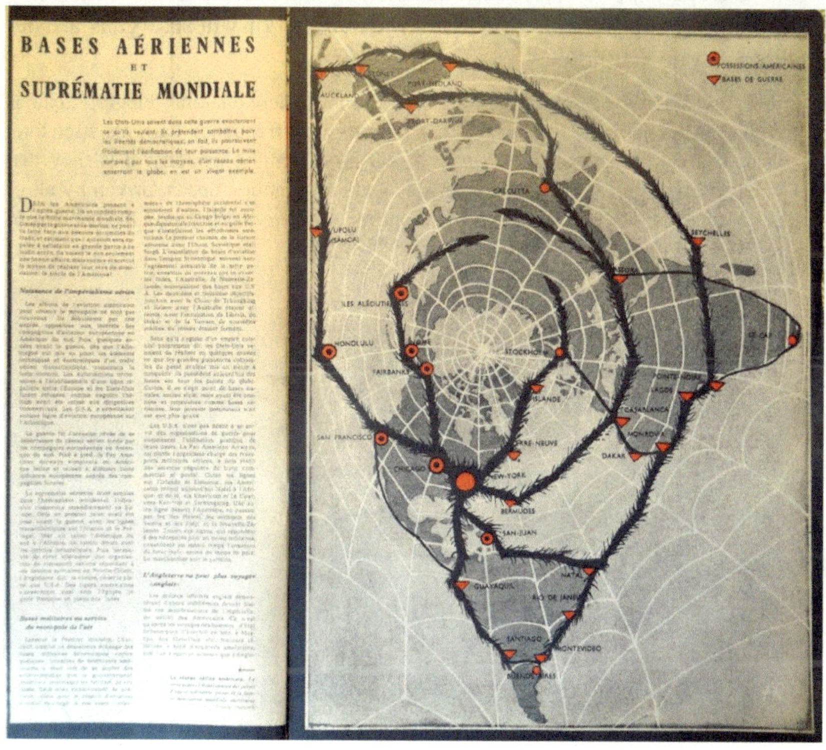

BASES AÉRIENNES ET SUPRÉMATIE MONDIALE

Ill. 6: "Bases aériennes et suprématie mondiale (les Etats-Unis)" (Airbases and Global Supremacy, the United States), in: *Signal* 9 (1943) (May): p. 4 – 6, here 4/5.

The image of American networks as a web threatening to devour Europe stood in opposition, in the articles on European networks created by or planned under the aegis of Germany, to the image of the healthy body nourished by regenerating flows of blood; the notion of "arterial" networks[91] led to the systematic depiction of infrastructure in red (Ill. 7). In

90 Wirsing, Giselher: „L'araignée et sa toile" (The Spider and Its Web), in: *Signal* 13 (1943) (Juli), p. 7f.

91 Kapeller: L'Europe, centre de la circulation aérienne, p. 41/42. This vocabulary was present from the very beginning of the magazine's publication. See Uber-

an organicist perspective demonstrating that the editorial board of *Signal* had embraced the concepts and language used in decision-making circles,[92] Europe was conceived of as a living organism that must develop according to the principles of a "vital order,"[93] all of whose organs are dependent on one another:

> Railways form the circulatory system of Europe; telephone and telegraph cables represent the nervous system; the thin lines of high-frequency currents stretching in bold arcs throughout the country depict its system of tendons: it is they that transmit energy. [...] The energy sources and consumption needs, driven by all of these systems, like the human body, appear to swing and balance themselves in harmonious proportions.[94]

---

lohde-Doesing, La 8e merveille du monde, p. 34, which evokes "roads that, like arteries, crisscross the Empire's immense body."

92 See for example Bauer, Raimund: "'Auch die neue europäische Wirtschaft muß organisch wachsen'. Walther Funks Rede 'Die wirtschaftliche Neuordnung Europas' vom 25. Juli 1940 im Kontext zeitgenössischer Europavorstellungen," in: *Themenportal Europäische Geschichte* (2016): <www.europa.clio-online.de/essay/id/fdae-1669>.

93 References to the "natural" or "biological order" were present everywhere, especially in: Anonymous "Plus de routes droites!"

94 Anonymous: Nouvelles énergies, p. 41.

Ill. 7: "Le rail collecteur européen" (The European Rail Collector), "Nouvelles énergies," in: *Signal* 18/1941 (September): p. 40 – 45, here p. 44.

4. *Conclusion*

Signal magazine made Europe a major topic throughout its publication, using it as a mobilizing slogan. The creation of a "European economic community" that would drive exchange, prosperity, and unity served to legitimize the war effort, as well as occupation methods and conquests. Networks offered both tangible examples and future prospects that would impact the everyday life of Europeans and bring them together, as well as present German hegemony as the work of benevolent coordination.

In *Signal*, trans-European networks were "symbol[s] of modernity and agent[s] of openness," performing a clear function of "symbolic integration"; they were especially deployed as "sign[s] of technological and economic collaboration,"[95] basically functioning as *proof by example* of the feasibility of European collaboration. They represented a concrete model for potential future cooperation in all fields, for they helped overcome fragmentation, particularism, and differing policies: "from the beginning, European traffic was [...] based on mutual confidence, a confidence of harmony that had never before been present in the political field."[96] Earlier trans-European realizations, which were the result of real cooperation in various domains, in addition to major investment by German authorities in networks on German soil (train, post, canals, telephone, air connections)—which helped to build Germany and again make it central to the (Central) European economy after 1918[97]—were ably staged and used, helping to sustain for *Signal*'s readers the "mechanisms of illusion"[98] garnering support for the "new Europe" project of numerous intellectuals.

It is difficult to assess the actual effectiveness of this propagandistic use of networks, or the general impact that *Signal*'s European rhetoric had on its readership. The articles on the subject, especially those by Kapeller aiming for closeness and support, clearly offered an attractive front through their didactic and entertaining form, as well as their content. In keeping with the continent's unification as a process, in which economic and human exchange preceded institutional and political organization, the reader of the time could see the almost "natural" legacy and accomplishments of earlier reflections and initiatives, just as today's reader can recognize the beginnings of the "functionalist" conception of Europe that led to the ECSC/CECA. Yet it is important to be clear that this was indeed the Nazi vision of History that way being diffused, with its rhetoric of a Euro-

---

95 Paraphrasing what Bruneteau: "L'Europe nouvelle", p. 107, said about the highways connecting Eastern Europe to Western Europe. On the integrating function of the "Reich's autostrada," which took on the dimension of a "myth," and which we can imagine the propagandists projected throughout all of Europe, see Reichel, Peter: *Der schöne Schein des Dritten Reiches. Faszination und Gewalt des Faschismus*, Frankfurt 1993, S. 280 ff.

96 Kapeller: Le trafic international, p. 43.

97 See for example Schröter, Harm: „The German Long Distance Telephone Network as a Large Technical System, 1919 – 1939, and its Spin-offs for the Integration of Europe," in: Caron, François / Erker, Paul / Fischer, Wolfram: *Innovations in the European Economy between the Wars*, Berlin 1995, p. 83 – 105.

98 Bruneteau: "L'Europe nouvelle", p. 77.

pean body in need of regeneration, and its opposition to the networks of others, replete with deadly spider webs and tentacles.

5. *References*

Aslangul, Claire: „Le magazine *Signal* (1940 – 1945). Propagande 'universelle' ou adaptation à des publics hétérogènes? L'exemple de la version francophone," in: *Matériaux pour l'histoire de notre temps* 1 (2020).

Aslangul, Claire: „*Signal* et la France: 'vendre' par l'image le rapprochement franco-allemand sous l'Occupation," in: Aslangul-Rallo, Claire / Krapoth, Stéphanie (eds.): *Les relations franco-allemandes en perspective: sources, méthodes et temporalités pour une approche des représentations depuis 1870*, Besançon 2016, p. 259 – 318.

Aslangul, Claire: „Faire peur, faire 'vrai': *Der ewige Jude*. Objectifs, procédés et paradoxes d'un 'documentaire' antisémite", in: *ILCEA. Revue de l'Institut des langues et cultures d'Europe, Amérique, Afrique, Asie et Australie* 23, Grenoble 2015. URL: https://ilcea.revues.org/3402.

Kotek, Joël: „Qu'est-ce qu'une caricature antisémite? Essai d'explication historique et politique," available at: https://isgap.org/flashpoint/quest-ce-quune-caricature-antisemite-essai-dexplication-historique-et-politique/ (accessed on August 4, 2020).

Aslangul, Claire: „Les publicités dans le magazine Signal (1940 – 1945) entre promotion commerciale et propagande politique: apports d'une analyse quantitative," in: Aslangul, Claire / Zunino, Bérénice (ed.): *Die Presse und ihre Bilder / La presse et ses images*, Berlin/Bern 2021.

Bauer, Raimund: „'Auch die neue europäische Wirtschaft muß organisch wachsen'. Walther Funks Rede 'Die wirtschaftliche Neuordnung Europas' vom 25. Juli 1940 im Kontext zeitgenössischer Europavorstellungen", in: *Themenportal Europäische Geschichte* (2016): <www.europa.clio-online.de/essay/id/fdae-1669>.

Bendig, Volker: *Die populärwissenschaftliche Zeitschrift Koralle im Ullstein und Deutschen Verlag 1925-1944,* Ph.D. diss., Ludwig-Maximilians-Universität München 2014.

Bruneteau, Bernard: "*L'Europe nouvelle" de Hitler. Une illusion des intellectuels de la France de Vichy*, Monaco 2003.

Burrin, Philippe: *La France à l'heure allemande: 1940-1944*, Paris 1995.

Huygue, François-Bernard: *Maîtres du faire croire. De la propagande à l'influence*, Paris 2008.

Jasanoff, Sheila / Hyun Kim, Sang (ed): *Dreamscapes of Modernity: Sociotechnical Imaginaries and the Fabrication of Power*, Chicago 2015.

Longerich, Peter: *Propagandisten im Krieg. Die Presseabteilung des Auswärtigen Amtes unter Ribbentrop*, München 1987.

Neulen, Hans Werner: *Europa und das Dritte Reich. Einigungsbestrebungen im deutschen Machtbereich 1939 – 1945*, München 1987.

Reichel, Peter: *Der schöne Schein des Dritten Reiches. Faszination und Gewalt des Faschismus*, Frankfurt 1993.

Rutz, Rainer: "*Signal." Eine deutsche Auslandsillustrierte als Propagandainstrument im Zweiten Weltkrieg*, Essen 2007.

Saur, Sébastien: "*Signal" et l'Union soviétique 1940 – 1944*, Parçay-sur-Vienne 2004.

Schröter, Harm: „The German Long Distance Telephone Network as a Large Technical System, 1919 –1939, and its Spin-offs for the Integration of Europe," in Caron, François / Erker, Paul / Fischer, Wolfram (eds.): *Innovations in the European Economy between the Wars*, Berlin 1995, p. 83 – 105.

A View from London – Some concluding Remarks

Julia Eichenberg

The Second World War was a territorial war and thus, it has always also been about infrastructure and resources. Hitler, the German government and High Command were looking to dominate Europe as a continent, to conquer formerly sovereign countries as German "Lebensraum", to control, take over or dismiss national governments, to suppress resistance. The Wehrmacht quickly conquered and occupied territory. Confronted with the German Blitzkrieg, without any restraint in face of International Law or Humanitarian Principles, European governments and political elites from all European countries saw no other option than to flee and go into exile to Great Britain to safeguard their statehood and defend their interests from abroad.

While Nazi Germany occupied the continent, European political, legal and diplomatic elites, including the cabinets and heads of states, were gathered in an enclosed setting: wartime central London. This created a microcosm of transnational European cooperation, opening new possibilities and opportunities of cooperation caused by close vicinity and the joint experience of the war: a "London Moment"[1].

The Europeans exiles in London were in a curious position vis-à-vis their home countries, the nations they represented. The continent and their national territories were occupied by German soldiers, stripped of national sovereignty (in some cases, of statehood altogether). Claims to power and to representing the national will were equally difficult, as monarchs had left their home soil, politicians had gone into exile and been replaced with puppet regimes back home, or alternative collaborating governments had taken over. With regard to the theme of this volume, they were also in the difficult position of having given up all access to and control over national infrastructure, as well as most national resources.

The aim of this book, as stated by the editors, "write a history of Europe where technological cooperation and conflict are thought of, not in opposi-

1 My remarks are based on findings within the research project "The London Moment", funded by a Freigeist-Fellowship and research group (VolkswagenFoundation) at the Universities of Bayreuth (2021-) and Humboldt Berlin (2014-2020).

tion", thus showing "how actors, institutions, practices and knowledge travelled from the interwar to the post-war through the wartime period". Building on existing research by Patel/Kaiser or Schipper/Schot's concept of "infrastructural Europeanism"[2], this volume focuses on the governance and uses of networked technologies (railways, motorways, waterways, and how to build and maintain them) as well as on people responsible for the creation and maintenance, to follow the continuities and collaborations throughout wartime.

The following conclusion aims to discuss the gap and yet interconnection between what was happening on the occupied continent, where conflict and cooperation went hand in hand, and London as the seat of European's exiled governments on the other hand, where an allied post-war order was planned from afar. Debates in London correspond to the broader topics discussed in this volume (communication, transportation, advertising cooperation, and the personal dimension) and the respective contributed chapters. Since exiles in London had almost no control over infrastructure, the relevant term of reference were national resources. In both cases, whether on the continent or in wartime London, debates about resources, infrastructure and cooperation should be read, as this volume has pointed out, as debates about power, control, and statehood as well as about the intertwined spheres of the national and the transnational.

The European exiles in London were in a delicate position and in dire need of legitimation – by their host country, by other Allies, by international law, but also by their people back home. The agency of these exiled representatives was thus restricted by their own precarious legal situation as well as by the lack of control over what is usually understood as the pillars of statehood: they neither had control over state territory, people, and state power, nor held a monopoly over the employ of physical force. Lacking these pillars of statehood endangered their legitimacy and threatened a lower status within the Allied hierarchy.

The European political exiles in London were a relatively small circle (very small if only counting the governments, counting up to a couple of hundreds when including the ministries, then surrounded by a larger circle of advisers, secretaries, translators etc), in which legal, political and diplo-

2 Schipper, Frank / Schot, Johan: "Infrastructural Europeanism, or the project of building Europe on infrastructures: an introduction", in: *History and Technology* 27 (3), 2011, pp. 245 – 264.

matic functions often overlapped. The state in exile was constructed by legal discourse and representation as well as by the exiles' practices of governance and performance of power. The London microcosm also featured various platforms of intense transnational exchange, providing the European exiles in London with a much needed sounding board for concepts to stabilize Europe. The interaction of exiles in London is not so much a story of the European integration of nations than rather a *histoire croisée* of European post-war plans. The London microcosm represents a transnational political space of governments, meaning it looks at transnational interaction without neglecting or denying the impact of the national or of the state. [3]

Legal recognition laid the foundation for legislation in exile, and was achieved and maintained by continuous lobbying of legal experts and advisors in and around the governments in exile.[4] In a second step, access to resources was essential to the agency of the exiled governments and to their capability to govern, not only in terms of diplomatic representation on an international level (even though this was essential), but also with regard to their own citizens – in so far contact was possible under the limiting circumstances.

Resources were important in a very broad understanding – extending to monetary and non-monetary resources of different kinds. Monetary resources are understood as resources which have a direct monetary value and/or can be directly exchanged against money. This includes raw material, gold, loans, credits, and commodities. Non-monetary resources on the other hand included aspects as access to infrastructure such as telecommunication, radio and cypher, the very obvious military support in terms of arms and munition as well as ships and aircraft, but also something more mundane like buildings to host governments. Besides military and welfare expenses, which had to be paid for, the daily logistics of government in exile also demanded these non-monetary resources. This problem was solved mostly outside of the discussion of war credits and re-payments, but in a more straightforward way: The British government provided the allied exiled European governments with (or helped them find) much needed

3 Budde, Gunilla / Conrad, Sebastian / Janz, Oliver (eds.): *Transnationale Geschichte. Themen, Tendenzen und Theorien*, Göttingen 2006; Patricia Clavin, "Introduction: Conceptualising Transnational Thought and Action between the Wars" in: Laqua, Daniel (ed.): *Internationalism Reconfigured. Transnational Ideas and Movements Between the World Wars,* New York 2011, pp. 1 – 14.

4 Madsen, Mikael R.: "Unpacking Legal Network Power: The Structural Construction of Transnational Legal Expert Networks", in: Fenwick, Mark / Van Uytsel, Steven / Wrbka, Stefan (eds.): *Networked Governance, Transnational Business and the Law*, Berlin 2014, pp. 39 – 56.

commodities: real estate and significant parts of the running costs. Interallied collaboration was closely linked to space and locations in the city of London. In many cases, the provision of said places (in terms of offices and meeting space) were supported by the British host, who continued to do so during the war even through rough patches in political collaboration.

In wartime London, the British parliament passed legislation enabling the British state to requisition buildings and real estate for war purposes.[5] On the countryside, this usually meant commandeering land formerly used for agricultural purposes and repurpose it for military practice or airfields. In town, and particularly in London, this enabled the British government to house ministries and B.B.C. offices in formerly private buildings.

At the same time, war endangered European infrastructure on the occupied continent. This volume had set out to discuss the role of political, social, infrastructural, societal and similar reasons and their impact in cooperation, non-cooperation and integration on the continent. Its choice of examples engages with the important question of axis rule and infrastructure – did political rule entail technological domination? Or did technological knowledge and expertise from the interwar period (in particular with regard to France and French experts) persist? The larger themes of the volume are communication, transportation, advertising cooperation, and biographies or biographical continuities – and, of course, as a red thread throughout the book, transnational cooperation and its rupture or continuance during the war and times of conflict.

The first part focusing on communication engages with postal service, telecommunication and broadcasting. In the chapter on the European Postal and Telecommunications Union (EPTU), Proschmann engages with an institution founded during wartime, in October 1942 in Vienna. The founding date seems to indicate that EPTU was under German control und was initiated to "to dictate the continent's postal rules". However, the chapter makes a strong point for the equally important influence "of path dependency and technocratic traditions [which might have led] to an organisation without (geo)political influence?" All administrations involved had an interest in this cooperation, war or not. At the same time, war was the focal point for the diplomatic and foreign policy agents of this interaction, who were mostly interested in building up a functioning post-war postal organisation. Continuities from interwar cooperation were strong, while at the same time,

5 Emergency (Defence) Act 1939, strengthened by the Landlord and Tenant (Requisitioned Land) Acts 1942 and 1944.

language, currency and location were adapted to the new German (and, with regard to language, Italian) power, to a loss of formerly dominating France, laying the foundation for its use in propaganda to promote a 'New Europe'. Displaying the interconnections between different long-term framework and new, realpolitical power changes, the case study underlines nonetheless the often underestimated agency of occupied countries' administrations and evaluates the EPTU eventually as "big achievements in the standardisation of European postal infrastructure". These are further explored with the example of stamps, which were discussed under the German *Reichspostministerium* for all of Europe but eventually only nationally implemented due to financial and technical difficulties.

Moving from communication to broadcasting, the International Broadcasting Union (IBU) is described as having chosen a "'third way' of dealing with the wartime tensions": neither discontinuing their activities nor transforming into a new institution, the IBU is described in terms of continuity. This was enabled by two important protecting factors: firstly the protection of Swiss law and neutrality, and secondly, the impact of secretary general at the time, Arthur Burrows, who supported remaining on Swiss soil in April 1940. Despite Swiss neutrality, Germans tried to gain influence within the IBU and instrumentalised it for political purposes, in particular when dealing with broadcasting stations in occupied countries like Belgium, Denmark, France, Norway and the Netherlands, where broadcasting was soon under Nazi control.

Its role changed significantly in 1941, when members from ten European countries, including the BBC, left the IBU because of its collaboration with the Nazi authorities. The attempt to remain neutral had been unsuccessful – or too difficult. Its post-war reconstruction as two separate organisations was due to the effects of the Cold War. The IBU's interwar structure, vision and even the individual representatives survived the rupture during the war and continued their work within these new organisations.

In London, for the allied exiled governments, access to diplomatic bags was as important as to radio and telecommunication, aspects also intensely discussed on the continent. In many cases, radio was the only way to communicate directly (with news programmes and speeches, but also cultural broadcasts) or covertly (with hidden messages) between the exiled government and the population left behind on the continent. The fact that back home, communication was under German control was a constant topic in London, and trying to counter this monopoly on information was a reason for close cooperation between the exiled governments and the B.B.C., which turned out to be a foundation for in-depth wartime broadcasts in all kinds of languages. Eventually, this turned into the initiation of Radio Free Europe, which should become essential during the later Cold War period.

The second part of this volume concentrates on transportation, infrastructure in a very classic understanding: waterways, railways, motorways. With regard to waterways, administration and cooperation was, of course, more tied to the actual physical conditions (in contrast to the more "virtual" broadcasting and telecommunication). Accordingly, transnational administration of the Rhine, which had been (re-)established in the interwar period, became quite a challenge during the Second World. Reorganisation of the waterways was considered a priority and quickly taken over by German occupiers. In the Netherlands, a special department for inland navigation headed by a commissioner („Kommissar für See- und Binnenschiffahrt") was created for this purpose. In Belgium, the situation in inland navigation was similar, but slowed by a significant lack of ships. The occupiers Rhine policy was supported by the occupied administrations, but also by Switzerland. When the war ended, regulation mostly returned to a status more prior to the First World War, but close collaboration between national governments and lobby groups, a 20th Century phenomenon, continued. Most surprisingly, Thiemeyer stresses, "there was a continuity in terms of technical, legal and administrative standards in the navigation on the Rhine, even though the institutional system changed completely".

This kind of continuity was also seen in plans for the canalization of the Moselle. Again, the interests of the occupying power were essential and dominated the wartime plans, but were built upon and combined with prewar plans. Martial Libera evaluates Nazi policy as one phase in a "*longue durée* of the Moselle improvement project", but estimates that while it was "undeniably European by virtue of its route and implications, it was not at all in terms of its spirit". A truly European approach should only be reached in the 1960s, within a joint venture to do so.

On the Eastern side, the German occupiers pushed to restrict international administration to purely technical issues (hydraulic structures, customs, navigation police, and social security of the personnel). Jiří Janáč argues that in contrast to usual cesuras applied to Eastern European history, the focus on infrastructural systems linked discontinuity less "to the wartime regimes and organisations, but rather with implementation of the liberal international system during the interwar period". Following the careers of Czechoslovak experts underlined this approach.

Railways were maybe middle ground between the tech-heavy telecommunication sector and the very geopolitical immobile waterways. A framework of international agreements had been build up to ensure cross-border railway traffic. Again, military domination on the continent meant Germany controlled European continental railways, with other national companies (including formerly mighty SNCF) having to accept this. Just as in the case study of waterways, the author points out that "all of this happened in accordance with international law as established before the war [...] at least in the French-German case", which even encouraged further Franco-German technical cooperation, and joint operational standardization. Wartime cooperation in the railway sector can, the chapter argues, be characterised as continuity of the transnational circulation of rolling stock. Pre-war agreements remained valid, pre-war institutions stayed (at least nominally) in charge – very much unlike the postal and telecommunication sector. Post-war times saw continuation, but almost exclusively in Western Europe, with projects like a European wagon pool. With regard to motorways, the two decades between 1935 and 1955 were also first to introduce the import of foreign (then Italian and German) institutional approaches.

Exiled governments in London – as far as their notes go – were less concerned with these long-term trajectories, but more with three immediate problems of the occupation and control of infrastructure: Firstly, they worried in how far their own lack of control and the German gain of it would have impact on the war effort, indicated by discussions on the destruction or sabotage of this potential. Secondly, it posed one of many examples to ponder on collaboration in the negative sense: in how far could working with the enemy be excused as trying to save national infrastructure from destruction, and when did it turn into political betrayal of maintaining infrastructure for the enemy? Finally, infrastructure was a central topic when exiled allied governments discussed their plans for the economic and social reconstruction of their own countries and of Europe as a whole – as they did within so-called 'technical commissions' (meaning: experts working on specific topics such as war crimes trials or reconstruction) of the London International Assembly.

The third part of this volume points to the fact that infrastructure never purely consists of technology and material objects. It is intensely linked to its architects and caretakers (the people who invent, design and maintain it), but also to propaganda and communication surrounding it. The Signal Magazine was such an example, which served to introduce and lobby for the project of a "'new community of nations', one that reserved a special role for transportation, energy, and communication networks", when talking about what was actually "maximal exploitation of the continent's resources for the benefit of the German Reich". The technological subject gave cover for more political aims: claiming that economic prosperity and interaction were linked to a certain political future, while at the same time the past (older technology just as interwar politics) was discredited. Both were used "to legitimize the Third Reich taking over 'leadership of Europe.'" Alleged technical superiority was used as an argument "to legitimize political and economic domination." Enemies were discredited also with regard to their technology, and interchanged with Anti-Bolshevism, Anti-Americanism, both sometimes linked to a rising Antisemitism. As propaganda was an important factor during the war, this was of course met with allied counter-information. Unlike for the German side, journals and magazines were mostly off-limits for the Allies exiled in London, but shorter flyers and leaflets were dropped from airplanes or distributed by resistance members. All in all, radio remained the most important tool for national as well as for coordinated Allied propaganda, mostly in cooperation with the B.B.C. – providing the exiled governments with airtime and equipment to produce national broadcasts was thus an important provision of resources to the exiles,

The fourth topic of this book, the personal dimension, is a particularly interesting one, as it links all different kinds of infrastructure listed above (communication, transportation and advertising/propaganda) and reflects it under the light of a central question within entangled histories: the question of structure and agency, the impact of institutions vs. individuals. As is rightly pointed out, in the regarded examples "experts usually enjoyed long-lasting careers within the administrations, the organisations that they built turned out to be crisis-proof."[6] These biographies, just as the infrastructure they are upkeeping, thus provide long-term trajectories throughout times of war and crisis.[7]

A closer look on French cooperation within the framework of the EPTU by Valentine Adelbert shows the continuous influence and agency of French experts during the war, also, but not only, as a symbolic gesture to integrate the occupied administrations. 'Pre-war technocratic internationalism', established in international conferences, was, however, undermined by the German rejection of telecommunications advisory committees – probably for exactly this very reason.

Karel Paul van der Mandele is introduced in a biographical piece as a central figure in discussions about river improvement, one of many Bene-Lux agents (here as a Dutch lawyer) to do so. With a closer look at one of

6 Laborie, Introduction.

7 Compare: See also: Patel, Kiran Klaus ; Kaiser, Wolfram, Continuity and Change in European Cooperation during the Twentieth Century. In: *Contemporary European History*. 2018; Vol. 27, No. 2. pp. 165 – 182.

the main protagonists, the Italian Giuseppe Gneme "The Dean of telecommunication", Aldebert takes a closer look at continuity in biographies. Gneme had a strong background in telecommunication and was considered one of the leading interwar specialists. As such, he was consulted when founding the EPTU in 1942, but quickly lost his standing and was not reinvolved later in the war, proving the changing political frameworks.[8]

The balance between expertise and political connections is also discussed in the following chapter on two exemplary German protagonists: one with a long-time career in telecommunication, a key member of transnational expert community (Bornemann) vs. one with a wartime career in postal service based on political connections, who was very close to the German Foreign Ministry (Risch). Considering the steep political career ended quickly after the end of the war, while Bornemann's expertise-based career was able to transfer into the post-war world, the authors conclude that "the more technical an infrastructure system is, the more indispensable the experts become, as a high degree of specialist expertise is required" (which was more important for telecommunication than for postal service).

The biography of another French protagonist exemplifies the ways senior civil servants adapted to changing circumstances under occupation. Pierre Marzin was a staunch believer in technology, which he also regarded as the crucial decisive factor in warfare. While he himself did not participate in the French resistance actively as many others did, Griset argues that Marzin nonetheless contributed significantly by covering for his colleagues involved instead of telling on them. In this chapter's very generous estimation Marzin's collaboration with the Germans was purely based on his eagerness to serve technology as a greater good, not on ideology, also enabling him to continue his career in the post-war period.

To contribute a concluding comment to this volume with a view from London seems fitting, as the volumes understands Europe as the European continent, and mostly the Nazi-occupied Western European one, although the occasional example for Eastern Europe is included. Linked to this definition of Europe is an understanding of infrastructure and technical collaboration referring to infrastructure physically linked to the European continent (or Western Europe): railways, rivers, motorways. During the war, all of these are under German political and military occupation, and presumably under German control. It is all the more interesting to see how the actual day-to-

8 Although he retired only in the 1950s after having served again in international organisations.

day practice of maintaining cross-border infrastructure was seemingly less affected than one could have imagined, and the omnipresent dominance of the German Reich and its control over infrastructure was sometimes balanced out by long-term trajectories in form of biographies, institutions and practices of collaboration. As such, the contributions to this volume have pointed out change and continuity alike, ranging from German exploitation to continuation of interwar cooperation to the creation of new multilateral structure. Sometimes, ironically (and surely without intention) this should mean laying the foundation for later European rapprochement.

Bibliography

Brandes, Detlef: *Großbritannien und seine osteuropäischen Alliierten 1939 – 1943. Die Regierungen Polens, der Tschechoslowakei und Jugoslawiens im Londoner Exil vom Kriegsausbruch bis zur Konferenz von Teheran*, München 1988.

Budde, Gunilla / Conrad, Sebastian / Janz, Oliver (eds.): *Transnationale Geschichte. Themen, Tendenzen und Theorien*, Göttingen 2006.

Clavin, Patricia: "Introduction: Conceptualising Transnational Thought and Action between the Wars" in: Laqua, Daniel (ed.): *Internationalism Reconfigured. Transnational Ideas and Movements Between the World Wars*, New York 2011, pp. 1–14.

Conway, Martin / Gotovitch, José (eds.): *Europe in Exile: European Exile Communities in Britain 1940-1945,* Oxford 2001.

Eichenberg, Julia: "Macht auf der Flucht. Europäische Regierungen in London (1940–1944)", in: *Zeithistorische Forschungen /Studies in Contemporary History* 15 (3), 2018, pp. 452–473. DOI: https://doi.org/10.14765/zzf.dok.4.1291.

Loeffler, James / Paz, Moria (eds.): *The Law of Strangers. Jewish Lawyers and International Law in the Twentieth Century*, Cambridge 2019.

Madsen, Mikael R.: "Legal Diplomacy: Die europäische Menschenrechtskonvention und der Kalte Krieg", in: Hoffmann, Stefan-Ludwig (ed.): *Moralpolitik. Geschichte der Menschenrechte im 20. Jahrhundert*, Göttingen 2010, p. 169–195.

Madsen, Mikael R.: "Unpacking Legal Network Power: The Structural Con-struction of Transnational Legal Expert Networks", in: Fenwick, Mark / Van Uytsel, Steven / Wrbka, Stefan (eds.): *Networked Governance, Transnational Business and the Law*, Berlin 2014, pp. 39–56.

Patel, Kiran Klaus ; Kaiser, Wolfram, Continuity and Change in European Cooperation during the Twentieth Century. In: *Contemporary European History*. 2018; Vol. 27, No. 2. pp. 165-182.

Plesch, Dan: *Wartime Origins and the future of United Nations*, London 2015.

Dan Plesch*: America, Hitler and the UN. How the Allies won World War II and forged a peace*, London 2011.

Prost, Antoine / Winter, Jay: *René Cassin et les droits de l'homme: Le projet d'une generation*, Paris 2011.

Smetana, Vít / Geaney, Kathleen (eds.) : *Exile in London: The Experience of Czechoslovakia and the Other Occupied Nations, 1940–1945*, Prague 2017

Zloch, Stephanie / Müller, Lars / Lässig, Simone (eds.): *Wissen in Bewegung. Migration und globale Verflechtungen in der Zeitgeschichte seit 1945*, Berlin 2018.